Elizabeth and Essex
Power, Passion, and Politics

STEVEN VEERAPEN

First published in 2019 by Sharpe Books.

ISBN: 9781099128189

TABLE OF CONTENTS

ACKNOWLEDGMENTS

In the Elizabethan period, the administrative and official New Year began on Lady Day (the 25th of March) according to the Julian calendar then in use. This meant that contemporary documents would record what we understand as March the 24th 1603 (the year of the queen's death) as March the 24th 1602, with the day afterwards being March the 25th 1603 – the first day of the new year. To further confuse matters, though, New Year's Day was celebrated at court (with gifts exchanged) on the 1st of January, despite the contemporary calendar continuing to show that the official new year would not begin for months. In order to minimise confusion, I have chosen to use the modern Gregorian system of dating throughout.

1: Love and the Virgin

When writing this book was suggested to me by my publisher, my immediate thought was 'Essex - not that tiresome, greedy madman!' The idea of writing about Elizabeth appealed to me very much; I never tire of reading about all aspects of her life and reign. Essex, however, has always left me cold. His literary efforts I found overblown and flowery, even by the standards of the age, and his political actions always struck me as representative of the worst kind of Elizabethan politician (and a type of politician sadly still familiar): the self-important, born-to-rule fool with little understanding and far too great a dollop of entitlement. As to the legendary relationship between the pair, I self-satisfyingly told myself that it was more myth than substance. He was a power-hungry user and she had become either addled with age or was simply enjoying a last stab at youth. Of course he never loved her, and the fact that she sent him to the block after his foolish and ultimately pathetic rebellion shows that she viewed him as no more than a failed attempt at cultivating a favourite. What more was there to be said?

However, when I began to research the book, I found myself revising my opinion of Essex, of Elizabeth, and of their relationship. Where I had previously been willing to see only the cold and familiar labyrinth of Tudor-era politics, full of back-biting and lacking in any real emotion beyond ambition, personalities began to sing from the pages of history. A relationship began to emerge that involved real people rather than cynical politicians feigning emotions. The gendered nature of the relationship struck me too, as I found a queen seeking a new role in the latter part of her life and a young man, callow but exceedingly well educated and almost running over with emotion and idealism, little of it well founded or directed. How different might things have been – and how differently might we look at the pair of them and their curious friendship – had she been an ageing and impotent king and he a tempestuous girl thirty years that king's junior. Would I then have been so determined at the outset that the relationship was a strictly cynical one?

The nebulous love life of Queen Elizabeth I has intrigued observers since the queen's days as Lady Elizabeth, when, as sister to Edward VI, her ostensibly romantic entanglements were a source of political import. Her relationships with a host of male favourites, few likeable or admirable, ceased to inhabit the realm of politics following her death in 1603. Instead they passed into the world of speculation, imagination, and fiction.

More than four-hundred years since the Elizabethan era gave way to the Jacobean, the life and loves of England's virgin queen continues to grip the popular imagination. Modern scholarly opinion holds, quite rightly, that it is unlikely that Elizabeth had ever the opportunity or the inclination to indulge in clandestine sexual affairs. What is clear, though, is that she enjoyed masculine company, reserving a particular affinity with the young, handsome gallants who flocked to her magnificent renaissance court.

In recent years, too, the queen's image has undergone something of a transformation amongst the scholarly community. Where once it was tantamount to iconoclasm to whisper criticism of this most successful and admirable of women, today it has become acceptable; indeed, we do Elizabeth the woman an injustice to view her as an infallible political titan rather than what she was: a remarkable, tolerant, intelligent, vacillating, vain, and occasionally petty, vindictive, and bloodthirsty woman. It is as well that she enjoyed male company, because she inhabited a world made by and for men. She was not above exploiting her femininity when it served her purpose to do so, and it is to her enormous credit that whilst she showered those men who were politically inutile with baubles, patronage, and attention, she reserved for an unusually loyal, reliable, and diligent band of men the business of government. In so doing she was mostly able to steer the ship of state through the stormy waters of rebellion, factionalism, aristocratic jealousy, and war. Occasionally, of course, the two groups collided, intermixed, and caused all manner of problems. Essex was to represent one such example of the challenges which arose when the queen's reliance on a dwindling band of hand-picked politicians met with resistance from those traditional advisers and statesmen: the nobility.

The earl of Essex was the last great reputed love of Elizabeth's life. Like the royal mistress he served – and ultimately betrayed – his image too has undergone reappraisal. In the early part of the twentieth century he was lauded as an heroic but doomed nobleman – a last and late blossoming of the chivalric ideal. As the biographer Lytton Strachey put it, he embodied 'the spirit of the ancient feudalism ... the flame was glorious – radiant with the colours of antique knighthood and the flashing gallantries of the past; but no substance fed it; flaring wildly, it tossed to and fro in the wind; it was suddenly put out'.[1]

This pseudo-romantic view of Essex gave way to a somewhat more cynical perspective in the later twentieth century, which saw him labelled as an empty-headed playboy. Robert Lacey's 1971 biography, which remains extremely enjoyable, is full of biting commentary on his deficiencies. More recently, the tide has turned again. Paul E. J. Hammer's exemplary academic study of the earl's political career up until 1597 is essential reading, and it has been accompanied by a slew of equally-excellent studies of the Essex circle, including Annaliese Connolly and Lisa Hopkins' edited collection, *Essex: The Cultural Impact of an Elizabethan Courtier*. These books focus heavily on reinterpreting the earl's literary and political contributions to Elizabethan public life and they present a much cannier figure than either the honey-tongued romantic or the dull-witted Icarus. In modern scholarship, Essex is a thoroughly political beast, steeped in the emerging debates about the absolutism or counsel-led theories of kingship which peppered late Elizabeth political discourse; he was no foolish rakehell nor truly a lover of the older queen. The problem is that Essex was all of these things at once, which is what makes him so interesting and enduring a figure.

Of Elizabeth, unwavering praise began to dominate after the religious divisions of her own era died down, and it has been

---

[1] Strachey, L. 1950 [1928]. *Elizabeth and Essex* (London: Penguin), p. 1.

the standard until relatively recently. Biographers prior to the later twentieth century tended to apologise for her short-comings – her jealousy and prevarication were seen as feminine frailties or politically-motivated affectations. As time passed, she was often held up as a feminist icon – and a feminist she was not – or, to those brave enough to challenge the image of Good Queen Bess, a weak-willed woman who stumbled from crises to crisis and survived thanks to good sense in selecting her statesmen. This image, too, is problematic and lacks nuance. Like Essex, Elizabeth combined a number of contradictory strengths and weaknesses, and like all humans she was frustratingly inconsistent, given to pipe dreams – such as the recovery of Calais – mood swings, and one of the best political heads in English history.

The relationship between these two iconic sixteenth-century figures has been one of fevered speculation, with interpretation differing according to the fashions of the age. In his *Elizabeth and Essex*, Lytton Strachey makes great play of the age difference, presenting an almost gothic story of a fright-wigged old woman preying on a younger man, whom she bests in every sense. Robert Lacey, too, paints his Elizabeth as a sour woman, toothless and bad-breathed even in her forties. Those who favour scandal and those who have axes to grind – particularly the more extreme of those involved in the spurious but frustratingly persistent Shakespeare authorship question – have gone ever further. To some, not only Essex but his friend and adviser Francis Bacon (as well as the earls of Oxford, Southampton, Henry Neville, Robert Cecil, Lady Mary Sidney, and Elizabeth Knollys) are Elizabeth's illegitimate children, Oxford born to her and her stepmother's husband, Thomas Seymour, and the rest fathered by her great love, the earl of Leicester.[2] One wonders how she had time to govern. Needless to say, these claims should be treated with contempt. The

---

[2] For an overview of these and other theories see Michell, J. 1996. *Who Wrote Shakespeare?* (London: Thames and Hudson); Shapiro, J. 2010. *Contested Will: Who Wrote Shakespeare?* (London: Faber and Faber).

relationship between Elizabeth and Essex is interesting enough without adding conspiracy and overtones of incest to the mix.

In hearing the names Elizabeth and Essex, casual readers will likely think of Bette Davis, fidgeting and blinking in *The Private Lives of Elizabeth and Essex* as she demands Errol Flynn 'take my throne! Take England! It is yours!' In 1930s Hollywood, the glamour of the court and the pairing of two stars mattered. There had to be romance and it had to be bursting with sexual energy. Though her performance is mesmerising and Flynn's very charming (the chemistry lights up the screen despite the notorious hatred she had for him), Davis's Elizabeth is overflowing with barely-repressed passion.

Although the popularity of the historical epic declined, the desire to see Elizabeth and Essex represented on screens did not. Most famous is 1971's sumptuous-if-studio-bound *Elizabeth R*. This captivating production is responsible more than any other for portraying the elderly Elizabeth as a white-painted, sharp-tongued terror. In the final episode, *Sweet England's Pride*, she is an anomaly at her own court, made-up to bizarre proportions and firing off commands like a well-oiled AK-47. Glenda Jackson's bravura performance in the title role needs no further praise. The image it presents, though, requires significant reassessment, and her interactions with a bombastic but ultimately pathetic Robin Ellis as Essex present the pair as lacking any real interest in one another. His Essex is just another upstart courtier – a footnote in the story of England's grand-dame. Though Elizabeth commends him as the magic mirror that makes her Gloriana, we see very little of this, and must rely instead on characters speaking of his apparent charm.

In the second part of the 2005 miniseries *Elizabeth I*, Dame Helen Mirren took on the role of Elizabeth, and portrayed the queen's often-overlooked emotional side and famously flirtatious nature – albeit in a script which had echoes of Hollywood in its depiction of a woman frequently overcome by love and reliance on men. Mirren's Elizabeth crying at the council table over the loss of her last chance at motherhood, and later screaming, 'I want Leicester! Bring him home!' particularly ring false. A fresh-faced Hugh Dancy played a callow, cruel, sex-crazed Essex and the result was a heavily sexualised queen getting up the hopes of a young chancer. Even their card games involved innuendo and heavy petting. The chemistry, again, was well portrayed, and the acting predictably stellar, even if the personalities as scripted seemed somewhat off the mark. The BBC's production of *The Virgin Queen* the same year pitted a heavily-made-up Anne Marie Duff against a brooding Hans Matheson as the pair; here, the older Elizabeth was again a visual horror of whom an ambitious younger man sought to take advantage.

So run the fictionalised versions of events. But what was the true nature of the relationship between the ageing queen and her dashing young favourite? A full-blooded May-December romance? A shrewd attempt by a man to use a woman? By a woman to manage, divide, and rule men? It will be the purpose of this book to reveal exactly what brought the two together, what soured their relationship, and the effect that the downfall of England's last Elizabethan hero had on a queen who had been given and lost one last kiss of youth. This will not be a story of an old woman preying on a young man, nor of an ambitious man taking advantage of a doddering and vain spinster. It will be one of two unique people, drawn together by an alien concept of love and a system that both encouraged and destroyed it.

2: An Inauspicious Beginning

The boy, twelve years old, was ushered through the guard chamber and into the presence chamber of Hampton Court Palace.[3] Everything about the palace was designed to impress, to cow, and to awe. Once belonging to the great Cardinal Wolsey, the complex of red brick buildings had been gifted to Henry VIII by the falling prelate in 1528. Henry, an enthusiastic builder, had beautified it, adding a tennis court, a hammer-beam-roofed great hall, and the famous gatehouse to the inner courtyard with its astronomical clock which, in addition to telling the time, marked out the phase of the moon, the quarter of the year, and the tide at London Bridge. By the time the boy arrived, during the Christmas revels of 1577-8, Hampton Court was a pleasure palace, set in extensive gardens filled with exquisitely carved heraldic beasts, columns, and statuary.[4] It

---

[3] The date of Essex's birth is a conundrum, with contemporary sources unable to agree on either the year or the date in November. I have opted for the earlier date (10th of November 1565) rather than November the 10th (or 19th) of 1567. The later date makes his scrupulously correct academic record unlikely. As G. B. Harrison (who favours the later date) points out, however, the actual date is largely immaterial beyond historical curiosity. A few years in either direction do not affect his deeds or the relationship he had with the queen. See Harrison, G. B. 1937. *The Life and Death of Robert Devereux, Earl of Essex* (London: Cassell & Company), pp. 329-30.
[4] In his biography of 1971 biography of Essex, Robert Lacey places the earl's debut at Court in the early months of 1577. This would mean that he believes Essex to have arrived at Christmas 1576-7. More recently, Andrew Hiscock places the debut explicitly during the 1577-8 (modern dating) revels. The latter is correct, and the confusion is likely because of the peculiarities of the calendar meaning that the Twelve Days of Christmas runs over two years in modern dating, but one year in the Julian calendar. It seems unlikely that Essex would have been introduced to court in the period 1576-7 (modern dating) given that he was judged too weak and sickly to

was a sight grander than his own home of Chartley in Staffordshire, and grander even than his more recent lodgings at the under-construction Theobalds.

Only the previous year, the boy, Robert Devereux, had succeeded to the earldom of Essex, his father Walter having died under circumstances that would later give rise to gossip, innuendo, and outright calumnious tracts. It was his first appearance at the royal court, and the festivities must have been dizzying. The popular, gruesome sport of bear-baiting – in which trained dogs were set upon a chained bear, with spectators betting on whether the bear's strength would win out over the dogs' numbers, speed, and agility – was conducted in the palace precincts (the conveyance of the bear set the queen back 40s, with 60s spent on the dogs). The theatrical troupe

---

travel from Chartley to his father's funeral in Carmarthen in late November 1576. More obviously, a to Richard Bagot from his son-in-law dated February 1578 contains the following:

> At his first arrival in London, the Citie gave him
> £500. At his coming to the Cort at Whitehall,
> her Majestie shewed him greatest countenance;
> and upon his cominge, meting with him, offered
> to kysse him, which he humblie altogether
> refused; upon her Majesties brynging him
> through the grand chamber, into the chamber of
> presence, her M. would have him put on his
> hatt; which no-wise he wold; offering himself in
> all things at her Majesties commandment; she
> then replied, that if he would be at her
> commandment, then he should put on his hat.
> He expounded, that it should be in all things,
> saving in things to his reproche.

See Lacey, R. 1971. *Robert, Earl of Essex: An Elizabethan Icarus* (London: Phoenix Press), pp. 18-9; Hiscock, A. 2016. '"Achilles Alter": The Heroic Lives and Afterlives of Robert Devereux, 2nd Earl of Essex' in A. Connolly and L. Hopkins (Eds.) *Essex: The Cultural Impact of an Elizabethan Courter* (Oxford: Oxford University Press), p. 122;

known as The Earl of Leicester's Men performed on the 26th of December, with the Children of the Chapel Royal taking to the stage the following day, to be succeeded by The Earl of Warwick's men on the 28th. On the 1st of January the queen was given no fewer than 201 gifts from her courtiers, amongst them *A Book of the States in King William Conqueror's Time* from Sir Gilbert Dethick and a bible bound in cloth of gold garnished in silver and gilt with plates displaying the queen's arms. It was a glittering world.

Yet the stage onto which young Essex was making his debut was not without scandal. The day after Christmas, a woman was laid to rest having been 'slain in the court by two of the scullions of the kitchen'.[5] The royal court, which resembled nothing so much as a grand hotel chain with a moveable staff and guests and a number of beautiful locations, was a place of danger and intrigue. As an institution it resisted absolute definition: it was simply the conglomeration of people and places which surrounded the queen, the personnel unfixed save those with official positions in the more clearly defined royal household. As is the case when any large number of people gather, there were jealousies, love affairs, and the endless jockeying for better lodgings and greater notice from the head of both household staff and courtly guests.

It was that head that Essex had been taken to the audience chamber to meet. Queen Elizabeth had reigned for nineteen years. By the late 1570s, her position was as secure as it was ever likely to be. By any measure, this was remarkable going for a woman who had been illegitimated at the age of two. In 1536, her father, Henry VIII, had resolved to rid himself of her unpopular mother, Anne Boleyn. The means by which he set out to do so were remarkably callous, even for that most egocentric and monstrous of men. Spinning Anne's courtly flirtations into a web of lies, half-truths, and misrepresentations,

---

[5] Colthorpe, M. E. 2017. '1577' in M. E. Colthorpe (Ed.) *The Elizabethan Court Day by Day* (Cambridge: Folgerpedia), p. 40. The above letter comes from: Bagot, W. B. 1824. *Memorials of the Bagot Family* (London: W. Hodgetts), p. 30-1.

Henry and his ministers fabricated a tissue of allegations spanning adultery, treason, and incest. On the 19th of May, Anne was executed by a specially-imported French swordsman. One the eve of her death, however, Henry determined that she should lose not only her life, but any pretensions she had had to queenship; his archbishop of Canterbury, Thomas Cranmer, declared the Tudor-Boleyn marriage invalid.

Henry's only child by Anne – the child she had been carrying when they had been officially wed in January 1533 – was thereby legally rendered a bastard: overnight she ceased being styled 'princess' and was known instead as 'Lady Elizabeth'. The diminution in status is said not to have escaped the precocious child, who supposedly remarked, 'Yesterday my Lady Princess, today but my Lady Elizabeth'. Her quondam claim to the succession was, at any rate, quickly supplanted by the arrival of a half-brother, Edward, to Henry's next wife, the fragrant Jane Seymour.

Thereafter, Elizabeth was brought up by her governesses and tutors, honing an innate cleverness with the rigorous humanist education popular in the sixteenth-century, even for wealthy females: the 'new learning'. In time she would gain French (although her accent would be criticised, much to her chagrin), Italian, Spanish, Greek, German, Latin, and reputedly even a smattering of Welsh. Scholasticism was livened up with occasional invitations to court to visit her father and a succession of stepmothers, until a more lasting stability arrived in the form of Henry's last queen, the influential and intelligent Katherine Parr. Under this remarkable, reformist-minded queen, Elizabeth further developed her already-formidable intellectual credentials.

Henry VIII finally died in 1547, leaving his son by Jane Seymour, Edward, to succeed to the throne as a minor. Leaving behind him a will authorised by parliament, the old king did go some way to making amends for dissolving his first two marriages; the will declared that his daughters by those marriages should succeed in the event of the failure of Edward to produce issue. Elizabeth was once more in line for the English throne, albeit there were murmurs about the subversion of tradition and custom in a monarch naming his bastards as legal heirs.

As testament to the bond the Lady Elizabeth had formed with her last stepmother, she joined Katherine's household, which was shaken up by the dowager queen's rapid remarriage to Jane Seymour's brother, the lord admiral, Thomas. This handsome gallant was to set the mould for the men who would interest Elizabeth throughout her life: attractive, adventurous, charming, and not particularly well-endowed with political sense. Alarmingly, Seymour seemed equally interested in his and his wife's young charge, flirting with her shamelessly and even involving the dowager in their romps. Eventually, for decency's sake, Katherine was compelled to send the girl away; she herself had become pregnant for the first time, although neither she nor the child would survive the difficult birth long. In September 1548, Elizabeth lost the closest thing she had ever known to a mother.

More dangerous were the continued attentions of the merry widower, Seymour. Likely born of a jealousy that his older brother Edward had assumed the protectorate of England – and the country's de facto rule – during young Edward VI's minority, he developed a desire to insinuate himself into the corridors of power via marriage. Although he had flirted with the idea of marrying Henry's eldest surviving daughter, Mary Tudor, Elizabeth became his prize. Secrets, however, did not last long in any early modern court, and soon the lord protector learnt of his brother's machinations, which crossed a line when the admiral attempted to kidnap the king. With remarkable sang-froid, the young Edward VI willingly consigned his madcap uncle to the block, and the lord admiral lost his head on the 20th of March 1549. This was not without effect on Elizabeth who, at her own house of Hatfield, had been vigorously examined by the privy council as to her knowledge of Seymour's plans and plots. Throughout the ordeal of cross-examination, she remained at turns obdurate, cool, and cunningly evasive. At the age of fifteen, she was already displaying traits that would be with her until death.

When the furore around Seymour had died down, Elizabeth

might have looked forward to a quiet life, with the potential for an arranged marriage with a foreign ally of appropriate rank. This would not come to pass, however. Edward VI fell ill and died of a pulmonary complaint in 1553, and the usual jockeying for power ran its course, exacerbated by the fact that Edward had left a 'devise for the succession' ignoring his half-sisters and passing the throne to his cousins. Elizabeth, wisely, did not back any faction, waiting to see whether those promoting her elder half-sister, Mary, or her cousin, Lady Jane Grey (a granddaughter of Henry VIII's younger sister) would win the majority support of the nobility and take the crown. It landed on the passionately Catholic Mary's head, and Jane's would later land on the block. Elizabeth would, when Mary's triumph became inevitable, show herself her sister's partisan, secure in the knowledge that, should anything happen to the new queen, she had laid out the stall for her own rule.

Throughout Mary's reign, the Protestant Elizabeth had been forced to temporise, dissemble, and avoid being drawn into any hot-headed anti-Catholic plots. As she had donned severe Protestant black during the reformist Edward's reign, so did she request Catholic prayer books and profess herself eager to learn the old faith under her sister. Nevertheless, she found herself an unwilling pawn in the Protestant discontent that swirled up around Mary's marriage to Philip II of Spain. When Sir Thomas Wyatt – son of the famous Henrician-era poet – raised a rebellion, Elizabeth was once again interrogated, and this time confined to the Tower of London. Though nothing could be proven against her, relations with Queen Mary would never be repaired, and it was likely only the insistence of Philip that kept her head on her shoulders. What Philip could not ensure, however, was the production of an heir to England and Spain with Mary. Quite apart from the fact that his visits to his wife were brief – painfully brief, from Mary's perspective – the queen was in her late thirties at the time of their marriage, and her health was poor. Despite several phantom pregnancies, the last of which might have resulted from symptoms of ovarian cancer, Mary I died childless in 1558. At the close of her life and reign, she indicated her willingness for her half-sister to succeed her, with the proviso – which would be ignored – that she maintain the realm in the counter-reformation Catholicism she had violently established.

When she had attained the throne in 1558, at the age of twenty-five, few had expected Elizabeth to reign long, at least on her own. She had withstood decades of pressure to marry and had lived in a constant state of insecurity due to her anomalous status as an ordained queen approved by parliament but illegitimate by law. She had weathered a serious attack of smallpox in 1562, numerous assassination attempts by partisans of her cousin, Mary Stewart, and been dogged by scurrilous rumours that she had taken multiple courtiers as lovers, producing children and allegedly stuffing them up chimneys. Such rumours were designed, no doubt, to destabilise the queen's value on the international marriage market: and, during Christmas 1577-8, in her mid-forties, she was facing the endgame of her ability to silence scurrilous rumour and present herself as a marriageable and fertile potential bride. The man most commonly accused of being her lover, the handsome and athletic Robert Dudley, ennobled as the earl of Leicester in 1564, was to play an enormous role in young Essex's life. So too was the queen's secretary of state and right-hand man – or, more accurately, his offspring – William Cecil, Baron Burghley. Though he could not have known it at the time, the close-knit circle of people into whose company the little boy was being thrust were to set him on a path that would lead through glory and end in destruction.

When Essex was introduced to the queen during the Christmas revels, he came as a ward of Burghley, the latter being master of the wards (a position which gave him control over those whose fathers died before they attained the legal age of majority, and which would later allow him to begin something of a home-school for noble and wealthy boys who had lost their fathers). He came not only as the earl of Essex in his own right, but as the queen's chief minister's ward, and the son of one of her women: her cousin (a granddaughter of Anne Boleyn's sister, Mary Carey) Lettice Devereux (nee Knollys). Lettice, a noted court beauty, was the daughter of Elizabeth's beloved cousin Catherine Carey, the chief lady of the bedchamber who had died in 1569. Rumours since have abounded that one or both of the children of Mary Carey (nee Boleyn) were the illegitimate offspring of Henry VIII, although even the more likely candidate for royal bastardy of the two, Catherine Carey, was never recognised.[6] It is safe to say that promoting the idea of Lettice being the granddaughter of Henry VIII is not necessary in extolling the lineage of the young Essex. The boy who made his debut at court was descended from a quiver of ancient noble families: the Hastings, the Staffords, the de Ferrers, the Bonvilles, the Greys, and the Bourchiers. He thus entered the court as a young man of considerably blue blood. Suitably coached in the strict formalities of a royal audience as he must have been, it would have been unthinkable that he would make an error. And yet he did: two of them.

When he was brought before the queen, Essex committed the faux pas of keeping his hat upon his head. He compounded this error by refusing a kiss from the queen when she did him the honour of offering one. Exactly what prompted the young Essex to so embarrass himself will never be known: nervousness, a temporary lapse of judgement, or hints of a rebellious and

---

[6] Nicola Tallis puts forward a defence of Catherine Carey's claim to royal bastardy, citing numerous sixteenth-century literary allusions and contemporary gossip. Others are less sanguine about the possibility. The truth is that the only ones who might have known for certain were King Henry, Mary Boleyn-Carey, and William Carey. None of them made any pronouncements diverging from the two children being born to husband and wife, and so even contemporary and near-contemporary suggestions as to Essex's grandmother's royal parentage are at risk of being gossipy and scandalous on the part of moralists, and opportunistic and optimistic on the part of her descendants. The records of the day adhere to the accepted version of events: that Mary's son and daughter were her husband's rather than the king's, though the possibility of Catherine – the likelier candidate for royal bastardy based on the timeline – being a Tudor is interesting. See Tallis, N. 2017. *Elizabeth's Rival: The Tumultuous Tale of Lettice Knollys, Countess of Essex* (London: Michael O'Mara Books).

independent nature. It might also be that he found her personally unattractive enough to be unmoved by the aura of majesty she had always sought to project – or, indeed, frightened by it. Portraits from the mid-1570s, such as the Darnley portrait (by an unknown artist) and that by celebrated miniaturist Nicholas Hilliard, depict the queen as, respectively, thin-faced and sombre, and magnificently haughty. In both she is splendidly clad; throughout her life she understood the power of costume in drawing attention away from a face that was arresting rather than beautiful. On first meeting her, Essex would have been faced with a woman of forty-four, with dark, almost black eyes, a long, thin, slightly hooked nose, prominent cheekbones, and flaming red hair enhanced by hairpieces.

Elizabeth's eyes would have fallen upon a boy who was by contemporary standards on the cusp of manhood. In addition to his churlish refusal to be kissed by her and to doff his cap, the young Essex had been described the previous year as being 'rather weak and tender of body', with Burghley making the rather more positive observation that he was nevertheless 'very comely and bashful'. The comeliness, at least, betokened future development into what the queen liked in her male courtiers' physical attributes. The shyness hints that the best gloss put on his behaviour at court is that he was more overwhelmed than otherwise by the sight and attention of Queen Elizabeth.

Luckily, the queen was in a forgiving mood, and with the characteristic unpredictability of the Tudors, she laughed the entire incident off. Although his mother, Lettice, and his guardian, Burghley, might have wrung their hands at Essex's behaviour (despite the queen's taking it in good part), it was certainly an inauspicious beginning to what would become a close and intriguing personal relationship. At any rate, all involved would soon have greater difficulties pressing upon them.

***

If Essex was punished or reprimanded for his behaviour at court, there is no record of it. He was, however, returned to his studies at Cambridge, where he had matriculated as a fellow-commoner at Trinity College earlier in 1577 (students then beginning their studies at a far earlier age than today). The lifestyle appears to have appealed to him; he wrote in the spring of 1577 a humble and typically stilted letter of thanks to Burghley

for your lordship's care in placing me here in the university where, for your lordship's sake, I have been very well entertained, both of the university and the town.[7]

The reference to 'the town' is particularly interesting. It was quite usual for arriving nobles to be entertained by civic authorities, especially in towns which were to play host to them. Essex's decision to remember them to Burghley is touching; but it is also prescient. Throughout his life, the earl was to place great faith in people – whether in crowds or mobs – and his belief in winning the loyalty of commoners was of a piece with his eventual claim to a relatively new political force: popularity – a word which was to be coined in the last years of his life.[8]

He certainly displayed an aptitude for study, with Burghley having commented that at age eleven he could 'express his mind in Latin and French as well as in English [and was] very courteous and modest in his bearing, disposed rather to hear than to answer, given greatly to learning'.[9] Learning aplenty he was to be afforded; his accounts for 1577 include charges for his meals, a standing desk, his ink and quills, and a selection of books. For long over a century, a myth has endured that amongst these books was the 1577 edition of Raphael Holinshed's *Chronicles of England, Scotland, and Ireland*. However, the detective work of Aaron T. Pratt and David Scott

---

[7] Devereux, W. M. 1853. *Lives and Letters of the Devereux. Earls of Essex in the Reigns of Elizabeth, James I and Charles I 1540-1646, Volume 1* (London: John Murray), p. 167.

[8] Dory, J. S. 2016. *Shakespeare, Popularity, and the Public Sphere* (Oxford: Oxford University Press), p. 14.

[9] Devereux, *Lives and Letters*, p. 166.

Kastan has effectively put an end to this myth, recognising as it does that the supposed evidence on which it is based is an interpolation by Essex's Victorian descendent, Walter Devereux Bourchier, in his hagiographic *Lives and Letters of the Devereux Earls*.[10] The myth has likely gained currency as, much later in his career, Essex would hire an actor-playwright and his company to perform a play drawn from its history of English kings. The playwright would be William Shakespeare and the play his *Richard II*.

Ironically enough, whilst Essex was continuing his studies – without Holinshed to consult but certainly with Isocrates, Goslicius, Beza, Sturmius, and Ramus – the same Richard II was the subject of discussion at Elizabeth's court. Essex's grandfather, Lettice's father Sir Francis Knollys, is to be found writing in January 1578 of the queen's attempts to deprive the archbishop of Canterbury, Edmund Grindal, from office for his puritanical sympathies.[11] He was to ask

who will persist in giving of safe counsel if her Majesty will persist in misliking of safe counsel? Nay, who will not rather shrinkingly (that I may say no worse) play the parts of King Richard the Second's men, than enter into the odious office of crossing of her Majesty's will? If the Bishop of Canterbury shall be deprived, then up starts the pride and practice of the Papists, and down declineth the comfort and strength of her Majesty's safety. And then King Richard the Second's men will flock into

---

[10] Pratt, A. T. & Kastan, S. 'Printers, Publishers, and the Chronicles as Artefact' in P. Kewes, I. A. Archer & F. Heal (Eds.) *The Oxford Handbook of Holinshed's Chronicles* (Oxford: Oxford University Press), p. .37-40.

[11] The word 'Puritan', at first meaning one who opposed the Romish hierarchy of the English Church but later came to mean one who sought deeper and more strictly enforced reforms, has been dated by Thomas Fuller to 1655 in his *Church History of Britain*. See Pastoor, C. & G. K. Johnson. 2007. *Historical Dictionary of the Puritans* (Plymouth: Scarecrow Press), p. 2-3.

court apace, and will show themselves in their colours.[12]

One does not need to suppose (or invent) ownership of *Holinshed's Chronicles* to find portents of Essex's knowledge of a monarch deposed for arbitrary rule and a reliance on detested favourites. On the heels of his debut at court, his grandfather was invoking the name and example of Richard II.

Without the benefit of Holinshed, Essex appears to have settled once again to academic life. This life comprised sixteen terms to be spread over four years, during which the student would be instructed in the trivium of grammar, rhetoric, and logic, as well as having lessons in the quadrivium of arithmetic, geometry, astronomy, and music.[13] The university's statutes dictated that first years spend their time on rhetoric, with lectures on the texts of Quintilian, Hermogenes, and Cicero. Beyond this they would move into Aristotelian dialectic and Cicero's *Topics*, before turning to Aristotle's *Ethics* and *Politics*, Pliny and Plato. The study of Greek language and texts (including Isocrates, Demosthenes, and Euripides – the first two of which Essex certainly owned books on) would round out the undergraduate experience.[14] This was complex stuff, and it aimed to produce graduates who not only understood the wealth of classical literature inherited and prized by renaissance thinkers, but ones who could communicate well and effectively. What was also hoped was that those inculcated in the classics would emerge as virtuous and Godly. Of equal importance was the fact that it outfitted young nobles and gentleman for a life within renaissance courts, which demanded displays of learning, piety (however assumed), grace, and wit.

The godliness promoted by Cambridge's course of instruction

---

[12] Thomson, P. 1999. *Shakespeare's Professional Career* (Cambridge: Cambridge University Press), p. 137.
[13] Whitteridge, G. 1971. *William Harvey and the Circulation of the Blood* (London: Macdonald), p. 6.
[14] See Todd, M. 2002. *Christian Humanism and the Puritan Social Order* (Cambridge: Cambridge University Press), particularly pp. 62-4.

was, moreover, compounded by the religious zeal of its reformist vice-chancellor, Dr John Whitgift, who would become archbishop of Canterbury in 1583. Whitgift had been the master of Trinity College between 1567 and 1577 and had helped draft the university's statutes. The religious leaning, indeed, of the whole university was towards reform, and it is no surprise that the young Essex would later develop into his own idea of a champion of Protestantism and the Anglican Church, more motivated by ideas of military than religious glory.

Of his behaviour at Cambridge, little is known, save that little provision was made for him in terms of clothing during his first year, with the precocious earl writing in Latin of the necessity of proper attire and plate to be dispatched (Burghley presumably having dropped the proverbial ball in attending to his charge's wardrobe). Immured at Cambridge with a new 'broad riding hat' and 'five pairs of shoes', Essex was quite safe from the scandal brewing at Court. In this he was lucky, given that it directly involved his mother.

3: An Elizabethan She-Wolf in London

A great deal has been written on Lettice Knollys-Devereux, despite the scanty evidence of her personality.[15] As first cousin (once removed) to Elizabeth, Lettice must have expected, and was granted, close proximity to queen and court; and the fact that her mother, Catherine Knollys, was a favourite attendant of Elizabeth can only have helped. Yet if there was one fault that can be justly laid at Queen Elizabeth's feet, it was jealousy, and it appears that Lettice did much to inspire it. In addition to being ten years younger than her sovereign, she was, according to the Spanish ambassador Diego de Silva, 'one of the best-looking ladies of the court'.[16] Portraits depict a pleasant-looking woman who shares the fashions started by the queen, as well as the red hair (though whether this was real or false is debatable). It is likely the broad similarities in the women's appearance that later resulted in rumours that Lettice bore a marked resemblance to Elizabeth and enjoyed the attentions she received in the latter part of the sixteenth century from those who spotted her travelling and mistook her for the queen. The Spanish ambassador was certainly unambivalent; he would later write, 'she is as proud as ever, [she] rides through Cheapside drawn by four milk-white steeds ... so that it might be supposed to be

---

[15] It is likely due to the scarce contemporary evidence that, despite her featuring heavily in material on Elizabeth, Essex, Leicester, and many other great figures of the period, this long-lived woman (she was born in 1543 and died in 1634, thus witnessing the reigns of Henry VIII, Mary I, Edward VI, Elizabeth I, James I, and Charles I) has only one devoted biography: the excellent *Elizabeth's Rival: The Tumultuous Tale of Lettice Knollys, Countess of Essex*.

[16] Hume, M. A. S. (Ed). 2013. *Calendar of Letters and State Papers Relating to English Affairs, Preserved Principally in the Archives of Simancas* (Cambridge: Cambridge University Press), p. 472.

the queen or some foreign prince or ambassador'.[17] Lettice, like many of her class, was accused of being proud and prone to haughtiness: characteristics which would only be exacerbated by Elizabeth's later treatment.

In the early part of Elizabeth's reign, Lettice had indeed been a favoured member of the royal court. She had even been allowed to marry in 1560, the marriage of her ladies being something which the queen was not quite as opposed to as legend holds (what bothered Elizabeth were marriages which she had not condoned, and which took place in secret). Following the marriage, Lettice continued to receive gifts from the queen, notably '13 yards of black velvet barred ... for a gown, £16.18.0' in 1564.[18] Her first husband was Walter Devereux, Viscount Hereford, and their marital home was Chartley Manor, a moated timber mansion. Little is known of their relationship, other than it seemed to cause no waves at court. Walter was something of a clothes horse, and so we might assume that they had fashion in common. It was at Chartley that she gave birth to two daughters, Penelope (in 1563) and Dorothy (in 1564), but she appears to have made return visits to court. She was certainly in London in 1565 when, pregnant with Robert, she indulged in an extramarital flirtation with the queen's great favourite, the earl of Leicester. Predictably, this infuriated the jealous Elizabeth, with Burghley (then still humble Sir William Cecil) having to smooth matters.[19] This seems to have quashed the budding affair – but only temporarily. Whether the brief affair was of a sexual nature is not known, but it is important to note that the game of courtly love, then in full tilt, was perfectly acceptable and did not require (in fact, it abjured) sex. Instead it relied on the male courtier fawning over his unattainable, often married, mistress,

---

[17] Everett Green, M. A. 1872. *Calendar of State Papers, Domestic Series, Elizabeth and James, Addenda, 1580-1625: Volume 1* (London: Longman), p. 137.
[18] Jenkins, E. 1961. *Elizabeth and Leicester* (London: Victor Gollancz), p. 124.
[19] Jenkins, *Elizabeth and Leicester*, p. 124-5.

and, rather symbolically, focussing his passion into his pen and spilling verses full of ardour and disappointment.

This game, which was to play so large a role in the relationship between the queen and Essex in later years, requires a little more attention. Whilst the male lover was expected to express passion – preferably genuine – for the unobtainable woman, she was expected to go no further than offering him favours, tokens, and romantic sighs. The whole thing was designed to be sexless, making it an ideal feature of Elizabethan court life, with Elizabeth herself often assuming the role of the mistress. Of course, in practice, it devolved into a political game, with the male seeking out females well placed politically, whether through male relatives or actual proximity to the queen's person. Occasionally, too, the romances became sexual, breaking the rules of the game. Yet sometimes those rules were adhered to, as difficult as it can be to understand the concept from the perspective of a modern, secular society in which love and sex are so frequently intertwined. Our willingness to recognise only those romances which became sexual later (and to read them backwards) or those which were nakedly political does the period a disservice.

Leicester certainly fit the mould of the Elizabethan courtier-lover. A son of the duke of Northumberland, who had lost his head after failing to establish his daughter-in-law, Lady Jane Grey, on the throne, he remains enigmatic. He was reported to be handsome, at least in his prime; he was a patron of the arts; an expert horseman (a boon for a man who held the post of the queen's master of horse); and an aesthete. Yet he was also sympathetic to Puritanism; a largely incompetent military leader; and of dubious popularity (though he counted amongst his friends a great many notables). He was, though, popular with the queen, and until his death their relationship resembled that of an old married couple: close, affectionate, and at times fraught with jealousies and minor rifts. If the young Essex was to achieve a close and quasi-romantic relationship with Elizabeth, it would lie in the shadow of the great love that existed between her and Leicester.

Following – or perhaps as a result of – the brief liaison with

Leicester, Lettice returned to Chartley, where two more sons followed Robert: Walter and the short-lived Francis. In late 1569 her husband provided royal service in helping suppress the Catholic rebellion of the northern earls (which aimed at freeing the recently-imprisoned Mary Queen of Scots) and in 1572 he was elevated to the earldom of Essex. The following year found him in Ireland, where he was to gain a reputation as a merciless butcher of the native people whom it had long been the English crown's intent to bring to subjection.[20] Elizabeth was quite happy to sponsor his colonial efforts in Clandeboye, but less forthcoming with financial support; the earl, as a result, sold off many of his English estates, leaving rather an impoverished title to his eldest son.

During the elder Essex's time in Ireland, his wife appears to have lived a merry life, indulging in hunting trips, notably (on at least two occasions) on the earl of Leicester's grounds at Kenilworth Castle. Whether they resumed their aborted relationship at this time is unknowable, but in light of later events it is likely that they rekindled at least a glimmer of courtly romance. If they did, Leicester was not faithful to her; during this period (and perhaps from as early as 1566) he was also engaged in an affair with the widowed Lady Douglas Sheffield, by whom he had a son, Robert (born in 1574) and with whom he very likely took part in some form of betrothal.

Her hunting trips notwithstanding, Lettice was certainly present at the famous July 1575 'princely pleasures' at Kenilworth, laid on by Leicester for the queen. At the climax of the pageantry – fireworks; interactive tableaux involving wild men; staged tableaux on the lake complete with Triton, Neptune, and dolphins; tilting at the quintain – Leicester betrayed a lack of interest in the married Lettice by offering to the queen the following words:

Vouchsafe, O comely Queene, yet longer to remaine,

---

[20] For a full account, see Heffernan, D. 2018. *Walter Devereux, First Earl of Essex, and the Colonization of North-East Ulster, 1573-6* (Dublin: Four Courts Press).

Or still to dwell amongst us here! O Queene commaunde againe

This Castle and the Knight, which keepes the same for you;

… Live here, good Queene, live here![21]

Here was the real objective of the earl, as it had been since his own wife had died (in circumstances that still defy definitive explanation) in 1560. Whatever went on with Lettice during the period of her marriage to Walter Devereux, it was Leicester's dearest ambition to make Elizabeth his wife. Flattered and gratified the queen undoubtedly was, but she had no intention of saying yes to Leicester or, it would transpire, to any man. She bid Kenilworth (and the high watermark of Elizabethan pageantry) farewell after nineteen days of revelry and, interestingly, travelled on to Chartley, where Lettice hosted her. Whether little Robert, then nine, saw or met with the queen on this occasion is unknown. He was, however, resident at the house, and under the tutelage of Richard Broughton, 'the collector of the earl's causes'.[22]

It was at the end of 1575 that Walter Devereux returned to his flirtatious wife, and, thanks to a portrait painted around this time, we have an impression of what she saw: a narrow-eyed but handsome man with dark hair and a wispy moustache, clad in black-and-gold armour. One hand is depicted resting on his helmet, which lies on a table beside him, signifying his respite from war; but the hand is stiff and awkwardly posed: a reminder, perhaps, that his military adventures had gone awry.

Nevertheless, the queen had named him her earl marshal of Ireland (he is, in fact, holding the baton of that office in the portrait) and he was back and ready to harass the Irish in the

[21] Laneham, R., Gascoigne, G. & Batchelder, J. D. 1825. *Kenilworth Festivities: Comprising Laneham's Description of the Pageantry, and Gascoigne's Masques, Represented Before Queen Elizabeth, at Kenilworth Castle Anno 1575; with Introductory Prefaces, Glossarial and Explanatory Notes. Illustrated with Several Engravings* (London: Merridew), p. 70.
[22] Devereux, *Lives and Letters*, p. 137.

autumn of 1576. As it would happen, he did not get the opportunity. He fell ill and died following a banquet given in his honour at Dublin, leaving Lettice a pretty, provenly-fertile widow. Before his body was returned for burial at his estate in Carmarthen, a post-mortem was held which found that he had died of dysentery: a not uncommon and frequently fatal ailment. This did not stop later scandal-mongers declaring that Lettice and Leicester had colluded in poisoning him. However, there is no reason to believe them. It is, though, possible to trace their foundation. Henry Sidney, the lord deputy (who was married to Leicester's sister, Mary), wrote to the queen's minister, Sir Francis Walsingham, that

hearing … as well before his death as after, that he died of poison, I thought good to examine the matter as far as I could learn … For, in truth, there was no appearance or cause of suspicion that could be gathered that he died of poison. For the manner of his disease was this: a flux took him on the Thursday at night, being the 30th of August last past, in his own house, where he had that day both supped and dined.

Adding to the later rumours, though, was Sidney's enigmatic assertion that

when he was opened it could not appear that any entrail within his body, at any time, had been infected with any poison. And yet I find a bruit there was that he was poisoned; and that arose by some words spoken by himself, and yet not originally at the first conceived of himself, as it is thought by the wisest here, and those that were continually ahout him; but one that was very near him at that time, and whom he entirely trusted, seeing him in extreme pain with flux and gripings in his belly, by reason of the same, said to him, By the mass, my lord, you are poisoned?[23]

---

[23] Knox, V. 1842. *Elegant Extracts, or Useful and Entertaining Passages, From the Best English Authors and Translations; Principally Designed for the Use of Young Persons Originally*

The post-mortem seems conclusive, as does the account Sidney gives of the elder Essex succumbing to dysentery in his last days. It was common enough that rumours of poison would follow the deaths of noble figures; the accusations against Lettice and Leicester, however, appear to have been embroidered out of a mangled version of Sidney's report of Devereux having had implanted in his mind the idea of poison by 'one that was very near to him'. It referred, of course, to a servant who gave voice to the perennial cry of poisoning. Nevertheless, Catholic polemicists would later have a field day claiming that the dead man's wife and her lover had managed to pay one of his entourage to murder him.

With Walter Devereux's death, a multitude of Irish people might justly have given thanks, and Lettice found herself free to marry again. As her son, now the 2nd earl of Essex, was embarking on his university education, her thoughts certainly turned to wedding bells. So too did the queen's.

***

Elizabeth I had voiced her intentions with regard to marriage as early as 1559. Speaking to the House of Commons, she declared

and, in the end, this shall be for me sufficient, that a marble stone shall declare that a queen, having reigned such a time, lived and died a virgin.[24]

The House of Commons did not listen. Neither did the queen's ministers. Neither did the princes of Europe. It was, after all, the first duty of a monarch to secure the succession. Adeptly realising that speculation about – and demands for –

compiled by the Rev. V. K. A, a New Edition Prepared by J. G. Percival, Volume 3 (Boston: Benjamin B. Mussey), p. 63.
[24] Bell, I. 2016. Elizabeth I: The Voice of a Monarch (New York: Palgrave Macmillan), p. 63.

her marriage would continue regardless, Elizabeth decided to gain maximum political capital from the situation, coyly acknowledging that though a single life was her preference, she might well be induced to marry. By 1579, however, the bloom was, if not entirely off the rose, decidedly faded. Playing the marriage market, as she had done expertly for years, was giving increasingly diminishing returns. Still, it had to be played whilst it could, and one French prince was still willing to press his suit.

The duke of Anjou was not Elizabeth's type. She liked her men athletic and handsome; he was slightly bent due to a curved spine and scarred facially by smallpox. He was, further, over twenty years her junior, and the prospect of an age gap had given the queen cause for demurral in marriage matters in the past. Indeed, when Anjou had first been mooted in 1572, she had written of 'the absurdity that the general opinion of the world might grow to concerning this our choice'.[25] She was, therefore, sensitive to the views her society held of an older woman embarking on a relationship with a younger man. Nevertheless, with the menopause approaching, the Anjou match represented her last chance. The moment her childbearing years were behind her, she cannot have helped but know, her reign would be winding down and her country would be looking elsewhere for the future security of the realm.

Elizabeth threw herself into the long-distance courtship, and Anjou sent over a charming representative, Jean de Simier, who quickly managed to coax out the queen's flirtatious nature. One man who was not amused by the unfolding proxy romance was the earl of Leicester. In a reverse of the situation in 1565, Leicester, after flirting with the idea, came out decidedly against the match, and accordingly conceived a hatred for Simier. He gave open voice to his disapproval of the young man the queen was had taken to affectionately calling her 'ape', and his disgruntlement was echoed by the more xenophobic of her subjects. Elizabeth openly paraded her affinity with Anjou's proxy, spending hours each day with him and, scandalously,

[25] Marcus, L., Mueller, J. & Rose, M. B. (Eds.) 2000. *Elizabeth I: Collected Works* (Chicago: University of Chicago Press), p. 207.

visiting him when he was semi-dressed in his bedchamber. The French ambassador, an obvious advocate of the Anjou match, knew exactly what to say, waxing lyrical that the queen had 'become more beautiful and bonny than she was fifteen years ago' thanks to the likelihood of marriage.[26]

Although his nose might have been put of joint by the queen's last tentative dance around the altar, Leicester had his own secret to keep. On the 21st of September 1578, he had married Lettice Knollys at Wanstead Hall in Essex. Quite why he did so remains a subject for debate, with the possibility of her pregnancy suggested by the loose gown she wore (although Leicester had shown no such interest in securing legal validity for the match with the mother of his previous bastard). It is equally possible that the earl, by now aging, growing portly, and hoping for legitimate heirs, recognised in the handsome Essex, who would become his stepson, a short-term means of distracting the queen's eye from his other rivals at court, in much the same way courtiers had paraded loyal female relatives before Henry VIII in a bid to keep the monarch's ear. Certainly, Essex would become his protégé, trained up in the arts of the royal favourite. This was a role the queen had revolutionised. Favourites had long been a part of monarchical systems, but the word itself was loaded with negativity: it was a synonym for lovers, confidants, sycophants, flatterers; favourites were symptomatic of corruption at the highest levels. As a female ruler outnumbered by male courtiers, Elizabeth made favouritism an integral path to patronage, professionalising it and making it a key part of her domestic polity – albeit not without attendant anxiety on the part of her people.

At any rate, the marriage was kept secret, although it seemed to be an open one at court, with the queen kept in ignorance (or, perhaps, hearing vague rumours and hoping it was only the kind of deniable faux-marriage such as her favourite had undertaken with Lady Douglas Sheffield). It was, however, brought directly to her attention by Simier, who returned Leicester's dislike with

---

[26] Whitelock, A. 2013. *Elizabeth's Bedfellows: An Intimate History of the Queen's Court* (London: Bloomsbury), p. 176.

alacrity. The news threw Elizabeth into an almighty Tudor tantrum, which comprised three days of tears and recriminations at her great favourite's falsity, and accusations of bigamy thrown at him. It was partly as a result of it that she allowed Anjou to cross the channel on August the 17th, 1579, whereupon he set about wooing her in person. Both Lettice and Leicester were banished from court, the latter temporarily and the former for the rest of the queen's life. Against Lettice the queen is said to have hurled the insult of 'she-wolf' – a term that, in Ancient Rome, had come to be a byword for the lowest of prostitutes: the insatiable and predatory man-eater.[27] Her pettiness is telling. Throughout Elizabeth's life, one of her less attractive traits was that of vindictive jealousy, and it is reasonable to suppose that her later attachment to Lettice's son was partially inspired by a desire to get one over on his mother.

By all accounts Elizabeth was quite taken with the duke of Anjou, whose appearance belied a charismatic personality. The pair, despite the difference in age, became inseparable, likely helped by the fact that, although he was a Catholic and brother to the French king, Anjou was sympathetic to French Protestantism. Leicester, however, remained opposed, and so did a considerable number of English people. Published in 1579, political amateur John Stubbs' *The Discoverie of a Gaping Gulf Whereinto England is Like to Be Swallowed By An Other French Marriage* voiced their opinions, vituperatively attacking Anjou's perceived faults (and those of his family). Furious, the queen insisted that Stubbs be hanged, but the grand jury refused to indict him, and she had to be satisfied with his losing a hand. In the febrile atmosphere, and despite Stubbs' punishment and the ban of his book, dissent remained. As Simier astutely noted, Leicester was an active agent in fomenting it, the cloud of disfavour which hung over him

---

[27] See Mazzoni, C. 2010. *She-Wolf: The Story of a Roman Icon* (Cambridge: Cambridge University Press), p. 114. Anna Whitelock notes that 'she-wolf' was a 'byword for lewdness' and that the term was applied to Elizabeth herself: Whitelock, *Elizabeth's Bedfellows*, p. 189.

notwithstanding.

Not were Leicester and the unfortunate Stubbs alone in their indictments of the proposed Anjou match. Sir Henry Sidney's son, Philip, complained bitterly about the alliance in an open letter which circulated at court. Like Stubbs, Sidney launched an attack on the French, particularly its royals, and the country itself, which he personified as a sick man. Anjou was French, lamented Sidney, 'and desiring to make France great; your Majesty English and desiring nothing less than that France should not grow great'.[28] This was to become significant in later years; Essex has often been accused of aping Sidney throughout his career, but the young earl was never to become a religious radical (much to some of his supporters' disappointment) and he was, moreover, certainly never to evince Sidney's anti-Gallic biases.

Although a draft marriage treaty was drawn up and a medical examination undertaken to prove her fertility, the queen did not take Anjou as her husband. The putative marriage hung in suspended animation until, in 1581, the Dutch revolt in the Netherlands against imperial Spain caused the project to be resurrected. More founded on policy than affection this time, it was again to come to nothing. Elizabeth wisely continued to string Anjou along until his final departure for the continent in 1582. The courtship had simply fizzled out, as all of those preceding it had. Rather than a wife, he left England with a proverbial golden handshake; a loan of £30, 000 was made in September 1581 for the raising of a private army, with a further £60, 000 pledged prior to his departure the following February.[29] Famously, the queen penned a poem in commemoration:

[28] Sidney, R. 15801 [1862]. 'Sir Philip Sidney to Queen Elizabeth, anno 1580, dissuading her from marrying the duke of Anjou' in H. R. Fox Bourne (Ed.) *A Memoir of Sir Philip Sidney* (London: Chapman and Hall), p. 257.

[29] Hammer, P. E. J. 2003. *Elizabeth's Wars: War, Government, and Society in Tudor England, 1544-1604* (London: Palgrave Macmillan), p. 112.

I grieve and dare not show my discontent,
I love and yet am forced to seem to hate,
I do, yet dare not say I ever meant,
I seem stark mute but inwardly do prate.
I am and not, I freeze and yet am burned,
Since from myself another self I turned.

My care is like my shadow in the sun,
Follows me flying, flies when I pursue it,
Stands and lies by me, doth what I have done.
His too familiar care doth make me rue it.
No means I find to rid him from my breast,
Till by the end of things it be supprest.

Some gentler passion slide into my mind,
For I am soft and made of melting snow;
Or be more cruel, love, and so be kind.
Let me or float or sink, be high or low.
Or let me live with some more sweet content,
Or die and so forget what love ere meant.[30]

The text has been variously read as a lover's lament and a reflection on both love and Anjou. It is not. It is, rather, a recognition that with Anjou went the policy of the first twenty-three years of her reign. Thus the poem does not necessarily offer a window into the mind of a rueful woman; it presents a crisis of queenship. In the first stanza, Elizabeth meditates on the dual nature of her monarchy: the public versus the private personas it requires. From her role as a putative bride to be won – the role she had played with consummate skill – she would undoubtedly have to turn. Instead, she recognises, she must pursue a new course, losing the joys and pleasures she had found in the old. The second stanza, with its direct male

---

[30] Elizabeth I. 2004 [c1581]. 'Poem 6' in S. W. May (Ed.) *Queen Elizabeth I: Selected Works* (New York: Washington Square Press), p. 12.

references, does not speak of Anjou in particular; the 'him' is every suitor, from Philip of Spain in the early days through Eric of Sweden, the earl of Arran, Charles IX, and several more. He is marriage: the hopeful bridegroom who would never be. In the final stanza, the conjunction 'or' charts out the potential futures that a single, non-marriageable, heirless queen might expect.

Leicester had become young Essex's stepfather, and Elizabeth remained single, with the weapon of marriage no longer in her armoury when she battled in the arena of European politics. It was not that she lamented the finality of a definite lack of husband and children – there is no evidence that she had ever truly wanted either – but she very much sorrowed at the loss of the flattering attentions her various courtships had brought. There were, however, less personal considerations. Not only would her people have to accept that she would never provide them with an heir of her body, but she would have to consider the realm's future and her place in it, carving out a political role other than the prospective bride. For the sake of remaining relevant, she would have to refashion herself for an ever-shifting political scene. Essex, who had shown such gaucheness when a green arriviste, would be intimately bound up in that reinvention.

4: Elizabethan Self-Fashioning

Unlike her famously belligerent father, Queen Elizabeth hated war. Not only did she have a naturally irenic disposition, but she was parsimonious, and war was an expensive business. More pressingly, the theatre of war was a masculine one, and one on which she could only appear as a disembodied voice. Nevertheless, she had deployed troops abroad in the past. In 1560 the Treaty of Berwick, made between the queen and the Scottish rebels calling themselves the Lords of the Congregation, had caused English troops to join with the Scots in armed resistance to the regent of Scotland, Mary of Guise, and her French troops. On that occasion, the rebels had been triumphant, mainly due to Mary's death in June of the same year.

The Scottish campaign was to prove an anomaly, and one to which the queen only gave reluctant assent. She sanctioned the brief occupation of Le Havre from October 1562 to June 1563, hoping to exchange the port for Calais, but this venture ended in failure when her erstwhile Huguenot allies joined forces with French Catholics to dislodge the English. Thereafter, throughout the 1560s and 70s, she was urged by her more Puritanical ministers to take a more active role in dispatching troops to assist the Protestant Dutch in their war against their Spanish Catholic overlords. Elizabeth, however, preferred less aggressively militant tactics, especially during those years in which she sought to maintain a place on the international marriage market (which was studded with Catholic princes). With Anjou's final departure in 1582, her role as a prudent, eternal, and stalwart defender of European Protestantism beckoned – whether she welcomed it or not. In the early 1580s, the ineluctable unfolding of events would write the script of the newly post-menopausal queen for her, and a veritable army of poets, painters, and lyricists would help.[31]

Even defensive queens need knights, and wars need their heroes. Despite his start at court, young Essex looked ideal to be moulded into one of them. His education at Cambridge had proceeded well, unencumbered by the disfavour into which his mother had fallen or the arrival of a stepfather. He had, further, made friends there. In addition to the crowd of petitioners who could seldom resist currying favour with an earl had been a Welshman about ten years older than Essex, Gelli Meyrick. The association of the Devereux family with Wales was a long one, Essex's great-grandfather having been appointed a member of the council of Wales in August 1513 (and, it will be recalled, Essex's father had been buried on the family estate in Carmarthen) under the young Henry VIII. The Tudors, of course, boasted their own Welsh descent, which led Lodowick Lloyd to praise the queen as the Welsh Sydanen.[32] As the sixteenth century wore on, the formation of a pan-British identity would become a hot topic, with Elizabeth and Essex at the forefront.

As Elizabeth mourned the loss of her marriageable identity and looked towards encroaching menopause, her future favourite completed his studies. He appears to have been an able scholar, achieving his MA in July 1581 at the ripe old age of fifteen. Thereafter he retired to his family estate in Llanfydd (or Lamphey) in Pembrokeshire, where the greatest issue facing him was his spending habits. In response to criticism from Burghley, he wrote on the 13th of December 1582,

---

[31] We do not know exactly when Elizabeth dealt with the menopause. She was judged fertile during the Anjou marriage negotiations. Although childbirth was only one of many reasons listed by the earl of Sussex for the match, it seems reasonable to suppose that her fertility ended between 1580 and 1584, perhaps coinciding with the revised treaty between England and France in which marriage was not mentioned.
[32] See Schwyzer, P. and Maley, W. 2016. *Shakespeare and Wales: From the Marches to the Assembly* (London: Routledge), p. 24.

I hope your lordship in courtesy will pardon my youth, if I have, through want of experience, in some sort passed the bounds of frugality. I cannot but embrace with duty your lordship's good counsel, whose love I have effectually proved, and of whose care of my well doings I am thoroughly persuaded.[33]

This was typical stuff, but he was correct in pointing out both his youthful folly and his continual proof of duty (Cecil being a stickler for learning). It might or might not have indicated an inherently spendthrift nature; it should be noted, however, that lavish spending was a prerequisite for Elizabethan courtiers – even aspiring ones. Success at court depended on the ostentatious display of wealth, and although he probably did not know it, the young Essex was setting out his stall early. The frequent attribution of his future financial woes to his youthful spending does, though, provide us with an issue that has pervaded decades if not centuries of study.

The earl's biographers have often looked for evidence of his later attitudes and behaviours in his younger years, and in a way that is frequently problematic. One might consider, for example, the claim made early in Robert Lacey's biography that Essex and his sisters, 'having witnessed no warmth or affection in either of their parents … were emotional cripples'.[34] It is true that Penelope, by 1581 a court beauty, had been cynically married off to Robert Rich, 3rd Baron Rich. Yet this kind of arranged marriage was routine, and it was generally hoped that love might develop following the marriage. Dorothy Devereux had a more colourful first marriage, eloping in July 1583 with Sir Thomas Perrot and embarking on a clandestine wedding ceremony complete with a scandalised vicar who found his church broken into by the couple and an interloping minister.

---

[33] Essex, 1827 [1582]. 'Letter CCXIII: The earl of Essex to Lord Burghley upon his lordship's charging him with want of frugality' in E. Angleterre (Ed.) *Original Letters Illustrative of English History* (London: Bentley and Harding), pp. 80-1.
[34] Lacey, *Essex*, p. 23.

These marriages do not tell us anything about Essex's attitudes towards love and marriage, and if he was later to 'treat marriage as a social obligation that placed him under no obligation to the woman who gave up her life for him', that is because, to the aristocratic male courtier, that is sadly what it was.[35] Lettice might be accused of many things, but being an unloving mother is not one of them. Rather, she sprang from a clan which prized family. Essex would, until very near his death, share her clannish views. It is no fairer to say that his mother made him an emotional cripple than it is to say that his childhood spending foreshadowed his later indebtedness. The young Essex found himself constantly out of pocket simply because his father had left him one of the most impoverished earldoms in the kingdom and his station in life demanded significant financial outlays.

Essex continued to spend beyond his means – over £40 went on two suits of clothes for Penelope's wedding – and had cause for further expensive celebration when his mother produced Leicester's only legitimate heir, Robert Lord Denbigh, born on the 6th of June 1581. It was, in fact, partly due to the young earl's spending that he had been removed from Cambridge and sent to Llanfydd; that move not quite curbing him, he was eventually sent to spend Christmas with his grandfather, Sir Francis Knollys, *en route* to service with the earl of Huntingdon at York (it being common for young men to be trained in the households of other nobles). With him went Gelli Meyrick, the Welshman who had become his steward. The great affairs of state probably impacted little on Llanfydd and made limited waves at York, the de facto capital of the north.

As the queen considered her new position on the world stage, however, they certainly impacted on her. In 1582 her quondam fiancé Anjou arrived in the Netherlands where, as a Frenchman, it was his duty to resist the Spanish empire. Between May and August, the Protestant Robert Browne, a church separatist and kinsman of Burghley, arrived in Middleburg with his followers, augmenting the idea that resistance to Catholic Spain had English sympathies. Gradually, things in Europe were heating

---

[35] *Ibid.*

up, and the Spanish Netherlands looked set to become a theatre of war that England could not help but tread.

Spain had long been a bête noire to England, and vice versa. The empire, ruled by the fanatical Philip II (Elizabeth's former brother-in-law and one-time suitor) had been long been reaching across Europe and the Americas, and, following the death of King Henry in January 1580 the neighbouring kingdom of Portugal had been added to the emperor's already laden crown. Not everyone in Portugal was happy about this.

At the end of June 1582, a handsome, moustachioed man in his fifties stepped ashore in England. His accent and the cut of his clothes were unmistakeably foreign, and he was bent on seeing the queen, which, over the course of his visit – which lasted into July – he was to do. Dom António, Prior of Crato, was a charismatic gallant. A grandson of Manuel I of Portugal and an illegitimate son of the dead Prince Louis of Beja, António was determined to resist Philip's claim to the Portuguese throne. This goal was shared by Burghley and Elizabeth's spymaster, Sir Francis Walsingham. Although proclaimed king in Santarém (and thereafter cheekily referred to as the king of Portugal in English dispatches), he became embroiled in a bloody war of succession, and his mission in England was to win Queen Elizabeth to his cause, as he had managed with Catherine de Medici in France (securing a fleet manned by Portuguese exiles, and French and English enterprisers, which was defeated in the battle of Ponta Delgada prior to his visit.

Elizabeth was sympathetic to the pretender, but not quite ready to assume the role of a warrior queen. She did, however, offer limited aid in the form of allowing him to issue letters of marque to English privateers. This had the effect of partially legitimising what had previously been English piracy, easily deniable by the queen as the acts of her renegade subjects.[36] Thereafter, she backpedalled, and an almost comic period of court wrangling involving the Spanish ambassador attempting

---

[36] Quinn, D. B. 1979. *England and the Azores, 1581-2: Three Letters* (Coimbra: Revista da Universidade de Coimbra), p. 209

to proceed against 'pirates' in England's courts followed. Yet the notional peace that existed between England and Spain was inevitably eroded. Dom António would quixotically seek Portugal's crown, with occasional English support, for the rest of the decade, and his cause would be helped in 1589 by Francis Drake, John Norris, and a bright-eyed and adventure-seeking earl of Essex.

Outright war with Spain was not inevitable, but it was likely. In January 1583, Anjou attacked Antwerp, but he was roundly humiliated in what became known as the French Fury. He died at twenty-nine on the 10th of June the following year.[37] If Elizabeth was saddened by his death – and the fact that she had continued to correspond with him after 1581 and immediately went into mourning on learning of his death suggest she was – she did not take up her pen in verse. It did allow her, however, to further build solidarity with Anjou's brother, Henry III (a former suitor) and his successor to the dukedom (and new heir presumptive to the French throne), the future Henry IV.[38] Anjou's disappearance from the scene did not, though, mark the end of Elizabeth's courtly love affairs. Instead it represented a new stage to them. Henceforward, her chaste romances would be grounded in domestic polity; but they would be no less

---

[37] There is some dubiety about the date of the duke's death. Loades and Hammer claim that he died in May 1584, which is supported by the Salisbury papers. These papers have, however, been emended. Sutherland opts for the 10th of June, identifying the cause of confusion as the old-style dating. Mack P. Holt provides definitive proof in the form of an eyewitness account of the death dated as the 10th of June. See Holt, M. P. 2002. *The Duke of Anjou and the Politique Struggle during the Wars of Religion* (Cambridge: Cambridge University Press), p. 208; Loades, D. 2009. *The Making of the Elizabethan Navy, 1540-1590: From the Solent to the Armada* (London: Boydell Press), p. 172; Hammer, *Elizabeth's Wars*, p. 112; Sutherland, N. M. 2002. *Henry IV of France and the Politics of Religion: 1572 - 1596, Volume 1* (Bristol: Elm Bank), p. 65.
[38] Paranque, E. 2018. *Elizabeth I of England Through Valois Eyes: Power, Representation, and Diplomacy in the Reign of the Queen, 1558--1588* (London: Palgrave Macmillan), p. 9.

romances for that.

Tensions abroad would only increase with the assassination William of Orange, the great hero of European Protestantism, by a Burgundian Catholic in 1584. It was therefore in a world of strained Anglo-Spanish relations and turmoil in the Netherlands that Essex was to return to court in 1585. He had left York in late 1583 and become a stalking horse for his stepfather, Leicester presumably grooming the young man as a placeholder favourite until his own heir, little Robert, could come of age. Essex and Leicester spent a great deal of time in each other's company during the summer of 1584; however, the revelry of travel did not last. In July news arrived that the infant Robert had died.at Wanstead. Leicester had lost his only legitimate heir (and, as he suspected, any chance of continuing the Dudley line) and Essex had lost a half-brother. The former wrote to the queen's vice-chamberlain and the man known to be the queen's vice-favourite, Christopher Hatton,

I do most heartily thank you for your careful and most godly advice at this time. Your good friendship never wanteth. I must confess I have received many afflictions within these few years, but not a greater, next her Majesty's displeasure: and, if it pleased God, I would the sacrifice of this poor innocent might satisfy; I mean not towards God … but for the world. The afflictions I have suffered may satisfy such as are offended, at least appease their long hard conceits: if not, yet I know there is a blessing for such as suffer; and so is there for those that be merciful.[39]

We need not doubt Leicester's grief, but his letter, with its somewhat on-the-nose 'next to her majesty's displeasure' indicates that he had not lost his political acumen, and that it, in turn, had not lost its primacy in his thoughts. Without an heir,

[39] Leicester. 1847 [1584]. 'The earl of Leicester to Sir Christopher Hatton' in N. H. Nicolas (Ed.) *Memoirs of the life and times of sir Christopher Hatton, including his correspondence with the queen and other distinguished persons* (London: Richard Bentley), p. 382.

his hopes of continuing to dominate the queen's affections rested solely on having a well-favoured and loyal young man to offset the new crop of courtiers – notably Sir Walter Raleigh, who had arrived in 1581.

Essex, however, was not quite willing to be touted by a Pandarus-like stepfather – not, at least, at first. After his stepbrother's death, he visited York and Chartley before returning to Llanfydd, mulling over his future role: that of a country-based earl or that encouraged by Leicester and Lettice – the grasping courtier. The former meant relative political obscurity. The latter promised reward, riches, and excitement. Essex was yet a poor and indebted young man, and the queen had in her gift all the great offices – and perks – of state. So too, though, did it offer dangers. Political intrigue was unavoidable in the life of a courtier, but a more invidious threat was soon made manifest: the prospect of becoming a figure of vituperation, slander, and opprobrium.

In 1584 a text which did just that for Leicester gained widespread currency and a considerable readership, circulating as it did in both printed and manuscript form. *The Copy of a Letter Written by a Master of Art of Cambridge to His Friend in London*, commonly titled *Leicester's Commonwealth* was responsible for resurrecting claims that Essex's father had been poisoned and pointing the finger directly at his stepfather. Framed as a letter ostensibly written by an anonymous scholar at Cambridge, it presented the great favourite as a rapacious murderer, who, having killed his first wife, had been behind a number of high-profile murders. Efforts were made to destroy all extant printed copies, but the handwritten manuscripts continued to be passed around. What Essex made of it is unknown, but as Paul E. J. Hammer contends, it probably strengthened the bond between stepfather and stepson.[40] If this seems counterintuitive, it should be noted that such attacks – anonymous, insulting, and scurrilous – were not just attacks on

---

[40] Hammer, P. E. J. 1999. *The Polarisation of Elizabethan Politics: The Political Career of Robert Devereux, 2nd Earl of Essex, 1585-1597* (Cambridge: Cambridge University Press), p. 37.

individuals, but an affront to those whose stations required them to uphold the existing social order.

It was thus in late 1585 that the twenty-year-old Essex reappeared at court, mentored, preened, and peacocked by his stepfather. He had chosen his role, and it was assuredly not that of the quiet country magnate.

Much has been written about the young earl's allegedly vertiginous rise (indeed, even the date of his return suffers from the usual dating complexities). Essex's biographer, Robert Lacey, is unequivocal:

He succeeded so brilliantly not through any greater wisdom or effort or skill but simply through the power which his personal attractions exercised over one elderly, vain, and capricious woman ... He was only seventeen [sic] when he first began seriously to attend to the work, ceremony and play that made up the daily routine of the royal palace of Whitehall, but already the ladies of the court found his charms irresistible.[41]

This reading is rather unfair on both Essex and Elizabeth. In his study of Essex's role in Elizabethan politics, Hammer is more restrained, noting that 'initially, Essex made little impact at court ... [He] could hardly have picked a worse time to enter upon the political stage ... the court was lost amid the frenzy and diplomacy of martial preparations' due to the coming war with Spain.[42]

The difference in opinions lies, probably, in the disagreement in the dating of Essex's return. The reality of his success (or lack of it) as an adult courtier probably lies somewhere in the middle, and it is worth noting that both historians elide the complexity of what the royal court was. When Essex arrived at the loose and constantly-shifting assemblage of household officers, domestic staff, politicians, administrators, noble guests and attendants, and hangers on, it was not a definite joining of a stable institution. In heeding his mother and stepfather's

---

[41] Lacey, *Essex*, p. 24.
[42] Hammer, *The Polarisation of Elizabethan Politics*, p. 37.

advice and attending on the queen, he was not necessarily making a permanent decision, but rather tasting courtly life. It is unlikely that he did so only out of a desire to make money (as Lacey would have it); indeed, he was actually to spend at least £4000 in his next adventure. Instead his decision to experience the court as an adult was predicated on a combination of reasons, from war fever and maternal encouragement to a chance to flaunt a variety of new clothes (making his grandfather Knollys grumble) and was at any rate reversible.

Tall, slim, and handsome, he undoubtedly made a favourable physical impression on his queen. With his sense of fashion and his swept-back auburn hair, he likely aroused interest other than the political amongst the female (and probably some male) attendees of the court. His problem was that political issues were currently at the forefront of court life and as a new arrival he had no real role in them. His reflection later that 'he had … few friends' is best read as his having had little political influence rather than as a comment on his popularity or personal charm.[43] Given that he wrote the comment later, it is even possible that he was attempting to play up the magnitude of his rise to power and influence. At any rate, the queen the fresh-faced earl had glimpsed during the awkward 1577-8 Christmas debut was gone. In her place was a new Elizabeth, and this one was an altogether different animal.

The queen had been compared to the moon goddess Diana – the perpetual virgin, innocent and pure – for some years. In 1575, Leicester had staged a dramatic interlude at Kenilworth featuring the goddess, albeit her arguments were trounced by the arguments of the married Juno. Then, the goal had been to indicate to Elizabeth the virtues of marrying – and marrying Leicester.[44] In 1578, in St Thomas's churchyard in Norwich, she was first openly celebrated as the Virgin Queen; then, Elizabeth was intimately involved in the festivities, which saw a maid dressed as Diana handing her a bow and arrows. According to

---

[43] Essex. 1598. *An Apologie of the Earle of Essex* (GB 1953 BTMS/23).

[44] Laneham, Gascoigne, & Batchelder, *Kenilworth Festivities*, p. 31.

Bernard Garter's account, 'the virgin's state Diana did praise'.[45] What joined these allusions was the fact that, at the time of their production, Elizabeth's virginity was placed in a political context in which she might yet yield it. She was not Diana herself, but, in turn, supposed to ignore Diana or subject to praise *by* her. With Monsieur Anjou's departure, she had become more intimately linked with the goddess – she had, in effect, become a living Diana, and it was this ethereal creature to whom Essex was expected to pay court.

Gallons of scholarly ink have been spilled on the artistic efforts spent on turning Elizabeth into Diana (and her proxies Artemis, Selene, and Cynthia). Virtually all studies have focussed on the fetishization of the queen's virginity, especially those which consider the visual images that show the queen holding a sieve (a common symbol of vestal purity), which cropped up with frequency between 1578 and 1583.[46] Nor have critics been slow to point out the so-called 'mask of youth' which was used by the queen (and her attendants) in order to present her to the world as a painted, unchanging icon, the better to curb tongues that wagged endlessly about who would succeed following a visibly ageing woman's inevitable death.[47] Less attention has been given to the more militant aspects of Diana. The goddess was a keen huntress, vengeful, and willing to punish perceived injustice (counting amongst her victims the peeping Actaeon, the proud Niobe, the boastful Adonis, and the thieving Agamemnon). She did not abjure the company of men; indeed, in Endymion, 'whose love of [her] was often interpreted as a as an … allegory for divine inspiration' lay the model for a sexless but loving relationship.[48] The other virginal goddess

---

[45] Archer, J. E., Goldring, E. & Knight, S. 2007. *The Progresses, Pageants, and Entertainments of Queen Elizabeth I* (Oxford: Oxford University Press), p. 139.

[46] Doran, S. 2002. *Monarchy and Matrimony* (London: Routledge), p. 171.

[47] See Whitelock, *Elizabeth's Bedfellows*, pp. 301-3.

[48] Berry, P. 2004. *Of Chastity and Power: Elizabethan Literature and the Unmarried Queen* (London: Routledge), p. 47.

often associated with Elizabeth, Astraea, was likewise a proponent of just causes. In his acrostic verses directly comparing the queen to Astraea, *Hymns to Astraea* (1599), John Davies is explicit:

> By love she rules more then [than] by law,
> Even her great mercy breedeth awe;
> This is her sword and sceptre:
> Herewith she hearts did ever draw,
> And this guard ever kept her.[49]

Here, then, is something more than the divine virgin scholars have long identified. Whether she intended it or not, Elizabeth was moving towards a role in Europe which was not simply that of an eternally youthful and chaste queen, but a bow- and sword-bearing goddess ready to right wrongs.

This, at least, was the Elizabeth who held sway at the English court and was projected across the world as the realm's queen. It is important, however, to note here that it was an image that did not, as is often assumed, form a cult which swept up the people of England in blind admiration. On the contrary, few outside of the London and summer progress circuit would ever see the defensive new virgin goddess, and instead had to rely on invocations of her name in civic courtrooms and municipal areas. On the 1st of April 1585, a labourer from Kent named Jeremy Vanhill was sentenced to hang for colourfully stating, 'shite upon your queen, I would she were dead that I might shit on her face'. In 1584 Peter Moyes declared the queen a 'rascal' and in 1577 the mayor of Doncaster had reported speeches against her so vile he was frightened of repeating them.[50]

---

[49] Davies, J. 1599. 'Of her Justice' in F. A. Yates (Ed.) *Astraea: The Imperial Theme in the Sixteenth Century* (London: Routledge & Kegan Paul), p. 68.

[50] The preceding cases of slanderous speeches made against Elizabeth are drawn from David Cressy's excellent 2010 book *Dangerous Talk: Scandalous, Seditious, and Treasonable Speech in Pre-Modern England* (Oxford: Oxford University Press), pp. 76-7.

Elizabeth might have frequently predicated her rule on the mutual love that existed between her and people, but the truth was that, then as now, there were those perfectly willing to flout authority. The role of the people, who were fickle, obstreperous, and potentially dangerous, was one quite different from the role of the court and its multitude of politicos. Essex and the queen would, in time, test the loyalties of both.

Essex, when he arrived at a court readying itself for a just war against an aggressive, imperialist, Catholic Spain, found at its head a queen readying herself for the role of the virtuous protectress of the true faith. If he wished to succeed, he would have to play Endymion, transforming himself into a knight of chivalry worthy of such a creature's divine love.

5: The Pursuit of Fame

The fleet of English ships cut through the choppy waves of the English Channel, or the Narrow Sea, as it was then called. It was December 1585 and the queen of England had given the first indication in decades that she really was prepared to go to war in defence of Protestantism. Prevarication, promises, and avoidance had availed her nothing. Typically, it had been framed as a defensive war, never even declared outright by Elizabeth. That mattered little to the men cocooned in the timber frames of the battleships. For the first time since the minor invasion of Scotland, made at the invitation of a clutch of Scottish rebels, and the failure of Le Havre, England's fighting men were sanctioned to set foot on foreign soil and prove themselves soldiers equal to the armies of Spain. Amongst them were Elizabeth's favourite, the earl of Leicester, given command of the army, and his stepson, Essex.

It was a war begun not with a bang but with a series of whimpers. The queen's long-term policy of official neutrality in European conflicts – often buttressed by unofficial financial aid to Protestant powers and a blind eye and expectant cap turned to English pirates – had begun to slip with her official sanction of some English harrying of Spanish ships. Throughout the Anjou affair, she had been engaged in high-level diplomacy, encouraging friendship with France to counterbalance the dominance of Spain, but careful lest the French grow too powerful. The assassination of William of Orange, long seen as Protestant Europe's blue-eyed boy, had left a space for a figurehead to stand against the Catholic empire. The Dutch rebels wanted Elizabeth; in fact, between May and June 1585 they pressed her to accept sovereignty of the Protestant United Provinces – in effect asking her to invade in support of their resistance, with the prize being her suzerainty over them and their lands. She was uninterested. The queen had never been covetous of other realms, preferring to focus the more militaristic and bloody aspects of early modern governance on territories she viewed as being rightly owned by the English crown (Ireland and Calais, for example). Yet the problem remained that for her to stand with rebels, even just as a sponsor and supporter, meant supporting a group which opposed their sovereign lord, King Philip. The decision to go to war would not be an easy one.

Complicating matters was the makeup of the English government, and chiefly of the privy council, its executive arm and administrative heart (though not, it should be stressed, the sole locus of political debate). Essentially, the country had long been ruled by a small, privileged Protestant coterie, with Elizabeth as its chief. She had learned from the ponderous council of sister to keep her band of male advisers small. Even so, there were varying shades of fervency amongst the group. The queen was a moderate, who inclined towards frugality, conservatism, and low-key interference. On her council, however, men like Walsingham and Leicester were in favour of active intervention in the name of religion, and Burghley proved to be as noncommittal on the issue as his mistress habitually was. Against the weaker voices of the non-interventionists, the interventionists' counsel won out.

With his stepfather a key proponent of military engagement, it is unsurprising that Essex was included in the campaign to the Netherlands. He, of course, was not a member of the council, which numbered only nineteen men.[51] It might even be, as Hammer suggests, that he joined the court due to the possibility of anti-Catholic military action; his father had been a staunch Protestant, and in his boyhood he had had as a companion Gabriel Montgomery, son of the exiled Huguenot count of Montgomery. In the earl of Leicester, further, he had an ultra-Protestant mentor. However, given his later career, it is more likely that Essex was motivated by chivalric goals – he wanted to be a hero – rather than religion. Further, given Leicester's clout in war matters, it is difficult to see that Essex's attending on the queen would be necessary in securing him a junior military position. Following the Treaty of Nonsuch in August,

---

[51] Haigh, C. 2014. *Elizabeth I* (London: Routledge), p. 84.

his stepfather had been widely accepted as the man to lead any campaign; and even after the provisions of the Treaty (which committed England to financial and military aid to the Dutch), the queen hoped that war could be avoided. It is clear that Leicester viewed himself as a great champion of the cause and agitator for war; of Essex's desire to play soldier there is less evidence, at least at this stage. What is clearer is that his conception of soldiering was limited to caparisoning himself like a warhorse; to that end he spent £1000 out of an already parlous personal treasury. If the idea behind his inclusion in the campaign was to provide a cheap tour of Europe (such as that undertaken by the 6th earl of Derby, who had travelled the continent in 1582 with a paid tutor as a companion) then Essex was disinclined towards the parsimonious aspects of it. Predictably, his grandfather remonstrated with him, decrying the 'wasteful prodigality' that had sunk other nobles.[52] The money did not all go on clothes and armaments, however. Tellingly, Knollys noted Essex's having levied a 'furnished band of men, needless and causeless'. This was, of course, how private armies were raised in the period – but for a young and inexperienced earl to do it raised eyebrows. He would raise them further during future attempts to secure and lead private forces.

Whatever the complexion of Essex's attitude to the war, his first impressions must have been favourable. Before the ships had left port, the earl and his troops went with Leicester to Colchester and then Harwich. Joining a quiver of other notables and their followings (amounting in total to over 1500 men) Essex bore witness to the grand civic pageantry and entertainments laid on for men of state. The ships were launched from Harwich to a cacophony of cheers and music. This was beyond anything seen at the Elizabethan court; it was the fanfare due a crusading monarch, of which England had been bereft since Henry VIII's death in 1547.

The ships arrived at Flushing (Vlissingen) on the 8th of December. The city's governor was Leicester's nephew, the

---

[52] Devereux, *Lives and Letters*, p. 178.

dashing Sir Philip Sidney, by now an extraordinary soldier-poet in the new mould, and formerly an ardent admirer of Essex's sister, Penelope. Leicester immediately set out on what amounted to a royal progress of the type Elizabeth undertook each summer in England. It had long been his goal to mount a holy war against Catholicism, and he appears to have milked the opportunity; from Flushing to Dort and Rotterdam, to Delft and the Hague, he led his stepson and both their followings on a tour worthy of a reigning monarch, with fireworks and entertainments at each town. The queen's arms were displayed throughout, but the star of the show was Leicester, performing much the same role as Elizabeth had done at his own Kenilworth festivities. In religious tableaux and scripted entertainments, this time it was Leicester who was welcomed and feted, handed tokens of peace, welcomed by the Roman god of war, celebrated as King Arthur, and even given fishing nets commanded to be filled by a man representing Christ.[53] In case native entertainments waned, along for the ride was the earl's theatrical troupe, including up-and-coming comic Will Kemp, ready with a joke and a jig to delight both Leicester and the people who were evidently coming to view themselves as his subjects-in-waiting. The expectation of the Dutch burghers could hardly have been more incompatible with the new role Elizabeth had envisioned for herself and her servant: he had been commanded to 'rather … make a defensive than an offensive war'.[54]

At the beginning of January, representatives from the United Provinces visited Leicester at his lodging in the Hague, and he invited them privately into his bedchamber (again, the kind of behaviour more typical of an early modern king). They had come to offer him the role of governorship of the United Provinces: in effect, they were offering to make him their ruler.

---

[53] A detailed summary of the entertainments laid on for Leicester and his men can be found in Harrison, *Life and Death*, pp. 11-12. A modern study of this remarkable pseudo-royal progress is overdue.
[54] Cruickshank, C. G. 1966. *Elizabeth's Army* (Oxford: Clarendon), p. 43.

Wisely, Leicester temporised, pointing out that he was unsure of Elizabeth's wishes, she having sent him as a servant, not a would-be potentate. The demurral did not last long, and it certainly did not dampen his enthusiasm for the lifestyle of a prince. He went to Leyden, again enjoying the welcome of a monarch, before turning to the Hague and appointing Essex colonel-general of the horse (a nominal but significant title; Leicester had got his own start as the queen's master of horse). Throughout the month, further entreaties were made regarding the governorship of the provinces; at the end of January, Leicester, seated under a cloth of estate, accepted the role without Elizabeth's approval. These were the heights to which, rightly or wrongly, an Elizabethan favourite could climb. Essex could not help but imbibe the lesson.

When the news reached England, the queen was livid. She laid out her thoughts, in all their passion, in a letter which left no doubt as to who was the ruler and who the subject:

How contemptuously we conceive ourself to have been used by you you shall by this bearer understand ... We could never have imagined (had we not seen it fall out in experience) that a man raised up by ourself and extraordinarily favoured by us above any other subject in this land would have in so contemptible a sort broken our commandment in a cause that so greatly toucheth our honour ... you may not therefore think that we have so little care of the reparation thereof as we mind to pass so great a wrong in silence unredressed.[55]

No matter how great her personal affection for Leicester or any favourite, Elizabeth would not hesitate to put her sovereignty first. Anything that impinged on it would always take precedence. The remarkable thing is that Leicester, knowing her, would have dared to behave as he did. It is possible that he thought that long affection and the fact of having been 'raised up' gave him abilities and rights beyond the command of the woman who had done the raising. This would

[55] Elizabeth I, *Selected Works*, p. 163.

be a pattern Essex would follow. Yet Elizabeth too must face criticism; she would make the same errors in raising up the young favourite as she had with the old.

There followed a semi-comic back-and-forth in which William Davison, a diplomat favoured by Leicester, took the blame for giving the earl bad advice. The queen, incensed and fearful that Lettice would soon sail to join her husband and hold court as a de facto queen consort, dispatched the reluctant Sir Thomas Heneage to command Leicester to give up his pretensions: something Heneage decidedly dragged his feet in doing. Amidst this wrangling, the war was still ostensibly going on.

With a new title, Essex involved himself in displaying his military prowess in martial exercises. There was no time for battles, however, until he left Leicester's feting and dramas and took to the field. This he did in April at Niekerken, and thereafter followed a period of intermittent fighting. It was hardly the stuff of glory, and throughout the campaign Leicester and Sir Philip Sidney complained of the queen's meanness in providing financially for her troops (Sidney heaping debt upon debt to make up for her cheapness). This inglorious beginning was not helped by the factional disputes which grew in the English camps, centred on those, like Essex, who declared themselves Leicester's men, and those who followed the leader of the infantry, Sir John Norris (whom both Leicester and Sidney accused of profiteering).[56] The grand beginning – the feasting and festivity – had given way not to the supposed glories of war, but to infighting and petty jealousies. Across the channel, Elizabeth continued to berate everyone: Sidney for his financial demands and Leicester for continuing to hold the hated title of governor-general of the United Provinces. Her attention, however, was not confined to her first real foray into war. She

---

[56] Motley, J. L. 1860. *History of the United Netherlands from the death of William the silent to the Synod of Dort, with a full view of the English-Dutch struggle against Spain, and of the origin and destruction of the Spanish armada* (Oxford: Oxford University Press), pp. 32-3.

was also looking north, and inadvertently creating a future friend for Essex. She was attempting to buy Scotland.

***

James VI of Scotland had been, as he would later boast, a cradle king. His coronation, however, had been a rather shabby affair, conducted with few elite guests. It had come about, on the 24th of July 1567, as the result of a coup against his mother, Mary Queen of Scots. Following the murder of her husband, King Henry (known as Lord Darnley in England), Mary had married the earl of Bothwell with indecent haste. Bothwell had almost certainly had a hand in killing the king, and his co-conspirators (chief amongst them the earl of Morton) had taken advantage of Mary's descent into depression to accuse the queen of conspiring with Bothwell to kill the hapless young Henry.

It is unlikely that Mary had had any inkling of the plot to kill her husband. The common means by which murderers seek to get away with killing their spouses (the appearance of an accident or natural causes, or even the identifiable scapegoat – the 'bushy-haired stranger') were all absent. Instead, Mary seems to have broken down sufficiently following the accusations against her to be bounced into Bothwell's bed – forcibly, if her claims are true. At any rate, the Bothwell marriage gave a sufficient number of Scottish nobles cause to rebel against her, ultimately forcing her abdication and flight into England. She left behind a divided country, hoping to return swiftly with aid from her cousin, Elizabeth. Instead she found a semi-legal show-trial for Darnley's death followed by imprisonment. In Scotland her considerable number of supporters was forced to fight on against those who had deposed her in a civil war that did not end until 1573. Her son, declared king by the coterie of rebels led by Mary's half-brother, the earl of Moray, had thus the strange position of a king not fully recognised by the world. Even Elizabeth had refused to recognise it until January 1572.[57]

By 1586, Mary had been imprisoned for nearly twenty years. She had grown stout and was frequently ill. Yet still she was, in many eyes, Elizabeth's heir: as a direct descendent of Henry VIII's older sister, Margaret Tudor, she was indisputably the next monarch according to the ancient laws of primogeniture. However, the English parliament cavilled. Heir she might be, but a Catholic queen they would not accept. To justify their opposition, members invoked the common law rule against alien inheritance, derived from a 1351 statute against foreign-born individuals inheriting English property. Politics is, however, the art of the possible. James VI, who was by then nearly twenty, had been raised a Protestant. Not only that, but he was a proven king, having assumed the reins of power at twelve, dispensing of the then regent, Morton. If Mary could be got rid of, the opposition to a Stewart succession would melt away.

Elizabeth did not like heirs to her throne. Moreover, she made no bones about it, treating every potential successor with cold disdain or outright malevolence. The Grey sisters, siblings to the short-lived Queen Jane, had been roundly maltreated. After each married without permission, she was imprisoned. On the subject of Mary Queen of Scots, she had once asked,

Think you that I could love my winding-sheet? Princes cannot like their own children, those that should succeed unto them... I know the inconstancy of the people of England, how they ever mislike the present government and have their eyes fixed upon that person that is next to succeed. More men love the rising sun than the one that sets.[58]

Mary, of course, would find little love from her cousin in England – instead she took on the complexion of an unwelcome guest, too dangerous to be allowed to leave. Throughout the

---

[57] Weir, A. 2011. *Mary Queen of Scots and the Murder of Lord Darnley* (London: Random House), p. 493.
[58] Whitelock, *Elizabeth's Bedfellows*, p. 57.

interminable years of captivity, she would be shunted from country house to country house, under a succession of wearied aristocratic hosts (with even Chartley, Essex's home, suggested as a suitable prison in 1584, much to his annoyance).

James VI, however, was somewhat different, and Elizabeth would give him more indications of favour – no more than indications – that he was likely to be her heir. He was in some ways an unlikely one. Raised by a succession of keepers and tutors, he lacked any kind of parental affection (though that by itself was a not unusual method of raising early modern monarchs). He was by the mid-1580s a suspicious, gangly, awkward young man, and would develop into the type of powerful figure who delights in making off-colour and ribald jokes, safe in the knowledge that his inferiors will be unable or unwilling to berate him. On the credit side, this meant that he was not particularly imperious, but generously and almost pathetically paternal. He was probably what would now be called bisexual, with a preference for men, and if Elizabeth so chose, it would undoubtedly have been easy to blow rumour into slander and rule him out as an heir to England.

As king of her neighbouring realm, however, she could not afford to debase or disgrace him. Neither, really, did she wish to. Instead, she preferred that he keep his mouth shut with regard to his claim to the English throne – something which, as the years passed, he would prove singularly unwilling to do. In return she would give tacit approval to his succession claim.

In May 1586 she went further. The previous year she had been writing to her 'dear brother' of a foiled Catholic plot to free his mother. On receiving assurances that he deplored the conspiracies that had long swirled around Mary – and, crucially, the rumours that Scots were fighting in Ireland against the English colonists – she wrote in June of her joy at James' 'gladsome acceptance of my offered amity together with the desire you seem to have engraven in your mind to make merits correspondent [i.e. to return the friendship]'.[59] This amity matured with the offering of a greased palm of friendship. The

---

[59] Elizabeth I, *Selected Works*, p. 160.

Treaty of Berwick, signed on July the 5th 1586, pledged Anglo-Scottish amity and mutual defence against the Catholic powers of Europe. For his trouble, James was to be awarded £4000 a year from England's coffers (a considerable but hardly bank-breaking sum).

Scotland had effectively been bought and need not – Elizabeth and her government hoped – continue be considered a worrisome postern gate for England's enemies. Coupled with the dubious Bond of Association of 1584, whereby anyone who might benefit from Elizabeth's murder or attempted murder could be summarily put to death whether they were privy to the murder or not, the stage was being prepared to finally get rid of the troublesome Mary Queen of Scots. Only when Mary was eliminated could James, bought, paid for, and an ally by treaty, squarely adopt the role of informal and unmistakably likely heir to England. Whether the treaty and James' pension – or, as he preferred it to be termed, his annuity – were designed to tacitly make him Elizabeth's heir apparent is debatable, but in future years, it would be to the king of Scots that men like Essex would turn as the sun of Elizabeth faded.

***

Towards the end of the year, events in the Netherlands began to heat up. The English had control of two towns: Brielle (or Brill), held by Burghley's eldest son, Sir Thomas Cecil; and Flushing, held by Sir Philip Sidney. What was sought, however, was a crushing English victory over the Spaniard, and Leicester was the man who wanted to reap its glory. Unfortunately, the hapless Sir John Norris continued to be a thorn in his side, and Essex, young and inexperienced as he was, recognised that 'our owne private warres ... [are] more dangerous then [than] the annoyance of the enemy'.[60] Whilst these private wars and Leicester's wrangling with the queen over the governorship dominated, the municipality of Grave had fallen to the Spanish (with its ostensible defender, Peter van Hemart, tried by a group

---

[60] PRO, SP, 84/49, folio 241.

of commissioners, including Essex). Then had followed the falls of Venlo and Nuys. About the only leader to emerge in unalloyed heroism was the dashing Sidney, who managed to capture Axel in late July. In September, victory looked likely at Spanish-held Doesburg, but here Leicester managed to claw humiliation from its jaws.

Splitting command of the attack on the city between Count Hollock (in Essex biographer G. B. Harrison's colourful view 'a notorious tosspot') and Norris – in an attempt to share command and ameliorate the jealousies that had riven the anti-Spanish forces all year – Leicester managed to win Doesburg's surrender. However, the condition was that the evacuation of soldiers and citizenry would be allowed unmolested. Unfortunately, fleeing women were set upon by the English soldiery, with Essex wading in to beat back the would-be rapists and plunderers. Neither this admirable attempt to prevent despoliation nor Leicester's own attempts to stop looting prevented the capture of Doesburg from becoming a scene of violent rapacity against the town's inhabitants. Worse was to come.

The morning of September the 22nd dawned misty, making the prospect of battle a deadly one to English and Spanish alike. The mist, as it swirled around the men parading in the English camp, can hardly have filled them with confidence; but they had their orders. They were to join up with Norris' infantry, which the night before had acted on a tip and garrisoned a road over a mile distant in the hope of cutting a Spanish supply line. It must have been a relief to make it to their position. That relief faded as the mist rose. Before the Englishmen were the Spanish forces: 3000 men and 1200 horses.

The musket fire came first. Essex threw himself into the fighting, wielding a lance as part of the cavalry. This was his first taste of real martial engagement, similar in physical action to the training given to young noblemen at university but different entirely in atmosphere. The Spanish forces were hurt, but far from crippled; despite losses, they managed to protect their supply line and carry it safely to its destination in the town of Zutphen. In the midst of the fighting, however, England's hero Sidney took a shot in the thigh. He was carried back to camp, where he made a will containing the bequest of his best sword to Essex – his 'beloved and much honoured lord'.[61] This is, it should be noted, the only evidence that there was much of a relationship between the pair, and it might well be that the dying hero bequeathed his sword (and, reputedly, the care of his wife) to Essex because the young man was his uncle's stepson. Whatever the truth of their attachment, Sidney lingered on in agony for nearly a month, but there was no hope of recovery, and he died on the 17th of October. Almost immediately, a haze of Protestant martyrology and encomium as thick as the Zutphen mist sprang up around the dead hero. His thighs had been unprotected because he had sacrificed his cuisses because his fellow soldier, Sir William Pelham, had been rendered unable to wear them, and heroes shared handicaps with their allies; as he lay dying, he had given away the chance of a blissful drop of water to another dying man, whose need he deemed greater. All of this – the glorious death in battle, the heroism, the willingness to die for country or friend – was the stuff of legend and would for the rest of his life be the kind of pose to which Essex would aspire in plotting his own course (although, it must be stressed, it would very much be his own course rather than a re-tread of Sidney's).

The battle of Zutphen is probably best remembered for being the site of Sidney's death. He was one of the first English sonnet sequencers, and one of the best lyricists of the golden age of the English renaissance courtier-poet. He left behind the first real piece of literary criticism in English – the *Apology For Poetry* (or *Defence of Poesy*), which celebrated poets as 'the least liars' whose job it was to 'teach and delight' through fictional writing; *The Countess of Pembroke's Arcadia* in both old and new versions; *Astrophel and Stella* (often unfairly reduced to an autobiographical account of the writer's love for Essex's sister); and *A Discourse in Defence of the Earl of Leicester* (which responded to the calumnies of *Leicester's Commonwealth*).

---

[61] Sidney, P. 1586. 'Will' in A. Feuillerat (Ed.) *The Prose Work of Sir Philip Sidney* (Oxford: Oxford University Press), p. 316.

After his death and throughout the 1590s the mantle of literary greatness would fall to the university men and middle-class playwrights (the latter boasting some of the former in its ranks, or vice versa) and a bustling and intellectually energetic literary class would bloom in London. Sidney would not see it, but Essex would, and would engage with the older class of writers and the newer. But Sidney left behind not only a legend and a poetic legacy; he left an attractive young widow – and Essex's eye would in time turn to all three.

For the moment, though, the immediate outcome of Zutphen was material: Essex was one of four men to receive from Leicester the knight banneret: the highest chivalric knighthood. This granted him full access to the administration of his estates (or, it might be fairer to say, the full financial burden of administering the indebted estates his father had left him). The campaigning season over, it was time to return to England, and for Leicester to finally recapitulate the governorship so hated by his queen. Both were in England in November 1586. The older earl, seeking favour after his offensive behaviour abroad, would take his stepson – who was more in need of money than ever, but gifted with military honours and a majority to help him gain it – back to the royal court. This time he would enjoy a rise every bit as meteoric as his biographers have sometimes wrongly assumed his previous sojourn to have witnessed. However, he would return with a surfeit of chivalrous notions honed on the battlefield; in fact, he would never learn a healthy scepticism and would remain throughout his life hopelessly gullible when it came to lofty romantic ideals.

6: 'This affection seemeth strange'[62]

In the dying days of 1586 the queen was in desperate need of diversion. As soon as Elizabeth had secured the friendship of James VI, her counsellors eagerly began plotting to rid England of the presence of Mary Queen of Scots. In late 1585 she had been moved to Essex's moated manor house at Chartley. It will be remembered that Elizabeth had proposed Chartley as a prison for Mary in 1584 and Essex had been nonplussed; things had changed by the time he was himself tasting court and martial life in late 1585. Although he was still not happy about the deposed queen's entourage flooding his house and doubtless despoiling the land around it – in fact, he tried to obstruct the move by begging his grandfather and stepfather to intervene – he eventually bowed to the queen's will.[63] Mary's keeper was the ultra-Puritan Sir Amias Paulet, a man she found infuriatingly immune to either charm or storms of tears. With the ink barely dry on the Treaty of Berwick, the English government swung into action.

The desire to get rid of Mary had been present in the minds of Burghley and Sir Francis Walsingham for decades. To them she was a constant and present danger: a cancer in the body politic. She drew to her the loyalties of discontented Catholics, who had been freed from their allegiance to Elizabeth by Pope Pius V's papal bull of 1570. Following that ill-advised document, the English government had begun a brutal repression of Catholicism that had hitherto been unknown under Elizabeth. Holy war raged, and the chief minister and spymaster wanted to

---

[62] Lyly, J. 2014. [1588] *Endymion* in G. Walker (Ed.) *The Oxford Anthology of Tudor Drama* (Oxford: Oxford University Press), p. 541.
[63] Bain, J. (Ed.). 1898. *Calendar of the State Papers relating to Scotland and Mary, Queen of Scots 1547-1603, Vol. VIII* (Edinburgh: H. M. General Custom House), p. 102.

claim the greatest scalp of all: the Scottish queen's. Jesuits smuggled from the continent were hunted down, and in March 1586 York residents witnessed the horrific spectacle of Margaret Clitherow, a protector of priests, crushed to death. This monstrous punishment was reserved for those who refused to plead – which Margaret bravely did, knowing that such a refusal would save her children from testifying at a trial and prevent the confiscation of her goods. She was laid supine on a small, sharp rock, and the door of her house placed over her body. Four beggars were then induced to begin placing heavy stones on the rock, the justices unwilling to do it themselves, in the hope that she would plead before death. This she did not do. Her back was broken, and the breath crushed from her lungs within a quarter of an hour. Elizabeth herself expressed horror on hearing of it – probably as much to quell the anger the execution threatened to raise in the north. However, Margaret's death provided yet more fuel for Burghley and Walsingham. Such horrors were the result of keeping the Scottish queen safe: she was the magnet for conspiracies and her continued existence gave those who would protect priests succour. After all, what else did the Margaret Clitherows of the world hope for but a return of English Catholicism under a Catholic monarch? Elizabeth was unmoved and would not move against Mary unless the Scottish queen could be proven to be at work against her. The English government determined to prove just that.

Much has been written on Mary's involvement in the Babington Plot: a hare-brained attempt by a priest called John Ballard to use a witless young Catholic gentleman, Sir Anthony Babington, and his friends to help spring Mary from prison. In no dispute is the role of an English agent provocateur, Gilbert Gifford, in winning Mary's trust in order to report her actions and words to the queen's spymaster, Sir Francis Walsingham, and his team. Walsingham is often considered a shady and malign figure, though recent biographies have been more sympathetic to the old workhorse. He was, at heart, a fervent

Protestant, and a dedicated servant of the Anglican state.[64] In practice, it was his job to work with Burghley in advancing and protecting the Protestant cause, and in doing so he amassed a motley crew of genius cryptographers, fly-by-night underworld figures, and chancers. Gifford was one of the latter, but Mary, cut off from the real world for so long, embraced him and gleefully looked forward to being able to communicate with her supporters again.

Disagreement arises as to whether the Scottish queen did involve herself in the plot, believing it all to be real, or whether she abjured the whole thing as a nonsense from the start and Walsingham's den of spies and codebreakers forged her assent. The weight of modern historiography falls on an interpretation somewhere in between: the Catholic plotters were real enough, and Mary gave her cautious assent to the plan, which was not just to free her, but to kill Elizabeth. This is exactly what Walsingham hoped would happen. An inveterate enemy of Mary – he called her the 'bosom serpent' – he knew all about the plot, and had Gifford encourage Mary's belief in a secret channel of communication via letters smuggled in and out of Chartley in beer barrels. Thereafter he allowed the first Catholic plot that arose to run as far as he safely could: just far enough to get written proof that Mary assented to Elizabeth's assassination. That proof came in the form of a reply from Mary to Babington which advised that he and his friends should, when foreign troops were amassed, 'set the Six Gentlemen on work, taking good order upon the accomplishment of their discharges, [so that] I may be suddenly transported out of this place'.[65] The 'work' was taken to mean Elizabeth's assassination. Mary, if she wrote it, was doomed. Elizabeth, however, was not happy

---

[64] The term 'Anglican' is not contemporary, but it is now the conventional means of describing the Elizabethan religious settlement.

[65] Higgons, B. 1753. *The History of the Life and Reign of Mary Queen of Scots: And Dowager of France. Faithfully Extracted from Original Prints, Records, and Writers of Credit, with Marginal References* (Dublin: Philip Bowes), p. 227.

about it, nor about the exultant cheers of those men about her who had brought the whole thing about and were now baying for the Scottish queen's blood.

It was to a court sweating in this heated atmosphere that Essex returned. Mary had been lodged in his house when the Babington Plot had been uncovered (or encouraged, or allowed to run its course), but his hands were clean by virtue of his having been abroad. Further, he was in the prime position of having been able to demonstrate and be rewarded for valour without having to take responsibility for the futile and internally divided nature of the campaign. Thus it was that he could appear at the Accession Day tilts on the 17th of November unsullied by the mire of the domestic politics of 1586, and rather caparisoned in glory as a fresh-faced military hero. His motto, *par nulla figura dolori* (nothing can represent sorrow), inscribed on his sable shield, has been read, convincingly, as a threnody over Sidney's death.[66] However, even if that were its chief design, it should be considered also in the context of the queen's mood as Mary's ultimate downfall approached.

Though Essex likely fully supported the destruction of the Catholic queen of Scots, his choice was masterful in appealing to his own sovereign, who bitterly resented the responsibility of trying and likely killing her cousin and peer. His appearance at the tilts in a posture of sorrow provided a neat counterpoint to the unseemly joy - distasteful to Elizabeth - that had met Mary's downfall and spread from council to country. The motto itself was, according to tradition, impressed upon a pasteboard shield for the joust and the whole *impresa* thereafter put on display in the water gallery at Whitehall, to which the public had limited

[66] Hammer, *The Polarisation of Elizabethan Politics*, p. 56; Scott, J. 1812. *A Catalogue of the Royal and Noble Authors of England, Scotland, and Ireland; with Lists of Their Works: by the Late Horatio Wapole, Earl of Orford. Enlarged and Continued to the Present Time, by Thomas Park, F.s.a, Volume 5* (London: John Scott), p. 364

access.[67] Only a few days before, a less welcome Latin tag had come from Sir Christopher Hatton on another public platform – in the parliamentary prosecution which sought the death sentence: *ne periapt Israell periapt Absolon*: "Absalom must perish lest Israel perish".[68]

Essex had made a good start, and he followed it up with a New Year's present of a jewel in the shape of a rainbow over two pillars, one of them cracked. Again, the cracked pillar is often read as representing Sidney, the other Essex himself, and the rainbow Elizabeth. Yet the genius of early modern allegory lay in its multifaceted nature: the broken pillar, which does not disturb the rainbow or its twin pillar, might be whatever Elizabeth wished to consider it. He was playing the elaborate game of the courtier with aplomb. It was a game the queen had always enjoyed, given that she was its mistress, and Essex's skill in it was, again, a welcome distraction from the unfolding saga of Mary Queen of Scots, which was racing towards its endgame; parliament managed to obtain a public proclamation of the death sentence on the 4th of December. In short, if Essex's spell at court in 1585 had come during a period in which he was overlooked due to political events, his return in 1586 was fortuitous in coinciding with a time at which Elizabeth did not want to look at them.

The difference in age between the queen and the man who was swiftly becoming her new favourite did not matter. This is not because she had given up her ostensible distaste for an older woman being seen to be in love with a younger man; it was, rather, because all threat of marriage had safely passed. The age gap between her and Essex did not matter, because he was never a prospective husband. She had coyly voiced worries about multi-decade temporal distances mainly to keep Anjou in suspense – it was a way out, too, should she have needed it.

---

[67] Höltgen, K. J. 1986. *Aspects of the emblem: studies in the English emblem tradition and the European context* (Kassel: Reichenberger), p. 79.
[68] Stater, V. 2019. 'Hatton, Christopher, first Baron Hatton' in *Oxford Dictionary of National Biography Hatton*, p. 161.

Means of retreat from mooted marriages belonged to the old
Elizabeth. The new one could safely flirt with men of any age.
Nevertheless, it is clear that Essex, probably either directly
guided or indirectly inspired by his stepfather's career, had
opted to pursue the lifestyle and rewards of the polished,
chastely amorous, and fawning courtier.

***

There were essentially two paths to fame and position under
Elizabeth: the tortuous path of proving oneself - often thankless
and workmanlike; and the sunlit, well-flowered path of the
aspiring favourite, on which rewards were common and
attractions plenty, and the cost of which was playing the game
of courtly love. To be a valued and trusted man of state lay at
the end of one; to be a rich and well-connected man of luxury,
laden with household positions and lucrative monopolies, lay at
the end of the other. Elizabeth, more often than not, had a hand
in directing the men who came to her court down either
according to her own assessment of their abilities, looks, and
talents.

It has been suggested, quite unfairly, that the Elizabethan
system of patronage, insofar as it involved the queen, was an
increasingly grotesque one. Often too readily accepted is the
cynical caricature of the vain and ageing queen, surrounded by
increasingly younger men who, if they wanted to succeed, had
to fawn obsequiously. Cited as evidence are the terse letters of
Sir Philip Sidney during Leicester's campaign in the
Netherlands, in which he reveals a barely-concealed dislike of
the queen and her methods of governance. However, Sidney
speaks only for Sidney and, as we have seen, he was at a low
financial ebb and more disgusted by Elizabeth's parsimony than
the phony passions she inspired in her would-be favourites.[69]
His attitude towards the queen and court – jaded, scornful, and
desirous of an alternative, pastoral fantasy – was primarily the

[69] See Duncan-Jones, K. 1991. *Sir Philip Sidney: Courtier Poet*
(London: Hamish Hamilton), particularly pp. 16-7, 147, 177-8, 272.

product of his dissatisfaction and a wider, fashionable pose which raged in literary circles.

The idea that one had to fawn over the queen in order to gain her ear is a problematic one. Burghley and Walsingham – both statesman – seldom did, at least not to the extent of a Leicester or a Hatton, and nor did Burghley's up-and-coming second son, Robert. It is fairer to say that some men, sometimes of ability and sometimes not, preferred it as a means of short-cutting the toil and labour of proving themselves indispensable statesmen. The difficulty was that, once the path of the fawning favourite was chosen, it was difficult to switch to the path of the statesman. The problem with men who chose the favourite's path is that all too often they expected it to end in statesmanship. Such crossover could only happen – as it did to some extent with Leicester – after many years of trust. The favourite could take on some of the duties of a statesman and the statesman enjoy a degree of familiarity and affection from the queen, but not without decades of security in either role.

We should therefore dispense with the idea that the Elizabethan regime involved a lonely and vain old woman taken advantage of by self-seeking men. Elizabeth's system was as beneficial to her and her monarchy as to the men who sought her favour. Any monarchical and aristocratic system requires support from its nobility, and the nobility in turn require routes to patronage. These Elizabeth provided willingly, and this resulted in a mutual interdependence of queen and courtiers; and her method of managing worked well - until, that is, men who travelled the courtly road began to chafe and lock horns with the statesmen. A safe space existed for this. Successful graduates (that is, those who satisfied the queen that they were ready) of each of the two paths – confirmed statesmen and long-term courtly favourites – converged in the council chamber, where they were expected to work together collegiately, with the united goal of protecting England's interests.

Yet it was far from a perfect system. In theory, attractive and charming commoners could find themselves royal favourites and intellectual ones statesmen; likewise, clever but dull nobles could find themselves chained to desks whilst their handsomer peers enjoyed titles and positions of favour. All depended on the queen's ultimate judgement of individuals. However, she could hardly fill out her council chamber with only clever and capable men. She did not live in or want to create a meritocracy. Instead she had to balance the conciliar wing of her government, the privy council, between those born to high positions and those she thought capable of them. The paths of the favourite and the statesmen provided her opportunities to measure her picks for the top table. Yet, as the years went on, even the council could not achieve a harmonious balance between either favourites and statesmen or nobles and up-and-comers. Essex, as a high-born favourite who would increasingly wish to be recognised as a statesman without having spent decades as either, would be one of those who would upset the balance in the 1590s.

As he willingly skipped along the path of the favourite, Essex was no more exploiting an old woman than she was exploiting him. As sovereign and aristocrat, both had a deep interest in making the system which kept them at the top of society work. Elizabeth was deeply sensitive to this. The courtier Fulke Greville famously recounts an incident involving his friend, Sidney, in his moralistic biography of the then-long-dead hero. After Sidney had an altercation with the earl of Oxford, during which the latter upbraided him as a 'puppy', a duel looked inevitable. Elizabeth had to step in.

The queen, who saw that by the loss, or disgrace of either, she could gain nothing, and (like an excellent monarch) lays before him [Sidney] the difference in degree between earls, and gentlemen; the respect inferiors ought to their superiors; and the necessity in princes to maintain their own creations, as degrees descending between the people's licentiousness, and the anointed sovereignty of crowns; how gentlemen's neglect of the nobility taught the peasant to insult both.[70]

---

[70] Greville, F. 1907 [1652]. *Life of Sir Philip Sidney* (Oxford: Clarendon Press), p. 68.

Breaking the system was not only unseemly, but an incitement to public insurrection. There is therefore nothing particularly unseemly about the twenty-one-year-old earl doting on the fifty-three-year-old queen. For willing young men like Essex and his rival, Raleigh, to engage in chaste love affairs with an elderly woman is, further, far less grotesque than the veritable pimping of young women to Henry VIII, or the similar parading of handsome youths before a leering and often overly tactile James VI and I. Men like Essex knew the system as well as the queen, and it benefited them as much as her.

Essex continued on his path into 1587, continuing to provide diversion and amusement to the queen. It is impossible to know what lay behind his rapid rise, but one must assume that he was adept at performing the expected roles of a courtier as set out in Castiglione's influential *The Book of the Courtier*. This involved not only moderate speech and a cool head, but wit, charm, carefully held postures and poses, elegance of manners, and a sound classical knowledge. Using the example of the cardinal of Ferrara, Castiglione notes that

from his birth, that his person, his aspect, his words and all his movements are so disposed and imbued with this grace, that — although he is young — he exhibits among the most aged prelates such weight of character that he seems fitter to teach than to be taught; likewise in conversation with men and women of every rank, in games, in pleasantry and in banter, he has a certain sweetness and manners so gracious, that whoso speaks with him or even sees him, must needs remain attached to him forever.[71]

Essex might well have taken note; certainly, he must have learnt something to alter his behaviour from his twelve-year-old self to the able courtier of the post-Netherlands campaign. The reference in the book to the idea that a young man might, regardless of age, express and obtain a weight of responsibility

---

[71] Castiglione, B. 1903 [1528]. *The Book of the Courtier by Count Baldesar Castiglione* (New York: Charles Scribner & Sons), p. 22-3.

and respect seem to resonate particularly with Essex. In the years that followed he would expect continually to be taken seriously amongst his older contemporaries through sheer force of noble ideas, personality, and charm. Part of his emerging fascination with the middle-aged Elizabeth might, indeed, have stemmed from this expectation: he would become the youth who thought he was older than his years and was accordingly attracted to powerful, older figures.

At any rate, these were the things Elizabeth had always prized in her favourites, and it cannot have but given her a fillip to know that she was advancing the disagreeable Lettice's son - making him her own protégée and spending endless hours making merry with him in the hallowed places denied his mother. Lettice was a maternal woman from a close-knit family; what she would have, so Elizabeth would take. The result of the dowager countess's mothering was that Essex had known little else but complete adoration and approbation. As a result, he expected nothing less than the queen's full and undivided attention.

At the outset of their relationship, however, there was no love on either side, courtly or otherwise. For Elizabeth there was amusement and the chance to enact her traditional policy of rewarding a noble through the well-worn path to prestige. For Essex, there was material reward: when Leicester was invited, not this time with much enthusiasm, to return to the Netherlands, his stepson received the household title the great favourite had held since the beginning of the reign – the mastery of the horse.

Mary Queen of Scots went to the block in February 1587, with Elizabeth's council united in promoting the execution. Donning red under her outer garments, the Scottish queen presented herself as a Catholic martyr, not only because of a genuine spiritual resurgence which she had undergone in captivity, but because she consciously sought to reject the English government's narrative that labelled her a traitor. Mary was unswervingly vocal in pointing out that as a foreign anointed sovereign, she could not be a traitor to England or its queen. The legal validity of her argument carried no weight, and with two strokes of the axe and some gruesome sawing of the neck sinews, she was finally released from her captivity.

On hearing of the execution, Elizabeth flew into mourning, partly for the benefit of the outraged people of Scotland, and partly in horror at the enormity of what she had done. From the pulpit her Protestant preachers railed against what they viewed as self-indulgence: the dean of Peterborough, Richard Fletcher (father of Shakespeare's successor, the dramatist John) invoked the biblical precedent of Joab, who rebuked David's sorrow and lamentations over the necessary death of Absalom.[72]

The queen blamed Burghley and, absurdly and unfairly, the secretary who had carried the warrant, Davison. As a result, the chief statesman of England fell out of favour for months, leaving the new favourite – a non-counsellor free of responsibility – to receive the queen's pleasure. He took it, but throughout the year he voiced a willingness to leave the court and a longing to return to military service, as in January when he expressed an interest in fighting for the Huguenot Henry of Navarre in France. Nevertheless, he remained an attendee at court (within easy access of Leicester's townhouse on the Strand) when his stepfather sailed again for the Low Countries on the 25th of June. It was with some satisfaction that Essex's servant could boast that 'even at night my lord is at cards or one game or another with her, that he cometh not to his own lodging till the birds sing in the morning'.[73] Essex was good company, bright and enthusiastic. The queen prized such men and we should not expect every decision she made regarding friends and favourites to have been political – she would scarcely have been human if every relationship was predicated on political calculation. Every one did, however, have political

---

[72] McCullough, P. E. 1998. 'Out of Egypt: Richard Fletcher's Sermon Before Elizabeth After the Execution of Mary Queen of Scots' in J. M. Walker (Ed.) *Dissing Elizabeth: Negative Representations of Gloriana* (Durham: Durham University Press), pp. 134-5.

[73] Johnson, P. 1974. *Elizabeth I: A Biography* (Philadelphia: Holt, Rinehart and Winston), p. 368.

consequences.

Complicating any courtly love affair between Elizabeth and Essex was another man: Sir Walter Raleigh. Flagrantly a thorn in the side of his budding relationship with Elizabeth, he was in his mid-thirties, swarthy, and had the disadvantage of a comparatively humble birth. Elizabeth, fond of nicknames, called him 'Water' in gentle mockery of his Devonshire accent. Nevertheless, and despite his provincial accent, the queen had knighted the sharp and enterprising gentleman in 1586. Although his arrogance made him unpopular with the public and many of his peers – a positive boon in Elizabeth's jealous eyes – Sir Walter had, until Essex exploded onto the scene, been one of the court's leading favourites. It was therefore natural that a rivalry should spring up between the pair. This had long been part of Elizabeth's system of management – to play courtiers off against one another. Even Leicester had had his pre-eminence checked by Hatton in earlier years. It was a necessary evil. One of the main criticisms against monarchs was the reliance on favourites, and clipping their wings by promoting rivals was as good a means as any for maintaining the system of reward without opening the floodgates of criticism.

The problem with the Raleigh versus Essex rivalry was, though, that it seemed so terribly personal. Further, Essex was, problematically, revealing himself to be extremely jealous, and his deeply-held code of honour fast proving a handicap. It was small wonder that the queen reportedly began calling him her 'wild horse', playing on the associations of horses with nobility, and wildness with an invitation to be tamed. During the late summer, for example, the queen's progress took the court to the earl of Warwick's house of North Hall, where Essex's sister, Dorothy, was then lodging. Naturally, as a favourite, he demanded that his sister be treated with all courtesy; the queen, who did not like either Devereux girl, refused to receive her. The young earl blurted out his opinions to his friend, Edward Dyer:

Her excuse was, first, she knew not of my sister's coming;

and, besides the jealousy that the world would conceive, that all her kindness to my sister was done for love of myself. Such bad excuses gave me a theme large enough, both for answer of them, and to tell her what the true causes were; why she would offer this disgrace both to me and my sister, which was only to please that knave Raleigh, for whose cause I saw she would both grieve me and my love, and disgrace me in the eyes of the world.[74]

A number of things leap out at us from Essex's writing. Firstly, the outrage he perceives as having been committed against him and his family is paramount. Secondly, he was quite prepared to boast of his love for the queen. We ought not to be too cynical of this. Beneath the outraged sensibility is a very real jealousy. It is not difficult to believe that the presence of a rival for Elizabeth's affections promoted a courtly infatuation with the older woman – a queen, but one he was curiously unawed by. Essex was beginning to fall under her spell. This is hardly surprising; it is, after all, a spell that continues to be cast year after year. Elizabeth in life was as attractive, mysterious, and curiously irresistible as Elizabeth in death. Again, we must be careful not to approach their relationship with either too much Freud or too much cynicism. It was possible – indeed, required – under the rules of courtly love for him to love Elizabeth without wishing to have sex with her. Further, his was an age which celebrated display - he was himself a peacock - and Elizabeth was the most glamorous and ostentatious figure at court. Simply put, Essex could be as obsessed with her as any modern-day academic or reader of history, and even love her as a patron, woman, and – at least at first – as queen, without necessarily faking his amorous protestations.

The effrontery of Essex is also hard to ignore, and one may be forgiven for thinking that the queen had bitten off more than she could chew in advancing such a hot-head to the status of favourite. She, for her part, attempted to defend Raleigh, only for Essex to explode into a barrage of character assassination

---

[74] Tytler, P. F. 1853. *Life of Sir Walter Raleigh, founded on authentic and original documents* (London: T. Nelson & Sons), pp. 62-3.

against the hated rival, asking with some passion how he could be expected to do service to a mistress who was in awe of such a man. The fact that he was willing to speak so brazenly before her (especially in insinuating that he could not do her service as long as she favoured Raleigh) indicates the rash sincerity of his emotions. They would ever be thus. Elizabeth, nonplussed, attempted to turn the conversation to catty condemnations of Essex's mother, upon which the earl stormed off, gathered his sister from her immurement in another room, and attempted to leave England to re-join the fighting in the Netherlands. He was stopped from doing so by Sir Robert Carey, tasked specially with this awkward parley by the queen.

The entire episode, in all its distasteful invective and language of spurned love, is illuminating. Essex was quite prepared to leave England and his 'beloved' queen from motives of jealousy and hurt honour. His willingness to depart out of spite and anger towards Elizabeth (presuming he really intended to go) suggests that his feelings were immature. When his coy and hurtful mistress slighted his honour it was commensurate with that honour to hurt her in return. Elizabeth aroused his jealousy and governed his actions and it was she who had begun to soak up his courtly passions (which were no less loving for being alien to our concept of love). In short, Essex had by the end of 1587 and throughout 1588 (the period of his meteoric rise as a royal favourite) thrown himself into the game body and soul.

This should neither surprise nor disgust us. At fifty-three, Elizabeth had retained her gamine figure and was suitably made up and coiffed with a mask of youth before appearing outside her bedchamber; she was still a country mile away from the emaciated, semi-toothed caricature which her critics shook their heads over in her final years. She no longer had youth to commend her, and she had never had conventional beauty, but she did have a commanding presence and glamour. As an emerging icon, she was ripe for praise and adoration from a young man versed in the classical idea that to love a goddess was expected and laudable. Further, this type of love was taken in by courtiers with their food and drink, and Essex was proving himself a devotee of all that was courtly. Indeed, all that is surprising is how deeply and personally he seemed to take her showing favour to others. A goddess she was, but his success lay in part in his ability to love her as an icon – as a courtly favourite must – and yet be excited by jealousy on a human level. This she had probably not experienced since the early years with Leicester. Even the favourites in between had appeared only to excel in loving the queen rather than the person.

Essex's emotional outbursts of jealousy and the queen's subsequent anger, followed by demands that he remain by her side, set what would become a pattern in their relationship as it deepened still further: she wanted him around, despite, or perhaps because of, his ungovernable passions, and he wanted to be the chief man in her life – the premier and preferably the only favourite. Raleigh aside, even the bookish Sir Charles Blount (later Lord Mountjoy), who had caught the queen's eye and been given a gold chess-queen as a present, drew Essex's jealousy. The little favour he tied to his arm with a red ribbon. Seeing it, Essex remarked, 'now I perceive every fool must have a favour'.[75] The two men consequently duelled in Marylebone Park, during which Essex was wounded in the thigh. Happily, in this rivalry, the outcome was that the pair became firm friends: honour had been satisfied, Essex losing the duel fairly. The queen, however, laconically swore, 'God's death, it is fit that someone or other should take him down, otherwise there would be no rule with him'.[76]

It is impossible to know if Elizabeth enjoyed these strange, almost domestic dramas. On the one hand it is tempting to think that her comparative maturity led her to dislike them; on the other, it is equally as likely that she found them intoxicating, given how often she would replay them. Alison Weir has suggested, understandably (given the queen's quasi-maternal desires that her young favourite reform his behaviour) that Elizabeth developed a pseudo-maternal view of him. This seems unlikely. The queen had a multitude of godchildren and

---

[75] *Bacon Papers*, vol II, p. 191.
[76] Kearsley, 1793. *Harleian Miscellany*, p. 186.

showed no particular maternal longings or instincts during her lifetime; indeed, her 'think you I could love my own winding sheet' made plain her disinclination to motherhood. In correspondence with other monarchs and in parliamentary speeches she invariably preferred rhetoric which made her wife to her country and sister to her peers. In maternal language and a maternal attitude lay eclipse by the child. Rather than a surrogate son, she seemed to want a pliant and merry young man's company: a man who would pay her shameless homage and devote himself to her entirely, receiving in return what she deigned to give but not growing overmighty.

In short, Elizabeth wanted an Endymion to her untouchable Selene. She was as much an active player of the courtly love game as Essex; the difference was that she was in charge of it and knew it far better. The fact that he made what can only be described as 'scenes' probably only added piquancy and freshness to a game which had grown stale in the playing. Many before had played it cynically, feigning passion, but Essex, due to a combination of naivety, idealism, and innate emotional instability, threw his full, restless energy into it. As queen she had no choice in playing – it was part of the system required to shore up her monarchy, and the required route to patronage for certain young nobles; as a volatile youth with stars in his eyes, his reckless enthusiasm made it exciting again.

Whatever Essex and Elizabeth wanted from their newfound interdependence, events on the international stage would have to take precedence. In December 1587 Leicester returned from what would turn out to be his last waltz in the Netherlands, following another campaign in which he had singularly failed to achieve greatness and had in fact lost the port of Sluys. Raleigh left court, undoubtedly knowing full well that his favour with the queen could not withstand the combined opposition of Essex and his stepfather. Relieved of the need to battle his rival for the queen's affections, Essex was thus able to join Leicester in trying to prevent any intimations Elizabeth was making in favour of reaching a peace accord with Spain. He was, after all, now a seasoned soldier; fighting was his game, and it was the bread and butter of the would-be hero.

Throughout the year, rumours had circulated that Spain was preparing itself for an all-out assault on England, exacerbated by what Catholics considered the murder of Mary Queen of Scots. Further, not only had English ships under Sir Francis Drake continued to annoy the Spanish, but the infanta of Spain, Isabella Clara Eugenia, had a claim to the English throne through distant descent from John of Gaunt (a fact of which King Philip was all too aware). Elizabeth, disgusted by the failures and costs of having involved herself in the war against Spain was hoping for peace. Essex and Leicester's party were to prevail: 1588 was to be the year of the first Spanish Armada.

7: The Golden Stage

A 4 o'clock in the afternoon on the 19th of July 1588 a respectable man raised his taper, his sharp eyes having scanned the sea and widened. It caught the pitch-soaked rope that formed the beacon and the whole thing burst into flame. He and his partner – two trustworthy householders over thirty manned the beacons during the day and three by night – moved to light the other two ropes that formed the trio of flames. Those three lines of fire acted as a signal to the next set along the southern English coast, and then the next, and so on; inland, pairs of similarly-manned ropes were lit, until the chain of warnings licked up into the sky, around and within southern England. The Spanish fleet had been spotted off the Lizard in Cornwall; the ships were in the English Channel. Seeing them, the post horses rode for London, from whence the defence forces began their march to the appointed place at Tilbury.

Throughout the year the march to direct battle had been interminable, despite the queen's attempts at conciliation. Philip, quite simply, wanted to take the war which the English had embarked on to England. Still Essex and Leicester had pummelled her verbally since the previous year – Leicester in council and in the privy chamber, and Essex over the card table. On the 7th of November 1587 the elder favourite had begged for her to give the notorious privateer and naval hero Sir Francis Drake free reign and they had exchanged angry words (of a quite different complexion from the domestic quarrels Essex offered). The split between the two had lasted some time. Despite this, and the ensuing chimeric peace talks, Philip had continued to build up his Gran Armada, which eventually numbered 140 ships.

The goal behind the Armada was not to land soldiers direct from the Spanish ships, but rather to use the ships to take naval control of the English Channel, covering a series of flat-bottomed barges which would ferry the duke of Parma's (Leicester's chief opponent in the Netherlands campaigns) army from Flanders to England. Only once the land army had been seen safely across the water were the 18, 500 Spanish troops on the Armada ships to get their boots muddy. By any measure this was a foolish plan with far too many variables. It assumed that Parma's army would be ready and able to leave Flanders at exactly the right moment; it assumed that the Dutch rebels would not harry and harass their attempts to board the barges; it assumed that the weather would be fine enough for all to go according to plan; it assumed that the English would not be able to do enough damage to the protective Armada ships. Philip, naturally, believed God to be on his side. It was hoped too that England's Catholics would rise in support of their Spanish liberators. Had they not, after all, been oppressed and seen their priests ruthlessly butchered by the queen's spymaster and his minions?

Despite hoping for peace, Elizabeth had bowed to reality, and instructed her cousin and lord high admiral Howard of Effingham to get her fleet in defensive mode. His job was to direct ships around the south and east coasts whilst she allowed Drake finally to patrol the west. By April 1588 the pair had commandeered 105 vessels. Throughout the preparations, as John Guy has recognised, the unfortunate Burghley was still conspicuous by his absence in the decision-making process, despite over a year having passed since he had manoeuvred Mary Queen of Scots to the block.[77] This, as Guy attests, was Elizabeth's show, whether she had wanted it or not.

The preparation made, the spring of 1588 gave onto a summer of watching and waiting – the kind of nervous, fretful anticipation which is felt in any war prior to an expected enemy attack. This mood prevailed until June, when the ticking of the clock finally forced the queen to allow a suddenly more bullish Burghley and Leicester to have their way and assemble a rag tag army. England, of course, had no standing army in the period: local militias had to be called up having been on standby since May. The troops called up around London were put under

---

[77] Guy, J. 2016. *Elizabeth: The Later Years* (London: Penguin), pp. 102-3.

lieutenant-general Leicester's command. Tilbury was their rendezvous point and, once secure in the knowledge that the Armada was at sea, it was there that they built up earthwork defences as a means of securing the Thames Estuary against a Spanish landing. The de facto English army was not an impressive one, and it likely could not have withstood a land invasion; indeed, it has been referred to as having more in common with 'Dad's Army' than an effective fighting force by at least one commentator.[78]

Nowadays, few do not know how the Armada ended. However, in the tense days of July 1588, no one did. London and the rest of England were in a state of emergency. On the 28th the English at sea sent eight 'fire ships' – disposable vessels filled with combustibles and lit by fuses so that the small crews could leap to safety after directing them towards the enemy – into the stationary Armada (which had been stuck at Calais awaiting news of Parma's men). At the same time, on land, Leicester issued an invitation to the queen to inspect the troops still cooling their heels at Tilbury.

The following day, adverse weather sent the Spanish northwards and the combined shipping of Howard of Effingham, Drake, and Lord Henry Seymour gave chase. Battle was engaged and the Spanish were scattered, bruised, and bloodied. To compound the disaster, which was beginning to look like a band of dogs viciously attacking a lumbering bear, the Spanish commander Medina Sidonia found his ships blown hither and yon by violent gales. He was forced to salvage what he could and lead them up the coast of England, away from the Channel (and Parma), and attempt a circuitous escape around the British Isles and Ireland.

The Armada was now a busted flush, but the news of its scattering and that concomitant realisation had not yet filtered back to London. So it was that Elizabeth took her barge – a gilded and glazed confection manned by twenty-one rowers – to Tilbury, arriving on the 5th of August, acting finally on

---

[78] Herridge, D. M. 2005. *Surrey Probate Inventories, 1558-1603* (Surrey: Surrey Record Society), p. xv.

Leicester's invitation after a week of preparation. To John Guy, Leicester 'meant from the outset to choreograph Elizabeth's visit so as to refashion her for ever as the Warrior Queen she had never really been'.[79] This is a critical point. As has been seen, the menopausal Elizabeth had struggled to find a role other than the sought-after bride. The warrior queen had been implicit in the Greek and Roman goddesses with whom she had been associated for years – Leicester had not invented that. However, he was the first to find her a suitable stage on which to enact it: Tilbury. Further, it is impossible to ignore the fact that, again, the role was not of her choice. Elizabeth did not create her own mythos – it was created for her, and she only reluctantly stepped into it. It is far likelier that she preferred the chaste and virginal aspects of her various aliases, but these would not do in the present circumstances. Likelier still she would have preferred the role her successor tried to adopt: the peace-making Solomon (and she had been so represented during Princess Cecilia of Sweden's visit in 1565-6).[80] It was not to be. In fact, the visit to Tilbury would form probably the best-known piece of Elizabethan iconography, at least as far as her speech-making goes.

Elizabeth gave her famous Tilbury speech to her troops – a speech which survives in several versions – after staying the night at nearby Ardern Hall. Though we have no idea if she dressed in armour (this being a later legend), it was here that she declared that she had 'but the body of a weak and feeble woman, but … the heart and stomach of a king, and of a king of England too, and take foul scorn that Parma or any prince of Europe should dare to invade the borders of my realm'.[81] This was almost certainly her own invention: it rings true to her pretensions of being only a defensive warrior. At the subsequent dinner in Leicester's tent, news arrived from the earl of

---

[79] Guy, *Elizabeth*, p. 106.
[80] Martin, N. 2011. 'Princess Cecilia's Visitation to England in 1565-6' in C. Beem (Ed.) *The Foreign Relations of Elizabeth I* (London: Palgrave Macmillan), pp. 27-44.
[81] Elizabeth I, *Selected Works*, pp. 77-8.

Cumberland that the Spanish had been driven north, towards Scotland's east coast. The warrior had triumphed without the Spanish having managed to land a single man in England.

Elizabeth was a masterful actor, but she seldom got to write her own scripts. With the failure of the first Spanish Armada, however, English seamanship and naval prowess, coupled with her willingness to let men suited to their roles assume them, ensured that on this occasion, the queen got to play exactly the role she coveted.

***

Where was the young favourite during the harried year of the Spanish Armada? On the 29th of July, he had been gripped with the excitement of the day and wrote, 'it is not now fit for me to tarry here': he was then in York House in London, the use of which he had been given by the queen earlier in the year.[82] His was not the path of the statesman, which would have involved sifting of documents and managing intelligence, but in the period from late 1587 to mid-1588 the path of the favourite had proven predictably rewarding. In October 1587 he had received parsonages (and associated tithes from tenants) worth £300 per year; in April 1588 he was elected a knight of the garter with the combined sponsorship of Leicester, Burghley, Worcester, Howard, and Huntingdon; in June, the attainted lands of the Catholic Sir Francis Englefield were granted him. He was even made supreme commander of the cavalry: a position that was nominal, and would turn out to matter little given that the cavalry saw no action, but a significant one nonetheless.

Essex chafed continually for real action. Although a favourite and thus not taken entirely seriously in matters of international diplomacy, warfare, like the council chamber, was one area in which statesmanship and favouritism converged. Quite simply, the queen was a victim of the prejudices of her age, which held that men of suitable rank, whether they had embarked on careers as men of state or courtly darlings, had an innate ability to lead.

---

[82] Essex, *Lives and Letters*, p. 192.

The assumption of the early modern era was that nobility and ability were two sides of the same coin. It was of course a fallacy: Elizabeth had ennobled Leicester and, as her creature and an educated and polished courtier, it was axiomatic that he would be a great military leader; as we have seen, however, his campaigns in the Netherlands were hardly successful. Nevertheless, old ideas die hard. Essex knew, as Elizabeth and Leicester knew, that his nobility entitled him to a life in the saddle, leading men to victory. In addition to land, titles, and favour, the aristocratic favourite might reasonably and entirely expect to make his mark on the international stage by heading military campaigns.

In his role as horse master, Essex did help Leicester rally the troops bound for Tilbury. He had attempted to work with Drake early in 1588, but the queen had inadvertently stymied his secret negotiations by seeking peace; by the time conflict looked inevitable, the energetic seaman had other fish to fry. Overall, the peak of Elizabeth's martial glory as England's defender coincided with a period of only titular action for the eager young favourite. Returning war hero though he was, his ambitions of pursuing greater glories were denied him. The reasons for his fascination with warfare are not hard to find. Not only did the cut and thrust of battle fit with his chivalric ideals, but it offered a stage on which he might be taken seriously. Unfortunately, the queen did not take him especially seriously. Instead, the period between his return to court and the Spanish Armada was to be the story of the birth of his strange and obsessively jealous love for the queen and its corollary: his bitterness and frustration at being treated as the decorative favourite he had willingly become.

Early in 1588 a troupe of young boys had filed in to the palace of Placentia (now generally known as Greenwich), some dressed as women and some as older men. They were the Children of St Paul's (a theatre troupe made up entirely of youths sometimes stolen away from their grammar schools). They were there to entertain the queen and court with a performance of John Lyly's *Endymion: The Man in the Moon*. The play involves the young Greek Endymion's love affair with the moon, personified by the celestial body's goddess, Cynthia. It re-treads the myth, with the sleeping Endymion woken after decades by the goddess's kiss, only for him to admit that he loves her only chastely; in response, she restores his youth. In subsequent centuries, scholars have been quick to identify Cynthia as a representation of Elizabeth and Endymion as Leicester (along with similar 1:1 identifications of other contemporary figures).[83] W. R. Streitberger, however, points out that 'Lyly warns against too close an interpretation in his prologue', and the assumption is that it would have been unwise for a writer to have brazenly made contemporary references to influential figures on stage.[84] In reality, the system of Elizabethan censorship was loose, and playwrights were quite willing to engage in veiled contemporary discussions. They had at hand a range of strategies by which to avoid admonition, from claiming the innocence of their intent to blaming audiences for their evil minds if offence was taken. Lyly's prologue is a good example of using a perfectly acceptable and well-known myth as a means of commenting on the contemporary political scene from behind the veil of an indisputably innocuous and much-told tale. Crackdowns on literary matter deemed insolent, scurrilous, or overtly political were surprisingly rare; when they happened, the penalties could be harsh, but they tended to happen only at times of heightened political sensitivity. *Endymion* did not simply depict Elizabeth and Leicester; Lyly was far too subtle to comment on contemporary politics directly. However, his dramatisation offered a model by which an avowed and unquestioned virgin and goddess could embark upon a relationship with an exceptional young mortal. Endymion, old and then refreshed by young blood, was neither Leicester, Hatton, or Raleigh, or even Essex; and yet he represents all of them - he is an archetype for the type of ageing and replenished male favourites a chaste goddess-queen might

[83] Patterson, M. 2007. *The Oxford Guide to Plays* (Oxford: Oxford University Press), p. 137.
[84] Streitberger, W. R. 2017. *The Masters of the Revels and Elizabeth I's Court Theatre* (Oxford: Oxford University Press), p. 184.

acceptably love and be loved by.

At some point during Essex's rise, usually considered also to be 1588, Essex was painted by the celebrated miniaturist Nicholas Hilliard as 'the young man among roses'. The painting depicts him standing by a tree amidst the thorny branches of a rose bush. His head is tilted downwards in the dejected pose of a melancholy lover, and he holds one hand over his heart. Significantly, the hand is partly obscured by a black shoulder cape – the love he feels is forbidden. The thorny branches might be read as representative of the court – the Elizabethans were not shy about bawdy imagery, and the pricks surrounding him could conceivably be his male rivals. The profusion of white eglantine – sometimes known as the queen's rose – that surrounds him provides evidence that the painting was designed to link Essex with Elizabeth.

There is little doubt that Essex had formed a jealous and obsessive attitude towards the queen – it was not love as we know it, but certainly love as idealistic courtiers who bought into chivalrous ideals and fantasies knew it. Elizabeth, for her part, enjoyed his love and his company, and resolved to do what she could for him. It is here important to note that Elizabeth I was not her father. The uxorious Henry VIII probably never felt love in any meaningful sense; rather, he coveted women to differing degrees of infatuation, and demanded loyalty and obsequies from friends. His daughter was no such monster. Though her status elevated her, she had an active rather than a superficial conscience, and she formed deep and lasting friendships with men and women. When she behaved pettily and spitefully, as she frequently did, it was born of a perception of disappointment at those she loved leaving or betraying her.

The love of the queen's life was and always had been Essex's stepfather, however. In modern parlance, one is tempted to say that she led Essex on; probably, though, it is fairer to imagine that she assumed him to be going through the motions that so many of her courtiers had, albeit his genuine displays of passion offered a frisson with which few bothered to imbue their protestations of love and emotion. After the defeat of the Armada things would change. Leicester, with whom she had quarrelled, loved, hated, been jealous of, and ultimately depended upon as one of the constants of her reign, would die after a short illness. Essex would lose the stepfather who had guided him and, in the last months and years, modelled him as a successor. Elizabeth would be bereft not only of the man to whom she had been closest emotionally since the 1550s, but of the towering figure amongst the jostling men who pushed and shoved their way along the path of the favourite.

8: The Queen's Two Bodies

Leicester had aged alongside Elizabeth, but by late 1588 it was apparent that time had been unkinder to him. He had grown positively fat, the handsome 'gypsy' of their shared youth having given way to paunchy and red-faced middle age. He, like Elizabeth, had been unwell following the defeat of the Armada, and accordingly she had allowed him leave to recover away from court, though not before the pair enjoyed watching Essex show off at the Whitehall tiltyard.

At the end of August, the young favourite took up his pen and wrote to his stepfather from York House:

Since your lordship's departure her majesty hath been earnest with me to lie in the court, and this morning she sent to me that I might lie in your lordship's lodging [at court] which I will forbear till I know your lordship's pleasure, except [unless] the queen force me to it.[85]

Leicester's biographer reads into this a determination on Elizabeth's part to replace the ailing favourite with the new one, but historians are divided on whether or not Essex was being primed to succeed in Elizabeth's affections. To Kendall there is no question: the young earl was crowned chief favourite on the death of the old one and Elizabeth, foreseeing Leicester's death, was preparing the ground for transition. To Hammer, a hierarchy of favourites existed, with the forty-eight-year-old Sir Christopher Hatton looking forward to seniority as secondary amongst the glittering ranks. The truth, however, is that there was neither a smooth transition nor a pecking order.

Elizabeth's band of favourites, which Leicester had for so long headed, was more idiosyncratic than institutional. She was apt to advance or cut short the careers of those who had chosen the courtly path according to their behaviour, prevailing

---

[85] Longleat, *Dudley MSS*, II, 265.

political winds, and her own tastes and moods. Yet it is abundantly clear that she was continuing to shower Essex with affection, advancing him far faster along his chosen path than she did with most young men. Her motto was of course *semper eadem* – always the same. If time could not be stopped then it was enough for her that, for all outward appearances, nothing must appear to have changed.

En route to the baths at Buxton – a resort town known for its healing waters – Leicester and Lettice stopped at Rycote in Oxfordshire, lodging at the home of Henry Norris, 1st Baron Norreys (father of the leader of the infantry in the Netherlands). It was here that the old favourite laid his head on pillows in a bed that the queen had probably used on her multiple visits to the house, but not before he had penned his famous last letter to his sovereign.[86] In its playful thanks for the medicine she had sent him we can read something of the genuine affection between this ageing pair, whose bond ran far deeper than the occasional explosions of temper and pique that sometimes threatened it. The medicine, however, was evidently ineffective. The great favourite fell into a 'continual burning fever' and died on the 4th of September. The man the queen had affectionately called her 'eyes', or her 'sweet Robin' was gone.

When news reached court, Elizabeth's reaction was an echo of her response to the news of Mary Queen of Scots' death, albeit this time it was motivated by a real sense of loss rather than fear of divine and political repercussions. She shut herself away, eschewing politics in favour of the company of her ladies of the bedchamber. Though she had never consummated her relationship with Leicester (the public nature of her life would have made this impossible even if she had wished to) she was nevertheless in mourning for her lover. But Elizabeth was not the only one feeling his loss: Essex had lost a mentor and his

---

[86] Elizabeth first visited Rycote as a virtual prisoner during her sister's reign; in happier times, she visited with Leicester (then known only as Lord Robert Dudley) in 1566, 1568, 1570, and 1572. She would return in 1592. See Salmon, J. T. 1967. *Rycote Chapel, Oxfordshire* (London: H. M. S. O.), p. 5.

mother a husband. How the young earl reacted is not clear: over the centuries, it has been suggested, unfairly, that he had never really liked his stepfather, but the reality is that Leicester had been immensely useful to him and the pair had travelled together and fought alongside one another. Custom, as much as anything, dictated that he show respect and mourn the old man's passing. It was his duty to fill the departed favourite's shoes, to provide the queen with company, and to give succour to those of his stepfather's adherents, followers, and camp-mates who might want it. Beyond Leicester's immediate circle, too, the English ultra-Protestants (by now being referred to as Puritans) had lost their unlikely champion and would have need of a new one. All of this was entirely in keeping with Elizabeth's policy of maintaining her court as it always had been. The personnel might change, and that might be personally difficult, but the ship of state had to remain on course.

Despite Elizabeth's bout of depression and self-imposed seclusion, the business of government had to go on. One apparent beneficiary of Leicester's absence was Burghley. Whilst he and the old favourite had maintained a working relationship over the decades – if not exactly a friendship – the loss of the highest-regarded courtier must have seemed a triumph of statesman over favourite in the council chamber. Yet Burghley was himself ageing and training his second son (the hunch-backed but formidably intelligent Robert Cecil, who would never have made a favourite) as his successor. If he hoped that Essex, who had been his ward and always showed him respect, might become Leicester's spiritual successor and in time cultivate with Robert a similar relationship as he had himself achieved with Leicester, he was to be disappointed. For the moment, however, the explosive rivalry that was to dominate the 1590s was only a distant storm cloud. More obvious ones were gathering and, typically, they were of a religious hue.

1588 bore witness to one of the strangest outpourings of Puritanism in the movement's history (although rather than a movement it might be fairer to imagine a loose collection of unallied reformers). Under the pseudonym Martin Marprelate a series of tracts issued from a movable press, each of which lambasted the Anglican church hierarchy in scurrilous and personally offensive terms. This signalled a shift in public debate from the ponderous and mutually respectful disagreement that had long dominated the two wings of Protestantism to a scrappy, public, invective-filled literary brawl. Marprelate, whoever he was (and he was likely more than one individual) presented the authorities with a problem – how to engage with unknown writers who were willing to attack in personal terms. The whole episode, though, threatened to discredit more moderate Puritans. What they needed was a new, respected, noble protector, and Essex looked to fit the bill.

As Elizabeth might have told Essex, the burden of becoming a successful and famous person was the sudden influx of place seekers, some of whom came from the now-defunct Leicester camp. Being an important personage in Elizabethan England was essentially like being the monarch in microcosm: a royal favourite could expect to find himself beset by an influx of followers whom he was expected to promote and to whom he was supposed to provide patronage; in return he could expect their loyalty. Yet, as Elizabeth also knew, followers had a stake in shaping their patron. She had been moulded as a Pallas Athena in the 1560s, as a prospective bride (despite her claims of disavowing marriage), and lately as a warrior queen and moon goddess. Essex's band of followers were to be of a distinctly religious flavour and they, probably more than he, were the ones who wanted him to emulate Sir Philip Sidney as an anti-French as well as an anti-Catholic hero. Their first move was a misguided and fruitless attempt to have him succeed Leicester as chancellor of Cambridge (then a hotbed of reformist thought). In the event, Hatton got the job; but there would be more useful (and more material) rewards for the unsuccessful candidate.

In the immediate aftermath of Leicester's death, Essex found himself unofficially acting as the queen's lord steward, an office that had officially been Leicester's. This required hosting and allotting apartments at court to visiting dignitaries, and the following January he was awarded the farm of the customs on sweet wines, a hugely lucrative monopoly which Leicester had enjoyed (and which would be welcome to his spendthrift stepson). What is apparent is that the queen was not simply making the young man the new Leicester, but she was willing to let some of the lost favourite's roles and benefits pass to the new. This was not enough. Essex, as usual, wanted the chance to distinguish himself, preferably militarily.

The chance to carve out his own path was of enormous importance to Essex, and it was probably given added impetus by the return to court of Sir Walter Raleigh. The cocky rival had cut him to the quick during their previous entanglement by suggesting that the young earl enjoyed his position due to the good fortune of his birth and pseudo-filial link to Leicester. This was an assault on Essex's honour, and it was one he was determined to disprove by martial exploit. The problem was that there was little to be done in the wake of the Armada, and his boundless energy sought other outlets (it was around this time that he duelled with Charles Blount of the golden chess-queen).

The first Christmas at court without Leicester was a fraught one. The festivities took place at Placentia, and the queen received New Year's gifts including a gold, diamond and ruby necklace and matching earrings from Hatton, an 'oringed' pie from the serjeant of the pastry, and a macaroon from the master cook. Significantly, nothing is recorded as coming from Essex or Raleigh; both were reputedly engaged in bitter argument, causing the queen to travel to Richmond to cool their tempers. It did little good – there was talk of duelling within days.

In many ways it is unsurprising that two of the queen's favourites would embark on such a petty round of fighting; the wonder is why this kind of thing did not happen more often. Each was hoping to fill the void left by Leicester, and there was little other means to satisfy honour. Dispatches continued to pour in from the beleaguered Netherlands and the war with Spain remained very much on, but during the period of the Christmas revels news reached Walsingham from his contact, Villiers, that 'there are no preparations in Spain which threaten any danger for next year'.[87] What was a man to do when the defeated enemy proved disobliging in offering fresh battles? The answer, for Essex, was to hitch himself to those who wanted to cause them. Accordingly, he joined in attempts made by the more militant-minded of the queen's court to take the war to the Spanish. It was to be an act of revenge for the temerity of Philip II in sending his failed Armada; English naval superiority had, after all just been demonstrated. It was commensurate with honour that an affronted England must seek revenge for the attempt to take her.

***

In the spring of 1589 Essex took up his pen and wrote to his grandfather Knollys:

Sir,

What my courses have been I need not repeat, for no man knoweth them better than yourself. What my state now is, I will tell you: my revenue no greater than when I sued my livery; my debts at least two or three and twenty thousand pounds; her Majesty's goodness hath been so great as I could not ask more of her; no way left to repair myself but mine own adventure, which I had much rather undertake than to offend her Majesty with suits, as I have done heretofore. If I should speed well, I will adventure to be rich; if not, I will never live to see the end of my poverty. And so, wishing that this letter, which I have left for you, may come to your hands, I commit you to God's good protection. From my study some few days before my departure.

Your assured friend,

[87] Wernham, R. B. (Ed.). 1936. *Calendar of State Papers Foreign: Elizabeth, Volume 22, July-December 1588* (London: H. M. S. O.), pp. 386-404.

R. Essex[88]

The curious mix of headstrong confidence and desperation is illustrative of the young man's perennially contrasting nature. The letter was written a few days before Essex sailed with Francis Drake in a retaliatory raid on Portugal: a sequel to the famous commander's celebrated 'singeing of the king of Spain's beard' in the spring of 1587. Its contents are illuminating. Not only does it reveal the earl's anxiety about money matters (always a sensitive subject with his grandfather) but it recognises his dependence on the queen – a dependence he is keen to shake. Here is no young opportunist taking advantage of what would in modern terms be called a 'sugar momma', but a developing youth eager to make his way in the world on his own terms. A streak of the hysterical is evident, too, in his desire to 'adventure' or die in poverty. Above all is the almost pathetic need to be taken seriously. He addresses his grandfather as his 'assured friend' (rather than the 'son' or 'humbly at commandment' he had previously signed himself to Leicester and Burghley).

The Portuguese adventure promised that. It was an endeavour heartily encouraged by Dom António, the pretender who had been in exile first in France and then in England following his previous failed attempt to oust Philip and claim the Portuguese crown. Once again he was full of vim and vigour, promising Elizabeth that his countrymen would rise in his favour if she supported a fresh invasion. Following the Armada, she was more forthcoming than she had been in 1582. This was not entirely altruistic nor even motivated by revenge on her part; rather, she was hoping to make piratical profit and cut off Philip's Atlantic fleet at the knees. Accordingly, she assigned Sir Francis Drake as leader of the naval contingent and Sir John Norris as head of the infantry. Neither were nobleman, and she was singularly unwilling to allow members of her nobility to lend official weight to the cause. Naturally, Essex did not let that bother him. About a month before, his mother (presumably

---

[88] Devereux, *Lives and Letters*, p. 206.

not overly distraught about the loss of Leicester) had remarried. She had chosen Sir Christopher Blount, a distant cousin of the Charles Blount who caught the queen's eye. Lettice was then forty-five and her bridegroom in his early thirties, and presumably a far cry from what Leicester had been in his declining years. Essex was not best pleased with the apparent love match, although the extent to which having a new stepfather exacerbated his desire to leave the country can only be guessed at. Whatever his motivation, he decided to ignore Elizabeth's prohibition and set about secret planning to join the expedition, much as he had attempted with Drake in early 1588.

Throughout his career, Essex was to wilfully ignore his sovereign's express commandments. One might assume that he simply disregarded the pleas of an old woman whom he secretly held in contempt, but to do so would be to misconstrue him. He held the office of the monarch in high esteem – as a knight, he could not do otherwise. When his beliefs in the nobility of his own course of action met with opposition from the queen, however, he was to resent her, as holder of the office, for denigrating it by acting ignobly and breaching the age-old relationship with her aristocracy.

Further, she was by now, as we have seen, his courtly lover – his unobtainable mistress. The power of the mistress to decide the fate and actions of a man was limited to love matters, to the realms of the poetic and the emotional. For an idealised mistress to begin dictating her lover's political and military career was beyond the pale. In short, to Essex there were two Elizabeths: the queen, who was unfairly halting his ability to make his way in the world; and the woman, who was an ethereal and stimulating figure, more show than substance. He would never be able to reconcile the queen's two bodies. Instead he would imbue Elizabeth the queen with the worst traits of Elizabeth the woman – her vindictiveness and vacillation – and invest the woman with the best attributes of the queen: vigour, pomp, and seductive flare. This differed from Leicester, who had ultimately accepted his subservience to his sovereign lady, simmering silently or threatening to withdraw from court to his own lands when disputes arose. Essex, by contrast, saw it as his duty to defy her when her demands failed to live up to his expectations of how a monarch should act – in tandem with the desires of her male nobles rather than against their wishes. This defiance would percolate for years, and Elizabeth the queen's continued existence and often arbitrary behaviours would exacerbate it. In time he would begin to take seriously emerging ideas about the rights of subjects to resist tyrannous sovereigns, but only because they told him what he wanted to hear. At heart he would remain a conservative thinker harking back to what was his perception of the old ways.

For the moment, the chance to shine on the battlefield, as well as being personally attractive, offered the opportunity of one-upping his rivals for Elizabeth's affection. The angry and wrong-headed queen would give way to the woman, impressed by the manly ardour of her strong-minded young lover.

It was the queen who had declared that no noblemen should enlist in the unofficial strike against Spanish-ruled Portugal, and it was the queen that Essex hid his plans from. Only a few men knew of them: his younger brother, Walter, the martial-minded and hard-drinking Sir Roger Williams, Sir Philip Butler, and Sir Edward Wingfield. In his organisation we can glimpse the continuation of a growing following which held the role of the monarch in distrust if not contempt.

The plan Essex concocted was suitably baroque. He wrote a letter to Penelope's husband, Lord Rich, with an invitation to supper in his chamber. This he sealed up in his desk along with about forty other letters (one to the queen and many to his friends) before meeting his secretary, Reynolds, at St James' Park. Together they sped towards Plymouth and, when a good distance from London, a groom was sent back with the keys to his desk and instructions to invite Lord Rich to the phony supper date and distribute the other letters, each defending his sudden disappearance, to their recipients. All, it was hoped, would be confusion, and in the midst of it Essex rode pell-mell for the *Swiftsure*, which was ready to set off with the ships of the 150-strong English Armada. The subterfuge would turn out to be characteristic; until the end of his life Essex would conceive a passion for such intrigues which was by turns charmingly boyish and utterly dangerous.

After the runaway boarded on the 5th of April, the vessel put out to sea, leaving the others behind. It plied the waters, its crew having no sure knowledge of what Drake and Norris were planning, and eventually began to sail desultorily towards Cadiz. Weeks passed and they had neither news nor sighting of Drake and Norris' ships, and were instead reduced to capturing the occasional corn-carrying merchant ship unlucky enough to cross their path near Cape Vincent. It was a fool's mission – the entire thing had been the enterprise of an excitable youth with too much power to command and too many friends willing to make his wild dreams happen. Eventually, in May, the *Swiftsure* caught sight of the English fleet and Essex was forced to face the music.

After the *Swiftsure* had sailed out of Plymouth harbour, the earl's grandfather had followed, hoping to recover him. The queen, having learnt of what her young favourite had done, had commanded the austere earl of Huntingdon, too, to find him and demand his return. Probably of more distress to Essex was the discovery that, whilst he and Williams had killed time treading water in the *Swiftsure*, the main Armada had reached, breached, and sacked the poorly-defended town of lower Coruña. Norris had taken the infantry ashore, killing 500 of the town's defenders, and besieging the upper town; Drake had merrily burnt the merchant vessels that lay in the harbour. The former was ultimately unsuccessful – the upper town held out despite the slaughter in the lower, thanks in no small part to the spirited women inhabiting it, but weeks of destruction had unfolded. The fighting had grown fiercer with the approach of hastily-assembled Spanish troops, which were routed, though not without significant English losses. Thereafter the lower town and its surrounding areas were burnt to the ground as Norris' departing men sought to scorch the earth behind them. They had only left a few days before encountering the *Swiftsure*, intending to carry on towards Lisbon. Essex had missed the heat and passion of it all.

As the expedition's leaders, Drake and Norris were in a quandary about what to do with the newly-discovered Essex.

His support, and that of the *Swiftsure*, were welcome, but they had been given orders to send him home. Fortunately for them, the weather voted in favour of his remaining with the fleet, and on they went to Peniche. The adverse winds were music to the young warrior's ears; the phrase 'better late than never' could not have been more appropriate. Needless to say, all of this was a direct flouting of the queen's authority, and it adds yet further to our understanding of her visceral aversion to war. Simply, the unpredictable unfolding of events was something she could not control even by direct order. What her favourite loved about it – the autonomy it offered and the age-old exercising of noble rights – was exactly what she feared and distrusted.

If he cared about his queen's attitude to either war or his abuse of her trust, Essex did not show it. Instead he flung himself into battle with alacrity; he was amongst the first off the landing boats at Peniche, wading 'through the water up to the shoulders' to reach shore.[89] Splitting the men under them, he and Williams took the castle, scattering the defenders who had unwisely come out to battle only to find themselves outflanked. Almost immediately the young earl had a notch on his scabbard.

Thereafter, the English infantry began to march southwards towards Lisbon, plundering as they went. It soon became apparent, however, that Elizabeth had been sold the proverbial pup. Though the English cried the name of Dom António wherever they met resistance, they found themselves treated by the native Portuguese as invaders rather than liberators from Spanish tyranny. When they finally reached Lisbon towards the end of May, they were a weakened and ineffective fighting force, suffering from the usual casualties of hunger and desertion, their numbers hardly buoyed by the meagre forty Portuguese horseman who bothered rallying to their calls. Humiliation threatened when, after the English collapsed asleep outside the garrisoned city, a number of pro-Spanish Portuguese slipped out and began burning their enemy's supplies before retreating back behind their stout walls. In retaliation Norris had

---

[89] Dickinson, J. 2015. *Court Politics and the Earl of Essex, 1589–1601* (London: Routledge), p. 56.

Essex and the rest of the company burnt Portuguese grain stores which lay outside of the town. It was, again, siege warfare, not battle. It was hardly a glorious expedition, but this did not stop Essex making the most of it. Later he would claim to have made a number of his 'fast friendes colonels, and 20 at the least of my domestickes captaines: so as I might have authoritie and party enough'.[90] Needless to say he lacked the authority to do this. That did not matter; he would simply arrogate it in order to promote himself as a powerful figure who did what he could for his people.

When Drake's Armada reached the coast, it was decided to withdraw the infantry. Essex acceded, but not before making a typically futile but chivalric gesture. Taking his lance, he drove it into city's gates in direct challenge. The garrison was not moved by the display. Nor was Drake. Essex and the rest of the ground troops were re-embarked, just in time to relieve a fleet of sixty Baltic merchant ships at Cascais of their stores of dry goods. The infamous sea dog was, as ever, more motivated by profit than honour. As the booty was written up, supply ships arrived from England, and with them a letter from the queen:

Essex,

Your sudden and undutiful departure from our presence and your place of attendance you may easily conceive how offensive it is, and ought to be, unto us. Our great favours bestowed on you without deserts [i.e. your deserving them] have drawn you thus to neglect and forget your duty: for other constructions we cannot make of those your strange actions.[91]

This was Elizabeth at her most imperious, yet it could hardly have been calculated to breed more resentment in the favourite. The reference to his having not deserved her 'great favours' struck exactly the nerve that had hitherto driven his desire to prove himself and exposed him for what his own letter to his

[90] Essex. 1598. *An Apologie of the Earle of Essex* (sig. A3 r-v).
[91] Devereux, *Lives and Letters*, pp. 204-5.

grandfather had lamented: the kept man constantly pressing his suit. How Essex reacted on first reading the six-week old letter is not recorded but might well be imagined. He and Elizabeth were now locked in a strange game of power, each trying to exercise what they could over one another. With the weight of her position and the irresistible (to a chivalrous knight) lure of femininity, she might have felt confident in having the upper hand; with the lightness of his youth, the strength of his passion for her as an iconic mistress, and a growing lack of respect for her as a monarch, he might have felt equally confident.

What is instructive is that this time he acted upon her instructions and returned to England in June. The expedition had been rather a bust, but again his part in the action – the taking of Peniche – had been beyond successful in military terms if not material reward. The fault, besides, had been the groundless promises of the hapless Dom António, who would be given no further chances; the dashing old pretender would die in French exile, penniless and spent, in 1595.

Despite the failure of England's Armada to stir up popular support against Philp or even cripple his fleet, Essex found himself able to bypass the regal anger by courting the woman, with the support of her counsellors. More importantly, however, he found that he was again feted by the common people as a national hero – something that Leicester had never managed. If the Netherlands campaign had earned him his stripes, the wild dash to fight for England on Philip's soil had given him a badge of honour. The nature of the campaign – piratical and completely fruitless in causing a Portuguese uprising – mattered less than his willingness to risk censure to fight for his country. The lesson learnt was that it was worth risking a prevaricating and cautious queen's displeasure to win popular acclaim. As more and more men flocked to him, it became one that he would not forget.

9: The Queen, the Spymaster, his Daughter, and her Lover

Being a hero was a pricy business. So too was maintaining the band of retainers and followers that a great man required. Despite the hopes he had expressed to his grandfather of making his fortune in the Portuguese campaign, he had returned with relatively little to show for it – in fact, his steward (the Welshman Gelli Meyrick, who had stuck with him since his Cambridge days) later estimated that he had spent in the region of £10,500 on his part in the Armada. His future, therefore, remained as uncertain as ever. So, in fact, did England's.

In the wake of Leicester's death, James VI had sent letters south commiserating with Essex on the loss of his stepfather. Now, however, it was Essex's turn to begin writing to the likely future king. This was a potentially dangerous course of action, but it was one that increasing numbers of Elizabethan courtiers found themselves having to do. Elizabeth had only herself to blame; the myth of her eternal youth could not entirely efface the reality that any day she might die. She was, after all, approaching fifty-six, and her father had died at fifty-five. Eyes were certainly turning northwards. Indeed, although the date cannot be known with certainty, the university wit, Robert Greene wrote a fantastical tragicomedy for the popular stage the year after the Portuguese venture. Titled (inaccurately) *The Scottish History of James the Fourth*, the drama involved a Scottish courtier relating to the fairy king, Oberon, a tale of a leonine English king giving his daughter in marriage to a venal young Scottish king, only for the princess – after many troubles and adventures – to school and reform the young monarch. Though sufficiently couched in fantasy, the drama indicates that the perceived necessity of English influence on the Scottish monarch was a topic hot enough to warrant a popular play.

Accordingly, Essex and his sister, Penelope, wrote joint letters to James in late 1589. Their choice of messenger was, however, misguided: they chose, understandably, Richard

Douglas, the nephew of the Scottish ambassador, Archibald (the likely murderer of James' father, Darnley). Although James was impressed by the 'fineness of [Penelope's] wit' and her later portrait, he was simply not willing to place trust in the coded game (Penelope was 'Ryalta'; Essex was 'Ernestus'; James was 'Victor'; and Elizabeth was 'Pallas').[92] Nothing came of the affair, but it does require explanation. Was Penelope behind it? Politically active women certainly existed amongst the aristocracy. Was Essex? He had, after all, recently shown a predilection for intrigue that would only grow in future years. Above all, for the purposes of the present study, does the secret communication indicate that the young favourite had grown tired of Elizabeth as an idealised mistress-lover? Tantalising evidence suggests that this might be the case, and if so, Elizabeth's attitude towards his martial ambitions probably had more to do with it than her appearance or age.

Burghley was, as usual, fully abreast of what Essex and his sister thought they were doing in secret. In his briefings it was reported that the pair had told King James that 'hir Majeste cowde not lyve above a yere or ii by reason of sum imperfeccion'.[93] If this is true, then even the courtly love Essex had felt for the queen had dissipated or been temporarily lost. He could hardly have calmly and eagerly looked towards her death otherwise. Yet doubt must remain. If Essex had really spoken of the queen dying within a year or two, then he had walked into the murky world of illegal language. This would hardly be out of character for one so reckless, but the dangers were well known. A number of laws covered what Elizabethans could say, as we have seen in the case of the labourer Jeremy Vanhill (he of the scatological desires). Amongst others, the

---

[92] Smuts, R. M. 2016. *The Oxford Handbook of the Age of Shakespeare* (Oxford: Oxford University Press), p. 505; Daybell, J. 2011. 'Gender, Politics, and Diplomacy: Women, News and Intelligence Networks in Elizabethan England) in R. Adams & R. Cox (Eds.) *Diplomacy and Early Modern Culture* (London: Palgrave Macmillan), p. 116.
[93] *Cecil MS*, 18/51.

statute of *scandalum magnatum* forbade the spreading of false news about the kingdom's governors; false prophecies were outlawed; the Treason Act (1571) made it a crime to assert that somebody else had the right of succession to the throne; seditious words (those which might lead to a breach of the peace) were illegal. In short, Burghley had a number of ways of proceeding against Essex and Penelope had he so wished, and yet he did not. Either he did not trust the information, or he wished to keep the matter quiet, or both. As Essex had been unsuccessful in his initial attempt to win James over with promises to support his succession, the whole thing was dropped – for the time being at least.

There exists another possibility. Essex would always suffer from emotional immaturity, and it was exactly that which saw him swing from chaste passion for an ageing icon to spiteful disinterest, to hatred, and back again to obsessive jealousy. Elizabeth in full sail as queen was insecure yet regal, cold, and infuriatingly indecisive. Elizabeth in her leisure hours was flirtatious and witty, captivating and bright-eyed. Both were impressive, untouchable sovereigns, but Essex disliked one and loved the other. In her different guises the queen represented the best and worst of the period's skewed perceptions of women – as a ruler she was far too timid and given to prevarication, whereas as a woman she stirred passions whilst remaining sacrosanct. Whatever the truth of Essex's ostensible claims that she was near death, it appears on the surface that, fresh from his curtailed adventure and lauded as a hero, the young earl was looking forward to a time in which England was ruled by a king rather than a queen. That could only happen when Elizabeth died and, whatever he felt about her as a person, he was quite willing to make preparations for it.

1590 thus dawned with Essex back at court and unquestionably in favour and eager to make his mark. His tepid approval of Puritanism (he had been seen as successor enough to Leicester to have been approached by the Puritans in 1588) gave way to adherence to the old guard of Anglican counsellors. He wooed Burghley, Hatton, and Walsingham. Indeed, the older men had been instrumental in calming Elizabeth's initial anger at the wayward young favourite when he returned from Lisbon. Not only that, but he drew support from the countess of Warwick and Lord Hunsdon, his mother's uncle. Even Raleigh could not compete against such ranged supporters of his young rival and, as he had done when Leicester had been on the scene championing Essex, he fled the court, this time for Ireland. All might have been well, and he might quickly have settled into his old role as the petted darling of the court and city, but for the fact that he had not given up his dreams. Nor had he given up on his apparently on-again, off-again sexual relationship with Walsingham's daughter, the unimaginatively-named Frances.

Walsingham himself was by now at the end of his days. He made his will in December 1589 and had been suffering pains and difficulties in passing water for years. Nevertheless, he soldiered on until April 1590, passing away quietly at his house in Seething Lane. He had been one of the greatest Elizabethan statesmen, perfectly willing to outlay vast sums of his own money in order to create a network of spies and informers hitherto unknown in England (it rivalled the Catholic spy networks of Europe, which he often infiltrated). Elizabeth had trusted him greatly and formed a solid relationship with him, calling him her 'moor'. However, there is no reason to suppose that she loved the grave, serious-minded spymaster any more than a modern president or prime minister must love their head of intelligence. As a token of her gratitude to his long service, she forgave his debts and provided his daughter a small annuity. One suspects that that, along with the modest burial in St Paul's Cathedral he received, would have suited his tastes.

Walsingham thus left behind him not only a relatively poor daughter, but a motley mass of spies and informants who were bereft of a paymaster. In time Essex would gather up a share of the latter, but for the moment he drew closer than ever to the former.

The nature of Essex's affair with Frances Walsingham started obscurely and would continue so. Exactly when and how sexual activity commenced is unknown – undoubtedly because the whole thing was carried out in secrecy, although the suggestion has been long made that Sidney, on his deathbed, begged Essex to look after his wife and infant daughter. Allegedly, the pair even went through some kind of formal betrothal or secret marriage only six months after Sidney's death.[94] Frances had certainly been with Sidney at the time of his death at Flushing and returned to England thereafter, which would make it entirely possible that she knew Essex well even then. What is clear is that he was sleeping with her in 1590, for she would give birth to his son and namesake, Robert Devereux, in January 1591. A surviving portrait of Frances painted in 1584 by Robert Peake the Elder indicates an attractive woman, similar in the shape of her face to Elizabeth, but with far larger, more expressive eyes and dark hair. If she is not beautiful, there is something remarkably sharp and attractive about her, despite the stiffness of the composition and the overpowering dress and ruff. She stares off to her left with a hint of patrician displeasure, her eyebrow raised over the slightly larger left eye. Portraiture tells us very little about personality, however. It is entirely possible that Frances was a careful cultivator of noblemen, intent on making a marriage with the handsome favourite, or that she was entirely passive and seduced into the bedroom.[95]

What ought to be resisted is the notion that Essex had chosen her purely because of a desire to replace the dead Sidney (who had in any case been gone for three-and-a-half years). Whilst he shared Sidney's literary ambitions – which would soon see

---

[94] This claim is made by Sir Roy Strong, who writes, 'Essex in fact did marry Frances Walsingham six months after her husband's death, but the marriage was kept secret'. This seems extremely unlikely and one wonders if 'husband's' is not a misprint of 'father's'. October falls six months after Francis Walsingham's death and is certainly when the secret marriage was revealed. See Strong, R. C. 1986. *The Cult of Elizabeth: Elizabethan Portraiture and Pageantry* (Berkeley: University of California Press), p. 79.

[95] Despite the paucity of information available on Frances' personality, her proximity to two Elizabethan titans, Sidney and Essex, has resulted in no fewer than two novels in which she is the protagonist: Angela McLeod's *The Brilliant Stage* (2014) and *The Walsingham Woman* by Jan Westcott (1953).

action – and his martial tastes, he would quickly show a predilection for the French and was already growing cool towards the hotter brand of Protestantism. Nor, to his credit, did he marry her for money, she having only her modest annuity from the crown. The date of his marriage to Sidney's widow is unknown, and it might conceivably have taken place any time between 1587 and 1590. However, the fact that it only came to the queen's attention in October of 1590 suggests that the pair wed when it was apparent that Frances was pregnant. It was not, it would seem, a love match, but a required one. Love and sex appear to have been mutually exclusive in Essex's mind, though sex and marriage were not. This should not surprise us. Maturing in a culture which demonised sex and the women who offered it, and promoted instead the virtues of Platonic, Aristotelian, and Ovidian love, it is only surprising that more educated Elizabethan men were not emotionally stunted. Thus he entered into marriage with Frances having slept with her, probably repeatedly, beforehand and marrying only when her condition – and thus his honour and that of his coming child – demanded it. Love he continued to feel towards almost everyone else – towards the queen, sometimes now cynically and sometimes still obsessively; towards his friends and followers; and towards his family.

Predictably, the secret marriage reached the queen's ears, as they always did. Equally predictably, she raged volubly against the newlyweds. It is often written that Elizabeth had a pathological jealousy of marriage, but it is much fairer to say that her anger stemmed from the secrecy with which those at her court did it. There were sound political reasons for this. When it became news that her people had married without her permission and kept it from her, it risked making her a laughing stock: she was, clearly, a monarch who could not control her courtiers, and her courtiers in turn thumbed their noses at her. The pleasant fiction of the omniscient monarch who knew all and saw all was shown up for what it was by such illicit conduct. On a personal level, her inherent insecurity and neediness meant that she deplored emotional unfaithfulness in her favourites. Wives were a necessary evil – nobleman were expected to beget heirs – but they should spend as little time with their brood mares as possible and remain ever ready to dance with and entertain their first love, Elizabeth herself.

What is surprising about the revelation of Essex and Frances' marriage is how quickly the queen passed from anger to acceptance. Within a fortnight the young favourite was back by her side. It is possible that she saw in Walsingham's daughter a welcome stabilising influence and an acceptable outlet for his more extreme passions. So too is it possible that she knew or suspected that he had no emotional interest in his wife and had married her only due to her impending childbirth. From a political standpoint, too, she could no more afford to protract Essex's disgrace than she had been able to when he returned from Portugal. Her statesmen were firmly on his side, and her people continued to make much of him; to make too long and great a show of her anger risked redounding on her as a bitter old woman who fulminated against the natural behaviours of the young. Besides, she still enjoyed his company, his enthusiasm, and his energy. Even in her declining years the queen remained energetic, riding and dancing with the best of them, and in Essex she saw a kindred spirit, albeit one which needed tamed.

Notwithstanding the queen's reaction, the marriage offered Essex's rival favourites an irresistible chance to make mischief. Chief amongst them was, again, Sir Walter Raleigh, who can only have looked with green eyes at the popularity the younger man had enjoyed since returning to England. Their rivalry found voice in an outpouring of acrimonious verses, and in these Raleigh had the upper hand, being a talented poet and friend to the writer and soldier, Edmund Spenser, who, though he only sporadically visited London and the court, was busy writing his *The Faerie Queene*, a series of books celebrating Elizabeth's reign and realm. As Raleigh had been forced – or chosen, as he claimed – to flee to Ireland, where Spenser held office and considerable lands, the two men had had plenty of time to discuss the irksome rise of the headstrong and cocky Essex. When Spenser then travelled to London to publish the first three books in 1590, Raleigh contributed to the dedicatory verses which prefaced the publication. As Steven W. May has suggested, the poem beginning, 'The prayse of meaner wits' targeted Essex as a cuckoo in the following lines:

The Praise of meaner Wits this Work like Profit brings,
  As doth the Cuckoo's Song delight, when Philomela sings.[96]

Essex, in return, was to pen his own 'Muses no more but mazes', which contained the stanza:

Muses no more, but mazes be your names
  When discord's sound shall mar your concord sweet
Unkindly now your careful fancy frames,
  When fortune treads your favours under feet;
But foul befall that cursed cuckoo's throat
  That so hath crossed sweet Philomela's note.[97]

'Fortune' was a nickname increasingly assigned to Raleigh, who under Essex's pen becomes the cuckoo (a bird notorious for laying its eggs in other birds' nests). In later lines the speaker goes on to condemn the target of his opprobrium for showing spite towards love. This has led May to suggest that

Ralegh's "spight at love" could refer to his efforts to harm the newlyweds, while the queen's anger would be aptly described in lines 33-4: "Beauty must seeme to goe against her kinde,/In crossinge nature in her sweetest Joyes," meaning that the queen has displayed an unnatural opposition to the Earl's very natural

---

[96] Raleigh, W. 1829 [1590] 'On the Same' in W. Oldys & T. Birch (Eds.) *The Works of Sir Walter Raleigh, Vol. VIII* (Oxford: Oxford University Press), p. 718.
[97] Essex. 1814 [c1590]. 'Muses no more' in E. Brydges (Ed.) *Excerpta Tudoriana; or, Extracts from Elizabethan literature, with a critical preface by sir E. Brydges. 2 vols.* (Oxford: Oxford University Press), p. 33.

enjoyment of wedlock.[98]

This is a little less convincing. Essex never showed much love towards Frances and, if the poetic persona has one overriding interest throughout the poem, it is to condemn an unnatural world in which love has been subverted, horses mating with asses, phoenixes with crows, and dainty hills bowing to dirty dales. What appears to be a condemnation of Raleigh is as much a tacit condemnation of Elizabeth for allowing such a world to come about. She is the phoenix and Raleigh the crow, just as Essex is the phoenix and Frances the crow. It is a text spun from the idea of various wrong matches contributing to a woeful world and preventing true love's course. It is typical of Essex – even the orderly and unwavering iambic pentameter is symptomatic of his desire to do everything nobly. Raleigh, in his freer use of alexandrine and iambic heptameter, is the better poet.

Spenser, too, deserves his due for his books, which sought to provide interactive literary manuals for the shaping of the ideal, virtuous gentleman. Alas, although he would win a relatively paltry £50 annual pension from Elizabeth, he would ruin any chance at further advancement the following year when he reissued a revised version of his 1578-9 *Mother Hubbard's Tale* in his collection, *Complaints*. With its veiled attacks on members of the court, *Mother Hubbard's Tale* pre-empted what Spenser and Raleigh were to get up to in the prefatory verses of *The Faerie Queene*, but this time its satirical bent drew the ire of Burghley. Despite those attacks being predicated on the ten-year-old Anjou marriage project, Burghley's sponsorship of it, and the Elizabethan church's priests, its republication came at a time of heightened religious tension within Protestantism, with the chief secretary working with Essex and Raleigh (in a rare display of unity) later in the year to defend the Archbishop of Canterbury, John Whitgift, from the slings and arrows of the

---

[98] May, S. W. 1980. 'The poems of Edward de Vere, seventeenth Earl of Oxford and Robert Devereux, second Earl of Essex', *Studies in Philology, 77*, pp.86-88.

Puritans.

Such literary sparring is illustrative of the age, but it should not be disregarded as flummery. Essex as an historical figure can often seem grossly insensitive, even bull-headed, but in fact the opposite is the case. He was altogether *too* sensitive. The slightest dark look was a slap across the face, literary attacks a punch, and outright criticism a dagger in the guts. All were outrageous slights, and all cried out for revenge. What Elizabeth made of her favourites exchanging accusatory verses is not known, but it is to be hoped that she preferred it to physical duelling. In some ways it was a backhanded compliment: she was a victim of her own success in creating a court in which wealthy, creative, and ambitious men could flourish and compete for her favour.

In addition to his literary endeavours, the winter of 1590-1 saw the birth of Essex's son and heir, Robert, later to be the 3rd earl (another son, Walter, would follow the next year, but would die young). This was a bright spot, but a child to be fed, eventually schooled, and kept in appropriate state would hardly be cheap. Money matters continued to weigh heavily on the indebted earl, as they had dominated his mind in the year between his return from Portugal and the exposure of his marriage. Earlier in 1590, before the queen had discovered his clandestine marriage, he had been forced to sell his manor house at Keyston – despite it being 'mine of ancient inheritance, free from incumbrance; a great circuit of ground, in a very good soil … but I am so far in debt, and so weary of owing, that sell I must'.[99] Prior to that he had been complaining to Burghley about irregularities in his farming of the customs on sweet wines and begging for it to be corrected in his favour rather than that of the London merchants.[100] It was likely the want of cash as much as the thought of glory that turned Essex's head again towards warfare – evidently he had not learnt from his dashed hopes of making his fortune in Portugal that war cost a great deal more than it offered in return. Yet, thankfully for Essex,

[99] Devereux, *Lives and Letters*, p. 208.
[100] *Ibid.*

the disintegrating state of French affairs promised a soldier fresh opportunity to fly the flag of England and cement his position as the realm's leading military light.

10: Round Rouen and Home Again

France had been plagued by intermittent religious wars between Huguenots (French Protestants) and Catholics (headed largely by the powerful Guise family) for decades. The monarch was then Henry IV – a beleaguered Protestant who found it impossible to take control of his country's capital, Paris being a stronghold of Catholicism. As she was his coreligionist, he had appealed to Elizabeth for aid in September 1589 and thereafter the queen supplied money and troops intermittently – as always, she was driven by a desire to maintain Protestant allies whilst not allowing them to grow overly powerful.[101]

Essex was intoxicated by the idea of fighting in France, no doubt stirred further by the tales his brother, Walter, and his colleague on the Portugal raid, Sir Roger Williams, had told him; both men had ventured to Navarre to fight in April 1588. To ingratiate himself with the French king, Essex had set about courting the country's ambassador to England, la Nocle, immediately upon his return from Portugal; thereafter he had begun writing directly to King Henry (in the hopes, no doubt, of making a more favourable impression than he and Penelope had made on the king of Scots). The import of his writing to either king cannot be underestimated. Writing to foreign potentates was an unequivocal expression of independence: a bold announcement that one was a serious political player bent on asserting autonomy.[102]

---

[101] This was not a subtle tactic. Although he wrote years later, Fulke Greville asserted that this was Elizabeth's goal from at least the time of the Netherlands campaign.

[102] During his brief reign as an uncrowned king of Scots, Lord Darnley had, for example, addressed himself to the kings of Spain and France, and written under his own seal to the pope, all in a fruitless attempt to assert his authority as Scotland's king. Needless to say, Mary Queen of Scots was discontented.

An immediately noticeable aspect of the young earl's personality is the extent to which certain ideas became totemic, utterly blotting out all others and brooking no counter-argument. So it was with the notion of a French campaign. He begged Elizabeth to let him do what he had begun to claim was his duty in France early in 1590 and then again later, when the old hand Sir John Norris looked set to be made commander of a force allowed by the queen to go to Brittany (Norris, despite Essex's attempts to cajole, sweeten, and ultimately thwart him, was confirmed as commander and eventually went in the spring of 1591). In November 1590, not long after the queen's anger towards him had cooled, he had entertained the visiting viscount of Turenne to dinner at York House, offering money to fit out German mercenaries – this at the time he was selling off Keyston. The disastrous nature of his finances notwithstanding, he even borrowed money to buy the lease of an entire island in the English Channel, presumably to use as a base. It was during this round of pleading for generalship that Essex made his infamous plea three times on bended knee, for two hours on one occasion, before the queen.

Elizabeth was unwilling to let him go. It has been suggested that her motivation in staying him was that 'in [her] mind, Essex still seemed a young courtier, not a credible general'.[103] This is only partly true. In the period, age and experience mattered less – far less than they should have – than rank. Leicester had been little more than a seasoned courtier, recommended for the Netherlands campaign only because he had cultivated a friendship with William of Orange; Sir Philip Sidney had had little more than enthusiasm, familial heritage, and a grand tour under his belt to recommend him as general of the horse, which post he was given in 1583; and back in the first years of her reign, when she had been forced by the threat of Burghley's (then William Cecil's) resignation, she had opted to put the weak-willed, twenty-three-year-old duke of Norfolk in charge of the forces she was obliged to send to Scotland to aid the Protestant rebellion there. If she did not want to advance Essex

---

[103] Hammer, *The Polarisation of Elizabeth Politics*, p. 95.

to military command, it was not because of his youth (at twenty-five he was older than Norfolk had been and the same age Elizabeth had been on her accession). It was not what you knew in Elizabethan England that guaranteed commissions, but who you knew – and Essex had been cultivating the right people.

Rather than seeing him as an inexperienced youth unfit for command, Elizabeth seemed instead to enjoy the long-game of punishing him for his earlier abscondment and secret marriage, and, perversely, to need his company as one of the stars of her court. Without him, the place was decidedly dusty – Hatton was around fifty, and even Raleigh was pushing forty. The place was looking out of touch with the city of London, which, thanks to the high mortality rate and low life expectancy, was perpetually young. To keep up with the times, Elizabeth had to allow an influx of fresh young faces from good families, and they naturally looked to the handsome, glittering Essex as their unofficial leader.

The problem with trying to maintain young folk at her court was obvious and Essex played his role in ensuring that chastity did not reign supreme. Despite his protestations of courtly love for the queen – which continued, however earnestly – and with little care for the wife his new son had forced on him, he continued to indulge in casual, loveless sex. During the year one young maid, Elizabeth Southwell, was found to be feigning 'lameness in her leg'.[104] She was pregnant, and one Thomas Vavasour took the blame, voluntarily accepting a term of imprisonment. When the child, Walter, was born, however, it was placed in the care of the dowager countess of Essex, Lettice. With that scandal still brewing, it is little wonder Essex was desirous to be off, and any such opportunity would have the added boon of pleasing those disenfranchised soldiers who had looked to him following Leicester's death. The only roadblock was Elizabeth, but he had learnt that her anger could be offset by his absence, it tending to make her heart grow fonder. Later in 1591 came the chance.

---

[104] Haigh, *Elizabeth I*, p. 96.

***

The city of Rouen in France had a colourful history. The capital of Normandy, it was a key port city on the banks of the Seine and boasted one of the most magnificent cathedrals in the country. During the Hundred Years War it had been besieged and won by Henry V, and in 1550 it had borne witness to Henry II's formal entry festivities, which involved mock sea battles, Roman-inspired tableaux, and all manner of exotica. As 1591 wore on, however, it was once more a battleground fought over by the Huguenots and the Catholic League, and Essex crossed the Channel to join it.

Essex had fought hard to be the commander of the force Elizabeth sent to Normandy. Unlike during the Portuguese campaign, the joining up of Englishmen with Henry IV's army required a man of appropriate rank – Leicester, had he been alive and well, would probably have been the natural choice. The fact that Burghley, Hatton, and even King Henry himself – all of whom were cock-a-hoop at the thought of persuading Elizabeth to take up arms in common cause – supported his candidacy helped. Significantly, all were men Essex had wooed.

Yet Essex was not the only young man whose cause was being pressed on Elizabeth during 1591. Burghley's second son, Robert Cecil, was at the same time being promoted as a candidate for the post of secretary vacant since its former incumbent, William Davison, had fallen from favour as a scapegoat in securing the queen's signature on Mary Stewart's death warrant. Robert Cecil was, as his father had taught him, made for the path of the statesman. Possessed of a steel-trap mind and a physically malformed body, he was quite willing to use quill and parchment where Essex preferred sword and shield. The two young men certainly knew one another, Cecil being only two years older than Essex. Whilst it is possible that they first met during Essex's youthful visit to Theobalds, there is no record of it; more concretely, Burghley sent his son to Cambridge to witness the young earl's graduation in 1581, and in late 1587 Essex responded to a direct plea from Cecil in achieving the reversion of some of Burghley's offices. Nothing in their relationship suggested animosity, until Burghley appealed for his son to become the royal secretary. Essex, on this occasion, lent his voice – beguiling as it was – against his fitness for the post. Although this was probably not out of malice (the earl had long fought for Davison's pardon and restoration), it sounded a sour note. Despite his father's attempt to sway the queen (absenting himself from court in a surprisingly huffy manner), Cecil did not get the job, his path to greatness suddenly looking that much more tortuous. Although he did achieve appointment to the privy council – a huge step in itself for a man just knighted – Robert Cecil was not a man to forget those who had thrown obstacles in his path.[105]

It is unlikely that Essex gave a second thought to the disappointed Cecil – an aspiring pen-pusher – when he arrived in France. His mind had been on other matters. Ignoring the financial situation that had weighed so heavily on him during the period 1589-91, he spent £14,000 over and above the queen's allowance outfitting his troops in his distinctive orange-and-white liveries. The queen herself had inspected them at Covent Garden in July, although it had not inspired her to give her favourite a free hand in directing them. Instead, she had laid out a royal commission strictly delineating his actions abroad. From Elizabeth's perspective, Essex was under her generalship; he was not this time a heroic, freebooting renegade.

It is to be doubted how seriously he took his orders. What did the queen know about military matters? She had never been in the field. In fact, she had never been further from London than the midlands. It had, further, become clear to Essex that no matter how good the channels of communication between England's capital and his forces, he would have to think on his feet. As soon as he had arrived at Dieppe and struck camp at nearby Arques in August, he found himself and his troops cut off from Henry IV's men, whom they had been ordered to join. This was a disaster, not least because the queen's commands held that his men must stay put until the French king had

[105] Loades, D. 2012. *The Cecils: Privilege and Power Behind the Throne* (London: Bloomsbury), p. 226.

formally responded to the Anglo-French treaty underpinning the support. Essex did so, but the rumblings reaching him from his putative ally's camp were not encouraging him. Not only was Henry IV ignoring his messages, but it seemed likely he would not live up to his ambassadors' promises of payment. August arrived and still nothing. Eventually, in the middle of the month, Sir Roger Williams, Essex's old comrade and leader of the advance expedition, arrived, inviting the earl to meet with Henry at Compiègne – a location far distant through Catholic territory from both Rouen and Arques.

Surprisingly, Essex made it there, resplendent in an orange velvet coat dripping in jewels, his trumpeters announcing the arrival of the 200-strong cavalry force. This was no doubt the kind of style he had learnt at Leicester's elbow. King Henry wined and dined the dashing earl for four days, treating him to a two-hour audience before riding off for the German provinces to beg for further assistance and prevent mutiny by those already in his employ. The earl was appropriately charmed and delighted in making himself out to be far more urbane and influential than he was: in Henry was a man whose company he could enjoy on a personal level and a monarch whom he could respect and serve. What he did not realise was that he and Elizabeth had been thoroughly duped, the fresh English troops simply raised to keep Rouen's governor, Villars, safely locked up behind his town's walls whilst King Henry ran hither and yon amassing support where he could. The French king was not overly interested in besieging Rouen – the ostensible object of the mission from England's perspective – and the most he would promise was that his army would join the siege only if Essex prepared the ground. Worse, the earl had been abandoned by his royal host a hundred miles from his troops.

The return trip must have been an exercise in humiliation and fear, which not even tangerine velvet could have alleviated. Raiding parties had been released from Rouen and were roving the countryside, launching intermittent attacks, and it was a depleted party that Essex led towards Pavilly, fifteen miles from Rouen. It was here that he had ordered his troops to march from Arques, but what he found when his expeditionary cavalry met them was no more encouraging. Though the troops left at Arques had seen no real action, they had encountered the equally fearsome enemy of late-summer heat and boggy land. Disease was cutting swathes through the men – not all soldiers, but many formerly-healthy tenants drawn unwillingly from his lands.

Nevertheless, he insisted that they follow Henry IV's orders rather than Elizabeth's and begin the siege. He simply must avoid and could not afford another embarrassing English military venture begun in hope but ending in failure. He ordered a small troop to advance on Rouen, hopeful that King Henry would keep his promise of sending his own army to join in. Amongst those Essex selected for the expedition was his brother. The consequences would be fatal. As he rode towards Rouen on the 8th of September, Walter Devereux was struck in the head and killed by a sniper. Essex was crushed when he learnt of it. He kept to his tent in a deep state of depression compounded by a fever.

Once the fever had broken and the depression sufficiently lifted, the English had no choice but to fall back towards Arques. During the retreat, however, Essex did manage a considerable victory in taking the town of Gournay – a strategic place that the Catholic Leaguers had needed to provision Rouen. Yet would one win be enough to quell the queen's growing wrath?

***

Back in London, Elizabeth had begun to fret. The fretting had turned to regret and the regret to anger. She was a woman who, having eventually reached a decision, inevitably wished she had done otherwise and looked to cast blame where she could. Many of her counsellors, Burghley chief amongst them, had persuaded her to trust and support Henry IV, but the buck would have to stop with Essex. Such was the nature of military command. At the end of August she learnt of his ride to meet Henry IV and was so incensed that, if the catty Robert Cecil is to be believed, she wished her favourite dead.

In Essex's absence she had travelled to Portsmouth as part of her progress through Sussex and Hampshire; she had hoped that King Henry could be talked into crossing the Channel and meeting with her. In this belief she was encouraged by the fawning letters the French king had addressed to her: 'madam,' he had written, 'I beg you to permit me to go and kiss your hand as king of Navarre and to spend two hours with you so that at least once in my life I may have the honour of seeing her to whom I have dedicated my time and my life and whom I love and revere more than anything in the world'.[106] Such sycophancy made even Essex look circumspect. Elizabeth could not resist it. Unfortunately, her gallant Gallic lover did not show – he was even then looking for other marks.

Piqued no doubt by this and, more importantly, the fool that Henry IV was making of her and her favourite, the queen sent a stream of invective across the Channel. In scathing terms, she excoriated Essex for his manifold failures and demanded his immediate recall. She had even, presciently, suggested to Essex that he preferred to serve a king than 'a mere queen'. She was no mind reader, but sometimes her suspicious jealousy was well-founded. Nor was it entirely personal. To the French ambassador, du Plessis, she raged the following January that 'he [Essex] makes the king of France believe that he … ruled our realm.[107] This was always her real fear of her popular and internationally-active nobles. Elizabeth's notice of recall was making its way to Normandy even as Essex's news of the capture of Gournay – and a plea for an extended commission – was on its way to London via his messenger Robert Carey.

The queen's recall and Essex's plea for more time passed in the night. Carey reached the queen and, despite being exposed to blistering diatribes against his master – she 'vowed she would make him an example to the entire world' – he managed to

---

[106] Pryor, F. (Ed.) 2003. *Elizabeth I: Her life in Letters* (Berkeley: University of California Press), p. 107.

[107] Strickland, A. 1852. *Lives of the Queens of England: From the Norman Conquest, Volumes 6-7* (Philadelphia: Lea and Blanchard), 120.

inveigle her to write to Essex again.[108] Things were now becoming farcical. At the end of September, she had published 'A declaration of the causes that moved her Majesty to revoke her forces in Normandy' (which would be followed months later by 'Causes moving her Majesty not to consent to send any more forces unto Normandy'). This was, in modern terms, an exercise in public relations. A Protestant fight-back against the Catholic League had been popular with those of her subjects given to English bravado. On the 4th of October, with Carey waiting, she then wrote

but since our commandment sent for your return, which we doubt not but you have disposed yourself according to your duty to have performed, we have lately considered that since the winning of Gournay in so short a time whereof we are very glad, and that we perceive the attempt of Caudebec and the besieging of Rouen is also begun … we certainly understand that our people … are like to give great furtherance, and their revocation great hindrance…

In other words, Elizabeth had recalled her notice of recall, giving Essex leave to remain in Normandy and help effect the siege of Rouen. However, her note was not without asperity:

Having shewed and sent to you in writing very good cause which moved us thereto [i.e. to remain only for the original period of two months], such as if you have well weighed them with a mind and judgement not blinded with vain persuasions either of yourself or of such others as do accompany you with their glorious, windy discourses, you would have readily asserted thereunto …[109]

This rebuke of Essex – and willing recognition that he was

---

[108] Sands, W., Brymer, A. Murray, A., & Cochran, J. (Eds.) 1808. 'Review – Cary's Memoirs', *The Scots Magazine, Vol. 70* (Edinburgh: Archibald Constable), p. 916.
[109] Elizabeth I, *Selected Works*, p. 190.

surrounded by bad influences – was to be a theme of her letter. In addition to condemning the French king for his actions and, rather caustically, praising the success of those English forces who had actually made it to join up with the French and besiege Rouen, she had time to condemn Roger Williams' rashness. This, she suggested, had caused the 'loss of Devereux', the unfortunate Walter. It was a neat attempt to separate her favourite from his hot-headed friends, if not a particularly attractive one. Her rebuke, too, had a political function which would she would use with relish in ensuing years. Court gossip had always held that the queen was beholden to Essex – she was becoming a doting old woman in thrall to her young lover, and the positions he won from her made him responsible for blunders and military setbacks. This suited her. As long as the favourite could be blamed for failures abroad, she would not be.

Her letter commanding him to stay came too late. Carey was simply unable to return to Essex before the queen's original recall arrived. The beleaguered commander had, in fact, boarded a skiff for Rye just hours before his messenger arrived back at Dieppe with the letter cancelling the recall. It was with a heavy heart that he had done so. As he had warned Elizabeth in his earlier justifications of the Compiègne meeting, 'I wish to be out of my prison, which I account my life'.[110] He had not lost his sense of the dramatic.

After landing in England, he sent a messenger ahead to announce his return and, after hearing that the queen had humiliated the poor fellow, he took up his own pen and wrote, 'I see your Majesty is constant to ruin me; I do humbly and patiently yield to your Majesty's will'.[111] It is difficult not to sympathise with him. In this farrago, it was the twenty-five-year-old military leader who was acting with dignity and the excitable queen who was giving way to hair-trigger rages and sudden swings in mood and policy.

When Essex did appear at court, further, the queen softened, and her anger melted. It was ever thus. Decades earlier, in 1554,

---

[110] Devereux, *Lives and Letters*, p. 234.

[111] Devereux, *Lives and Letters*, p. 244.

the then Lady Elizabeth had written to her sister Mary

I have heard of many in my time cast away for want of coming to the presence of their Prince … I pray to God the like evil persuasions persuade not one sister against the other, and all for that they have heard false report, and the truth not known.[112]

Elizabeth not only knew the power of interpersonal meetings; she was deeply susceptible to them. Though she was capable of all the mercurial temper of her mother and father, she could not maintain it in the presence of those she loved. It was by now abundantly clear that she really did hold Essex, as a person, in deep affection. The problem was that affection and her desire to control the tide of warfare from afar were uncomfortable bedfellows.

Confident that he had regained her trust, Essex left Richmond and returned to Normandy. On the credit side, Henry IV had unloosed his purse strings and his general, Biron, was attacking the vicinity of Rouen like a shark circling a bleeding swimmer. Yet the English forces to whom Essex returned were even then sadly depleted. Plague, malaria, and dysentery had had their fun and around half of his men were dead or dying. He wrote explaining the death and desertion and asking for aid, including a personal note to the woman he had just left:

While your Majesty gives me leave to say I love you, my fortune is as my affection, unmatchable. If ever you deny me that liberty you may end my life, but never shake my constancy, for were the sweetness of your nature turned into the greatest bitterness that could be, it is not in your power (as great a queen as you are) to make me love you less.[113]

This had become bread-and-butter stuff, but it does indicate a playfulness that would always mark their relationship, however

---

[112] Strickland, A. 1843. *Lives of the Queens of England* (London: Henry Colburn), p. 91.
[113] Devereux, *Lives and Letters*, p. 250.

fraught politics made it.

On finally reaching Rouen, Essex did something extraordinary (and which would become extraordinarily typical of him). After riding uphill to overlook the town, he inspected his troops and arbitrarily dubbed twenty-four of his officers knights of the realm. This was, again, very much in the mould of Leicester. It was also against Elizabeth's orders that he reward only those who had won honour on the battlefield. However, it was not, as is often portrayed, the act of a foolish young man puffed up with pride and hubris. Essex knew the power the bestowing of titles had. It bound men to the person who gave them, and it was designed to restore morale which had understandably flagged during the weeks and months of misery and death.

With his new band of deferential knights, Essex joined with Biron in laying siege to the walled city. The plan was to begin on the 29th of October, and the English forces – bolstered by, surprisingly, a thousand men allowed by the queen to join from those stationed in the Netherlands – dug trenches in a hill overlooking one of the city gates. Henry IV arrived in early November, but his foot-dragging had brought Essex again to the temporal limit of his extension. Again, he had to return to England, leaving his soldiers dug in, and beg Elizabeth to give him more time, money, and men. The weather in France was turning colder and his soldiers were deserting. Elizabeth, assured that Rouen was on the brink of being taken, agreed to give him two more months, and he was back in France in mid-December. It would not be for long.

Once again, Elizabeth changed her mind. Essex had been quite right in complaining about the loss of men on the now-chilly fields of France. Having considered the losses at length, the queen wrote to him on Christmas Eve, 'we therefore, both in regard of our own honour and your particular reputation, do require you, upon the sight hereof, to make your speedy return'.[114] She had only recently lost another favourite, Hatton, who had succumbed to a long-term illness on the 20th of November. Another of the old guard had gone and another reminder that her court would perforce become a young man's world had raised its head. She wanted some good cheer and to stop spending money and men on a project which took away her cheerful young darling and was in any case sponsored by a guile-filled French king. On a less personal level, she wanted the leader of the young crowd back under her gaze, to be her eyes and ears in a court with which she was increasingly unfamiliar, and which had fewer and fewer men genuinely close to her. Essex was far better at her right hand than winning either acclaim or infamy on a stage on which she could not set foot.

Only a few days after the dispatch of this letter, Essex was engaged in what would be the most humiliating episode of the war. Using scaling ladders supplied by Biron, he set about an all-out assault on the town. After ordering his men to don white coats so that they might see one another during the moonlit attack, he had them cross the trenches and raise their ladders to breach the walls. It was during the attempt that the deficiency of the plan became clear. The ladders were eight feet shy of the ramparts' summit. As they retreated, no doubt mortified, Sieur de Villars' soldiers were easily able to pick off the highly-visible departing white coats. In a final stab at chivalry, their leader invited Villars to settle matters by means of personal combat, maintaining that 'the cause of King Henry is more just than that of your League, and my mistress more beautiful than yours!' Villars did not take Essex up on the offer.

The Rouen affair had ended in ignominy. The last, failed assault on the town had been entirely Essex's fault, but it was a folly born of months of stress and physical and emotional trauma. Taken in totality, the whole thing had been badly bungled by all involved. Henry IV's false promises, Elizabeth's semi-hysterical vacillations, and the favourite's incompetence

---

[114] Williams. C. 1759. *Collection of State papers relating to affairs in the reign of queen Elizabeth from 1571 to 1596* (London: William Bowyer), p. 651.

had all combined to produce disaster for England. As usual, it was the soldiers who suffered, sent into warfare in poor conditions under an inexperienced leader whose command was recalled, unrecalled, and reissued according to a distant ruler's whim. Essex would return to England in January 1592, not a broken man but a wearied one. He had, he felt sure, done his best under exceptionally difficult circumstances, responding to unexpected events as best he could. Before stepping off French soil he dramatically kissed his blade, no doubt appreciative that, however fruitless the enterprise, it nevertheless added to his growing experience. He had dined with a king, led men on minor victories, and bound over a number of knights. Moreover, he had seen again how mutable Elizabeth could be and how she might be disobeyed and then immediately won over by personal meetings. His latest stab at martial glory had failed and it was clear that he could not hope to succeed in the field as long as his strings were jerked by his queen. What he needed was a seat at the top table. If he wished for an escape for what he had called the 'prison' of his life, the man who had found himself cursing the day of his birth would have to achieve serious credit, respect, and responsibility. Only then might he hope to enjoy liberty under a woman who had had no compunction about berating him as a rash youth.

In subsequent years, Normandy's verdant fields would continue to be soaked in blood spilled by the Huguenots and the Catholic Leaguers. Henry IV would continue bilking his allies and attempting to gain control over his country until, in 1593, he supposedly shrugged his shoulders and decided 'Paris is worth a mass'. Whether he said it or not, convert he did. By this time, Elizabeth and Essex would have problems far closer to home.

11: The Spying Game

It is probable that the instantly-recognisable Ditchley portrait of Queen Elizabeth was produced in 1592. It is a remarkably honest portrait, notwithstanding the fact that she is depicted treading the globe. Her face is noticeably that of an older woman, the lines visible. Yet there is nothing haggard or grotesque about it. If it retains even a reasonable verisimilitude to the woman Essex gazed on daily after his return to court in January of that year, then it is fair to suppose that he still looked upon an attractive if imperious woman, approaching sixty but made up, dressed, and artificially coiffed to look younger.

It has become the norm in modern screen portrayals of Elizabeth to portray her in the 1590s as unrecognisable, almost frightening, beneath a thick, white, matte layer of makeup. Yet the Ditchley portrait is extremely recognisable as the same woman of her earlier years, albeit with a few wrinkles. Helen Hackett has recently challenged the stereotypical 'clown' appearance and there is good reason to do so. Although, due to the toxic nature of early modern cosmetics, no one could sensibly recreate authentic Elizabethan makeup, the portrait suggests that rather than appearing caked, head, bosom, and hands, in stark-white modern face paint, the overall effect Elizabeth achieved was more akin to having lashings of (admittedly toxic) talcum powder rubbed into her skin, with cheeks and lips blushed. It would be unnatural, to be sure, but far from monstrous. Her teeth, too, were probably very poor by this time, but so too would be most of those who had grown up in the late-sixteenth-century, when dental hygiene was poor and sugary treats a staple for the wealthy. Rich Elizabethans enjoyed twenty-first-century levels of sugar consumption but relied on mediaeval practices of dental hygiene, and so we can assume that the queen's teeth were hardly anomalous. In short, Elizabeth in full sail was still eye catching, especially to those easily dazzled by displays of grandeur.

1592 was to see one of Essex's most important associations

form: that between him and the Bacon brothers, Anthony and Francis – the 'golden lads' recognised by novelist Daphne du Maurier in her exquisite biographical studies.[115] It was clear immediately Essex returned from France that he had a new resolve: to be taken seriously as a politician. There would and could be no waiting for the honour to come with time and by proving himself militarily. This was not a radical idea in itself – as we have seen, courtiers could become statesmen – but the speed with which he expected it was problematic. He had only been a favourite since late 1586, but Hatton's death had left an opening on the privy council which he trained his eye on. As was always the case with Essex, when he had a goal in mind he pursued it with almost fanatical determination. This was not entirely born of natural impatience – the fact was that any man hoping to reach prominence in the 1590s knew it would have to be done quickly; he would not have the luxury of decades of growth because the queen did not have decades left. She might die at any moment and a new monarch raised the risk of having to start again – unless, of course, one had already proven oneself an indispensable tool of the state. Luckily, being a man of influence, even if only as a favourite, there were plenty of subordinate men who were willing to throw in their lot with him.

Anthony and Francis Bacon were the sons of Elizabeth's late lord keeper, Nicholas, and therefore nephews of Burghley (whose wife was sister to Nicholas). Little love was lost, however, between the Bacon brothers and their cousin, Robert Cecil. The boys were each blessed with unique talents: Anthony had spent years on the continent, building a network of contacts and, despite a brush with the law when he was accused of sodomy with a page boy and had to be rescued by the future Henry IV, becoming a first-class spymaster; Francis was a

---

[115] du Maurier's *The Golden Lads* (1975) and *The Winding Stair* (1976) are exceptionally readable nonfiction studies of the brothers. The only drawback are the intermittent forays into the Shakespeare authorship question - du Maurier flirted with the discredited but one-time fashionable 'Baconianism'.

brilliant polymath with diverse sexual tastes and considerable legal training. Neither had had much luck securing advancement and patronage under Burghley and it was Francis's idea to hitch their wagon to the charismatic favourite. Anthony had corresponded with Essex, writing in 1588 about the playwright and spy Thomas Watson. The relationship had not blossomed into anything, and although Anthony's health had seriously deteriorated in recent years, his formidable mind and contacts remained sound. More recently, Francis had approached Essex in early 1591, along with the unemployed codebreaker Thomas Phelippes, a former agent of Walsingham's who had been instrumental in destroying Mary Stewart. Again, the stars had not aligned particularly well, mainly because Essex, a novice in matters of state intelligence, was focused on other things. They did so in 1592.

In Elizabethan England, a man who knew things was a man worth knowing. If he had the queen's ear, so much the better. Essex, to his credit, had realised that he could not hope to reach the prominence his position in society deserved if he did not build an effective power base. This meant going beyond the place-seekers, adventurers, soldiers, and myriad other lobbyists who swore allegiance in return for his granting them what favours he could give (or induce the queen to give). He had not turned away from the military, but rather realised that if he were to reach his potential, he must have some autonomy – he must be in a position to shape the queen's foreign policy rather than simply being her tool in it. As a pair, Anthony and Francis Bacon were well placed to help the earl gain the prestige he needed to get a seat on the privy council and make his opinions matter.

With Walsingham had died the effective governance of the Elizabethan spy network. The old man had been the glue which held it together and its chief financial backer. In his wake he left a significant number of disenfranchised secret agents with impeccable contacts and means of gathering information. They continued to spy, but now their information was available to the highest bidder and was therefore dispersed amongst any patron or privy counsellor willing to pay. Essex, the Bacons assured him, might assume Walsingham's old role as the country's primary intelligencer. It would not be easy, of course. Although the spy network had been massive, it had also been leaky and fraught with double dealing, no English agent truly trusting his government and the government never truly trusting its band of cut-throats, gentlemen spies, or cryptographers. It was not unusual for double-agents to work both sides and, even when they had done good government service, to flee afterwards in fear of their masters throwing them to the wolves.[116] None of this deterred Essex. Central to his desire to earn serious credit was the importance of knowledge: if the queen dined at a courtier's house on progress, the cunning man would know what she was fed and how to better it; if a party of Jesuits arrived from Douai, the cunning man would know who housed them; if a cell of Puritans was working on seditious pamphlets, the cunning man could either encourage or denounce them. Knowledge made a man indispensable.

Essex was to pursue a place on the privy council with all the zeal he had pursued military adventure. He launched a charm offensive, assiduously courting even those who had been his enemies. Remarkably, he even managed a rapprochement with Sir Walter Raleigh. The queen, Essex knew, deplored petty rivalries unless she engineered them. She had done her best for Raleigh, providing him with an office – the captaincy of her guard – and granting him the manor of Sherborne. Ordinarily this would have infuriated Essex but, luckily, the older favourite had left himself desperately vulnerable. Despite the honours heaped upon him, he had engaged in a clandestine marriage to Bess Throckmorton, a senior and very pregnant gentlewoman of the privy chamber. Unlike Essex, Raleigh had very little popular and aristocratic support to offset the queen's rage

---

[116] Gilbert Gifford, for example, the agent provocateur who had encouraged Mary Queen of Scots to trust to Chartley's beer barrels as a means of smuggling letters, fled to France when the Babington Plot came to light. He did not have Walsingham's permission and apparently feared that he would be killed alongside the plotters. He would die, allegedly in a brothel, in November 1590.

should she ever find out what he had done. Finding the older man thus declawed, it was safe for Essex to be magnanimous and extend the hand of friendship.

His approach was, as usual, a case of feast following famine; Essex was as ever a man of extremes, and one was consequently either his best friend or his mortal enemy. Happily, as he was never a cruel man, he threw himself into the newfound friendship with real alacrity. The shared ignominy of illicit marriage no doubt gave them something about which they could smile and shake their heads together. In April he stood as godfather to Raleigh and Bess's son, Damerei (the unusual name a corruption of D'amerie, supposedly the name of a noble ancestor who linked Raleigh to Henry I). The earl then nominated Raleigh to join him as a knight of the garter. He would not receive it; in May Elizabeth discovered the secret marriage and Raleigh's credit sank to an all-time low.[117] Unlike with Essex, she could not be smoothed down nor did she feel the need to keep a man of provincial origins within her orbit. By the end of the month he and his wife found themselves clapped in the Tower of London. Raleigh did manage a brief reprieve after the Battle of Flores ended in August, when it was hoped that his presence might stop his captains stealing the immense spoils of the captured *Madre de Dios*, but he bungled it and was thereafter forbidden access to the queen and court (when Cecil attempted to recover the stolen loot he found sailors bedecked in diamonds and was able only to get a fraction of the booty back to London). Notwithstanding their recent friendship, Raleigh's fall from grace left the field open. Between the deaths and disasters of others, the path to fame was being swept clear.

Throughout the year, Essex would lobby hard for admission to the privy council. He showed contrition and maturity through his dealing with Raleigh; he grew closer to the ingenious Francis Bacon and visited his housebound but knowledgeable brother at Gray's Inn, where the pair plotted and ruminated; and

---

[117] She did not find out from Essex, but likely either from her lord chamberlain or his son. See Rowse, A. L. 1962. *Raleigh and the Throckmortons* (London: Macmillan), p. 160.

he even repudiated his flirtation with the Puritans. He was becoming an establishment man, and one who could offer something back. What, though, was Elizabeth to make of her young man's sudden development into a sober statesman-in-training?

***

In August, the court was treated to a visit by a balding, severe-faced man. He was Frederick, heir apparent to the duchy of Württemberg. The queen received him at Reading, and he dictated to his secretary afterwards:

Notwithstanding that her Majesty was at this time in her 67th [sic] year, seeing that she was chosen Queen on the 16th of November, 1558, in the 33rd year of her age, and has thus borne the heavy burthen of ruling a kingdom thirty-four years, she need not indeed – to judge both from her person and appearance – yield much to a young girl of sixteen. She has a very dignified, serious and royal look, and rules her kingdom with great discretion.[118]

Unless sixteen-year-old Elizabethan girls endured even harder lives than is commonly supposed, we must allow for a degree of diplomatic hyperbole here – Frederick was, after all, both a guest and one who thirsted for English honours. Yet the surprising pen portrait is revelatory in that it indicates that Elizabeth was capable of making herself appear youthful and animated – in fact, it was critical that she did so. Had she been willing to publicly appear old and haggard, it is likely that her ministers and her people would have turned their backs on her as very soon to be yesterday's woman. To Elizabeth, youth was an attitude of mind as well as makeup. She consciously sought to project youth whilst maintaining the magical quality of age-born wisdom. Essex, however, would prove a problem in that

---

[118] Wry, W. B. 1865. *England as Seen by Foreigners in the Days of Elizabeth and James the First* (London: John Russel Smuth), p. 12.

his youth required her to, on the one hand, keep up with his racing mind and ideas and, on the other, to rein him in with shows of superior age and authority.

Not only had the duke gazed, starstruck, at the woman on whom Essex poured words of love – and the queen who frequently drew his ire – but he also spent time with the earl himself. Indeed, still assiduously tending to courtly guests, it was Essex who had formally welcomed Frederick to England. Yet still formal admission to the privy council remained frustratingly out of reach.

Essex continued to do what he could. He formally began his tenure at Wanstead, formerly Leicester's grand country home; he also took over Leicester House in London when Sir John Puckering succeeded to Hatton's old role as lord keeper. It was renamed Essex House. His power bases were not just to be groups of people but physical and strategic locations which gave him speedy access to London's greatest thoroughfare, the Thames. All of this was part of his grand stratagem to make it look increasingly ridiculous that he, a man favoured by nature and breeding, and who counted foreign monarchs as his friends and knowledge-gathering spies amongst his confidants, was denied a place at his sovereign's council table where Burghley, a lawyer raised up by the queen's own hand, dominated.

The association with the Bacons immediately began to bear fruit. Through their work, he was able to gain reports from spies like Anthony Standen on the schemes of Catholic exiles abroad; on the movements of Spanish troops; on which Irish aristocrats had dealings with Philip of Spain. Essex could boast that he was saving the queen money and doing her loyal service by spending yet more cash himself on the deployment of men abroad - £900 alone went on trying to squirrel information out of the town of Lyons, from whence rumours sprang that the French king was making ready to betray his coreligionists. The earl's attempts did not please Burghley, who looked askance at the Bacon brothers' influence on Essex as a rising power block likely to far outshine his son. Yet it was increasingly clear that the earl would not be stopped.

Still Elizabeth demurred. Partly this was due to the power

balance she desperately sought to retain. If there was one thing she detested it was being bounced into decisions, especially by men who held what they did through her favour. When Burghley cautioned her against admitting Essex to the council until he had gained more experience, she accepted.

Ironically, it was likely the accusations, often made by Catholics, that the council – which had begun to meet daily due to the volume of state business, and often without the queen present – was becoming a *regnum Cecilianum*:

Tracts such as Richard Verstegan's 'A declaration of the true causes of the great troubles' (1592) and Robert Parsons' (or Persons') 'An advertisement written to a secretarie of my L. Treasurers of Ingland' (1592) were smuggled into the realm and collectively created the defamatory notion of "Burghley's commonwealth" or a *regnum Cecilianum*, in which Elizabeth and her realm were shamelessly manipulated for the benefit of the Cecil family and their supporters.[119]

This was a real problem, although in fairness it was the stuff of mischief-making. Burghley naturally sought to look after his family, but the makeup of the privy council was ultimately Elizabeth's choice and, if Burghley came to dominate, it was due to her chronic unwillingness to accept change. As was so often the case in the early modern period, however, criticism of the monarch was refracted through criticism of advisers. This allowed polemicists to position themselves not as radical rebels looking to sink the ship of state, but concerned subjects hoping to liberate it from corrupt hijackers.

Still, whatever the rights and wrongs of those who sought to blame Cecil for dominating the primary forum for conciliar advice, they certainly added weight to the idea that a new, aristocratic voice should speak for the traditional political classes. That other site of political debate, parliament, also had

[119] Bellany, A. & McRae, A. (Eds.) 2005. 'Essex, Ralegh and Late-Elizabethan Politics (c.1590-1603)', *Early Modern Literary Studies Text Series I.*

to be cultivated.

Parliaments were rare in Elizabeth's reign – once rubber stamps for giving legal power to the monarch's wishes, usually financial, in the second half of the sixteenth century the members had shown increasing bolshiness in their expression. Parliament offered a chance for the civic authorities and merchant classes to make their opinions heard, and the newly-sensitive Essex determined that he should have support amongst the elected representatives. For the first time taking a real interest in parliamentary procedure, Essex ensured that the men elected from his own lands – Lichfield, Stafford, Newcastle, and Tamworth – were pliable fellows loyal to him. Additionally, he could count on his stepfather, Sir Christopher Blount (who had won his friendship), loyal Welsh members, and Francis Bacon – member for Middlesex – himself.

Elizabeth's eighth parliament opened on the 19th of February, but Essex's diligent work had already paid off. His highly visible contributions to political life and his careful and surprisingly respectful lobbying had come up trumps. On the 25th of February 1593, only a year after he had set to work in earnest, Elizabeth admitted him to the privileged position of privy counsellor. Whether she had been broken down by his entreaties, convinced by his sudden zeal, or simply wanted to keep a close eye on his new activities, remained to be seen.

***

Much like a modern-day cabinet minister might do with a prime minister, it was the job of a privy counsellor to put forward arguments that would ultimately shape the government of the day. Unlike today, however, roles within the privy council were not circumscribed – there was, for example, no member of the select group charged with a brief on transport or education. Instead, counsellors argued according to their own strengths, or what they believed to be their particular strengths. Essex, as might be expected, jockeyed to be the voice of foreign diplomacy and relations.

The 1593 parliament rumbled on. It had got off to a bad start.

Long-term proponent of free speech, Peter Wentworth, had had the temerity to raise, again, a petition calling for the 'intayling the succession' to be presented to the queen by the Commons and lords. For this he went straight to the Tower, having learnt nothing from his sojourn there the previous year for writing a tract on the same subject. Nevertheless, Essex threw himself into proceedings, attending the upper house each day and thereafter attending committees aimed at discussing important bills. The heat of the battlefield had been replaced by the heat of debate.

The ostensible object of the parliament was to debate rumoured Spanish invasion and raise the queen money. It was the latter issue that provoked the most unrest and led to the first great clash between Essex and Robert Cecil. As a member of the Commons whose father was the leading privy counsellor, Cecil was essentially a government agent working through the commons. Given that Burghley was ill throughout February, a great deal of responsibility in making the institution deliver lay upon his shoulders. Over the course of the parliament he therefore sought to elicit as much subsidy money for the crown as possible. His tactic was to engage in a mutual agreement between commoners and lords that would see the largest possible financial package voted through, with credit going to the lords. Immediately this roused the objection of Essex's man, Francis Bacon. His argument won the day, leaving Cecil's nose out of joint. He went too far, however, in arguing for a lower subsidy, pleading the poverty into which the larger one would force taxpayers.

Quite why Essex and Francis were so cavalier in standing up against the government line requires consideration. Primarily there was principle involved, probably more so on the latter's part. More importantly, it made clear from the outset that although Essex had become a privy counsellor he would remain an independent and powerful voice. It was, unfortunately, a miscalculation. Probably the earl had intended only to establish himself as an alternative – and dangerously populist – power to Cecil and Burghley. In practice, Francis' obstruction of the smooth passage of a government-led subsidy annoyed the queen and she had no compunction about showing it. Francis found himself beset suddenly by his creditors, and it was made clear to him that his hopes of advancement in the law – the position of attorney-general would become vacant in 1594 – would be quashed.

Essex breezily waved this off. The queen never stayed angry at him for long and nor would she remain angry at his special friends. He set his mind to convincing her to appoint Francis to the role and appealed to Elizabeth directly and repeatedly, presuming upon the love he felt for her. Eventually she grew exasperated. Burghley had his own nominee, Sir Edward Coke, and in the end it was he who got the job. The queen had raised Essex up only to find that rather than being more of a puppet, he was becoming more strident in his demands. He would have to be cut down to size, and her cutting remark was that, 'if it had been in … her father's time, a less offence than that would have made a man banished from his presence forever'.[120] The offence was, ostensibly, Francis Bacon's, but it equally applied to Essex's presumptuous lobbying. Francis was simply collateral damage.

In the wake of the parliament, which drew to a close in August, Francis Bacon, ever a strategist, would make secret entreaties to the Cecils to see if they might provide securer means of advance. Cecil's advice was that he remain loyal to his loving lord. No outright hostility existed between the Cecil family and the earl; Robert Cecil was satisfied on his plodding path to statesmanship and he had no intention of being provoked into a feud with a man who outmatched him. He knew full well that Essex was the one who wanted factionalism to erupt, because the more popular favourite, with his own large following, would be the beneficiary. There would be time for that later. Essex did not find out about Francis's disloyalty, and for the next few years his future and the earl's would be deeply intertwined. It did indicate, though, that the love on the clever client's part was not invulnerable: Francis's career would

---

[120] Bowen, C. D. 1993. *Francis Bacon: The Temper of a Man* (New York: Fordham University Press), p. 70.

always come first. At the opening of the new century it would lead to one of the most tragic scenes in Essex's drama.

12: To Catch a Poisoner

On the 7th of June 1594, a baffled, frightened, but dignified old man was led up the steps to the scaffold at Tyburn. A traitor's death, in all its horror, awaited him. He turned to the crowd and pleaded that he loved his queen as much as he loved Jesus Christ. The crowd was thick – the man was no common traitor or Jesuit. His name was Roderigo Lopez and he had been Elizabeth's physician-in-chief since 1581. The people's response was cruel and derisive laughter. Of course the man had no love at all for Jesus Christ. Converted though he had been, a Jew was a Jew. Lopez was hanged, one hopes until unconsciousness, before his stomach was slit open and his bowels dragged out. The executioner, his arms stained in gore, tossed them onto a fire. A loathsome traitor and would-be assassin had died the death reserved for such monsters. Or so Essex believed.

Lopez was an unlikely traitor. Years later Francis Bacon would lay out the case against him, recalling that

this Lopez, of nation a Portuguese, and suspected to be in sect secretly a Jew, though here he conformed himself to the rights of the Christian religion, for a long time professed physic in this land … [was] of a pleasing and pliable behaviour; in that regard, rather than for any great learning in his faculty, he grew known and favoured in court, and was some years since sworn physician of her Majesty's household.[121]

Bacon was, naturally, attempting to blacken the man's name and posthumous reputation. In reality Lopez had studied at the University of Coimbra, settling in London in 1559 and

---

[121] Bacon, F. 1594. 'A Report of Doctor Lopez's Treason' in B. Montague (Ed.) *The Works of Francis Bacon, Lord Chancellor of England: A New Edition, Vol. 5* (London: William Pickering), pp. 293-4.

beginning a successful practice. In 1591 he was noted as being 'both careful and very skilful ... in his counsel in dieting, purging and bleeding'.[122] The attempts to link him to the secret practice of Judaism are typically antisemitic– God-fearing Anglicans considered Jews to be child-eating monsters. The stereotypes are then more fully indulged: 'being a person wholly of a corrupt and mercenary nature, and finding his hopes cold from that part [Dom António]; he cast his eyes upon a more able paymaster, and secretly made offer long since of his service to the king of Spain'.[123] Such was the official version of the man's life. In truth, he had achieved much from a humble beginning, counting Leicester amongst his patients. Indeed, precisely that association had led Catholic propagandists to suggest that he had been the earl's agent in the art of poisoning. Anyone wishing to destroy the doctor – and raise questions about the abilities of those who ought to have done so sooner – had fertile ground from which to grow a plot.

As a spymaster, it was up to Essex to discover plots and ensure the queen's safety. Whilst in council – which he continued to attend religiously – he worked with Howard of Effingham on defensive matters and considered the state of governance in Ireland. In matters of intelligence he was at the mercy of his agents. These were desperate men – the mysterious and venal Thomas Walton, the increasingly marginalised Thomas Phelippes, William Sterrell, Anthony Standen, Anthony Rolston. Throughout 1593 his reach grew: Antonio Perez arrived with the vidame de Chartres and would spend two years furnishing Essex with detailed information about the Spanish empire. Towards the end of the year he employed the Anglo-Florentine James Guicciardini who went to Italy with the intent of supplying his new master with the news out of Italy. With such a crew it was not surprising that rumours were sniffed out about dealings between Dr Lopez and the Spanish. It could not have come a moment too soon; the Cecils were operating

---

[122] Stephen, L. (Ed.). 1893. 'Roderigo Lopez', *Dictionary of National Biography* (London: Smith, Elder & Co.), p. 133.

[123] Bacon, 'Report of Doctor Lopez's Treason', p. 295.

their own intelligence service, and the queen had favoured theirs in her own key 1593 project: the building up of a pro-English party in Scotland to counter the Spanish king's wooing of Catholic Scottish nobles, which a disgruntled James VI was not doing enough to counter, especially since his pension had been slashed in 1592.

A great deal has been conjectured about Dr Lopez's horrific downfall. The weight of scholarly opinion is that he was certainly innocent of attempting to murder Elizabeth, and that his grisly death resulted from Essex's eagerness to achieve an intelligence coup over his rivals and a general antisemitic prejudice that infected Elizabethan society. The chain of events are these: in late 1593 Anthony Bacon, still a virtual invalid, picked up information that one Stephano Ferrera de Gama, a Portuguese, was communicating secretly with Spain. Ferrera was then lodging with Dr Lopez in Holborn. Essex had the fellow arrested and interrogated, before ordering all post arriving at the southern ports searched. Full of premature self-confidence, he burst into the queen's presence in early January and announced that her doctor was a traitor; he had seen the man now imprisoned now under arrest in deep conversation with Lopez the previous summer. Elizabeth was nonplussed, and she openly called him a 'a rash and temerarious youth'.[124] To a man approaching thirty, this was insulting precisely because he was not a youth. His bitterness – every bit as strong as Sidney's had been when the earl of Oxford branded him a 'puppy', made him more firmly determined to prove his case, whatever it took. Worse, Elizabeth made mockery of the damaging rumours of venereal disease for which Lopez had allegedly been treating him and, to add even further insult, she made clear that Burghley and his son, former patrons of the doctor, had already explored the possibility of Lopez's corruption and found him spotless.

The searches Essex had ordered of the ports at Rye, Sandwich,

---

[124] Aikin, L. 1818. *Memoirs of the Court of Queen Elizabeth: In Two Volumes, Vol. 2* (London: Longman, Hurst, Rees, Orme, and Brown), p. 352.

and Dover did turn up a shady man, Gomez d'Avila, carrying letters addressed to Ferrera concerning mysterious purchases. Fearing for his life, d'Avila requested that the news of his arrest be carried to Lopez – a man he knew to be in the queen's service. It was a fatal move and one that could only play into Essex's hands.

What Bacon and Essex had unwittingly stumbled into was a spy ring which predated their own. Lopez had been in Walsingham's employ from 1589, covertly passing on information about Philip's post-Armada designs. He had thereafter become embroiled in the world of Portuguese spies in London. In 1591 Manuel Andrada, another Portuguese agent, had travelled from England to Spain and used Lopez's name to try and trick money and jewels out of Philip with promises of assassinating Elizabeth. This had been done without the government's knowledge and Burghley had had Andrada arrested on his return, unsure whether the man was loyal or simply willing to be turned by the highest bidder. Andrada fled England, but Lopez remained.

Essex did not know of the existing spy ring. Instead, he dealt as he found, sending a man to Lopez with a supposed warning from Ferrera. Lopez panicked and wrote back advising Ferrera to prevent d'Avila coming to England for fear it might ruin them both. Ferrera was then intimidated into confession, at first admitting that a plot had existed but only to the detriment of the pretender to the Portuguese throne, Dom António. The goal was supposedly to convert António's son to Spain's interests, and the letters with the strange purchases – of 'amber, musk, and pearl' – had been written by Manuel Luis Tinoco, a Spanish agent in Brussels. The web was becoming ever more opaque: Tinoco had at the same time been lobbying Burghley in a bid to establish contact.

Still not sure of what they had, Essex and Bacon had to let Burghley in on developments. The old man was, after all, the country's key counsellor. Burghley had invited Tinoco across the Channel with a promise of safe conduct, and abruptly arrested him when he arrived in late January. Essex and Cecil then joined forces in interrogating him, drawing from him the admission that he had been to England to win Lopez to his cause. On his person were found letters addressed to Ferrera, requiring him to succeed the departed Andrada in the scheme to kill Elizabeth. Proof of a plot had been found. It did not take long for the dots to be joined, however hazily; the letters mentioning purchases had been coded, with the principle message being that the Spanish ought to attack and Elizabeth be killed. Lopez was to be the instrument, as had been agreed during his discussions with Ferrera during the summer. It was a crystal-clear case of conspiracy, and Essex had been the mastermind behind it.

Lopez, however, stoutly denied any wrongdoing save retaining some unwise contacts that might, he admitted, look suspicious. These had been investigated already by the Cecils. Certainly, he had been sent a jewel from Spain, but he had hoped only to bilk money out of the elderly Philip. Ferrera was simply his agent in doing so. It was about this time that Cecil could not resist making one of the passive aggressive digs at which he excelled. He pointed out that the upcoming post of attorney-general would likely to go to his father's nominee, Edward Coke, and asked if Essex had had anyone else in mind. He knew, of course, that the earl was backing Francis Bacon, and, when told, tutted that that was an 'impossible and unlikely' thing. This was to set the pattern for the relationship between the pair for some years: Cecil would keep his powder dry and make only the most veiled and seemingly innocuous of barbs; Essex would do what he could to surreptitiously undermine the secretary to anyone who would listen. Tension was clearly flaring between the two interrogators, and it drove Essex still further in his absolute certainty that Lopez was an assassin.

Burghley fell ill during February and the interrogation of the doctor fell almost entirely to Essex, who stage-managed it in earnest. There followed a flood of confessions, from Tinoco, Ferrera, and finally Lopez. Threatened with the rack, the doctor admitted that he had promised to poison the queen – a direct reversal of his earlier denial – but had not intended to carry out the promise. Again, he stated that he had no more aim in mind than getting money out of King Philip. This was enough and a trial was set, with Cecil and Essex standing in judgement as part of the fifteen-man commission. By the very fact of a trial, however, the outcome was clear – trials of this nature were opportunities for authorities to demonstrate how a guilty verdict had already been reached. Lopez was doomed. So were the other two, Ferrera and Tinoco, despite the assurances they had been given that turning queen's evidence against Lopez would set them free.

There followed a grim, three-month-long dance in which Elizabeth, who did not believe in the doctor's guilt, sought to find fair means or foul to spare his life. Against her were ranged Essex, Cecil, Burghley, and a bloodthirsty and antisemitic London populace crying out for justice. The queen failed to spare him and was eventually manoeuvred into signing the death warrants. Her only concession to mercy was returning the doctor's property to his widow, Sarah, and granting a small annuity for his son Anthony's studies. It was small beer in recompense for butchering a man she believed innocent, although admittedly more than was required of her. The death sentence, to Essex, was a singular victory – he had found and exposed a plot against the queen that even Burghley and his son had managed to miss. Or had he?

Agent provocateurs had long been employed in the Elizabethan spying game. However, they were rarely considered honourable, and it was understood that plots should only be encouraged and then exposed when the ends justified the means (as Walsingham and Burghley had decided they did in ridding England of Mary Stewart). Rumours persist – and have debatable documentary evidence – that Tinoco in particular was encouraged by Essex, who hoped thereafter to expose the scheme and win glory as Elizabeth's saviour.[125] This is difficult to believe. Although it is probable that the accusations against Lopez were massaged with false promises that the doctor's co-conspirators would go free, it seems unlikely that a man as bound to honour as Essex would engineer from the start the judicial murder of a man he knew to be

---

[125] Hammer, *The Polarisation of Elizabethan Politics*, pp. 159-60.

innocent. It is more likely that Essex became absolutely convinced that Lopez had intended to assassinate Elizabeth and, once convinced that it was true, he lacked only the proof. If that had to be bribed and forced, so be it – it simply meant hoodwinking and breaking down the defences of a small trio of evil traitors.

Lopez was almost certainly innocent of planning the queen's death. He was, however, utterly foolish in continuing to engage in secret schemes and practices following the death of Walsingham, even if he wanted no more than financial gain. The lives of all spies, however esteemed their public lives, were insecure. The guilt of the man's death is often, fairly, laid at Essex's door, but such were the dangers of loose speech and illicit contact with enemy nations in Elizabethan England. In fact, no one emerges from the affair well: not Essex, who convinced himself that Lopez was a traitor; not Anthony Bacon or the Cecils, who encouraged him for different reasons; not the queen, for allowing matters to proceed against her better judgement; not the people, who licked their lips at the thought of bloodshed; and not Lopez, Tinoco, or Ferrera, who played so tragically with fire. At the time, though, the earl achieved what he wanted – the people viewed him as having foiled a dastardly plotter and given them a delightful afternoon's entertainment.

If he hoped to win a victory over the Cecils by destroying Lopez, Essex was disappointed, for they shared a role in bringing the doctor down. If he hoped to secure Francis Bacon's place as the new attorney-general, he was similarly let down; as everyone knew would happen, it went to Coke. If he hoped to bowl the queen over with his heroism in saving her from certain death, then he had grossly misjudged her. Elizabeth despised plotters, but she equally disliked having to execute them, especially when she entertained doubts about their innocence. Essex's presentation of a trio of traitors to the scaffold might have won him further accolades amongst the people of London and it might even have cemented his role as a man of real ability, but it did nothing to endear him to his mistress.

13: In Fashioning, You Reduce

The mid 1590s saw the beginning of the end of the Elizabethan age. However, this would not have been apparent during the Accession Day celebration of 1595. Then Essex would run six courses against sixteen opponents, breaking fifty-seven lances. At thirty, he was no longer in the first flush of youth, but he was still a young man who had accomplished more than many twice his age. He had been tasked with organising munitions to be sent to Brittany in July, and his secretary reported that 'he hath bene much payned all this daye in his head, and yet he hath not spared hymself to peruse his dispatches'.[126] His life was one of business as well as pleasure: it was his job to consider how he might put his friends and adherents forward for offices; how he might make his ideas on everything from Ireland to France heard; and how he might please his queen. This he did well: at the celebrations of 1594 she had rewarded him with her glove. As always, however, she gave with one hand and took away with the other. Essex had again made it his mission to advance Francis Bacon – this time to the lesser post of solicitor-general, which had become vacant when Coke moved up to attorney-general. Elizabeth, no doubt with a twinkle in her eye, decided that Thomas Fleming deserved the job. Friend Bacon was still *persona non grata*. More than anyone she knew that Essex was the type who perceived everything someone else got as something taken directly from him. She could still display her power over her subjects when they looked like presuming on her favour.

But all was not well in Elizabeth's England. The war with Spain continued to be ruinously expensive and matters in Ireland similarly showed no signs of improvement. The year saw Shakespeare's *The Comedy of Errors* performed and the older *Titus Andronicus* published, but the first of three bad

---

[126] *Lambeth Palace Library MS*, 648, 100.

harvests had brought hunger to the realm. As the clergyman George Abbot would lament in late 1596, 'one year there hath been hunger, the second year there was a dearth, and a third, which is this year, there is a great cleannesse of teeth … our seed-times are no seed-times'.[127] The economic impact of poor harvests would only grow from 1594 onwards, making prices skyrocket and ensuring that the little money people had bought them less. Tensions would gradually increase across the country, from court to city to countryside.

In May 1595, the open secret of the paternity of Elizabeth Southwell's son, Walter, finally reached Elizabeth's ears. She furiously insisted that the earl acknowledge that he and not Thomas Vavasour was responsible for the boy, and Essex accordingly changed his will to include provision for his 'base and reputed son … begotten of the body of Elizabeth Southwell'.[128] He now had two children, one legitimate and one illegitimate, to provide for (Frances had given birth to another Walter in 1592 but the child had lived for only a month; and one 'maister Henry Devereux, third son to the earle of Essex', was baptised in April 1595 but appears also to have died young). Essex thus found himself immensely popular with the people and in the court yet still on a knife edge with Elizabeth. As always when news of her courtiers' sexual indiscretions came to her attention, her anger was not so much at the immorality as at the fact that the image of all-seeing omnipotence she liked to project was revealed as a fiction. Rather, knowledge was frequently and easily withheld from her until such a time as the more mischief-making of her subjects decided to make capital of it.

As a well-known man of influence with a generous heart, people continued to lobby the earl for favours. An 'Essex circle' had formed, comprised of gentlemen and lords, amongst them the dandyish earl of Southampton, still in his early twenties. These were not stupid people, but highly educated and

---

[127] Knight, C. 1843. *William Shakspere: A Biography, Book 2* (London: C. Knight & Co.), p. 360.
[128] Devereux, *Lives and Letters*, p. 475.

questioning ones, with even Henry Cuffe, Essex's secretary and a notorious Puritan firebrand, found reading Aristotle's *Politics* to Southampton.[129] Many were, however, steeped in the violence of the age. In late 1594 Southampton came to his illustrious friend with a problem: two of his close associates, the Danvers brothers, had shot and killed Henry Long, a minor scion of the rival Long family. After the murders, the Danvers had sought refuge with Southampton and, being a friend, he concealed them. Exactly what Essex did or did not do is unclear – but the Danvers were shuttled to safety in France and Southampton remained a pernicious but captivating influence in the Essex circle. Violence had become commonplace and disaffection a cause for concern. In 1593 the 'Dutch libel' had tried to rouse hatred of foreign immigrants interfering in domestic business and politics; the threat of riots, especially in the larger town and cities, loomed large; there was rioting over foreign labourers in 1593 and 1594, which put the government firmly on edge.[130] As often happens, the people, who lacked any means of safely criticising their government, far less changing it, had begun to turn upon one another.

In the summer of 1595 tensions further exploded when a thousand copies of a text published in Antwerp, *A Conference About the Next Succession to the Crown*, arrived. Written by the Jesuit Robert Persons (or Parsons) under the pseudonym Doleman, it engaged directly in discussion of Elizabeth's most persistent bugbear. The text lambasted the Protestant claimants to England's throne, from the obvious front-runner James VI to his cousin Arbella (the daughter of Lord Darnley's deceased younger brother) and all others whose bloodline qualified them. This was explosive stuff – forbidden stuff – and it naturally sold out quickly. Elizabeth might have been content to let God decide who followed her, but her people craved the stability of knowledge, especially at a time of economic depression.

[129] Hiscock, 'Achilles Alter', p. 106.

[130] Forse, J. H. 1993. *Art Imitates Business: Commercial and Political Influences in Elizabethan Theatre* (London: Popular Press), p. 147.

Elizabeth was naturally furious, but so too was James VI. In Scotland his wife Anne had only just proven her fertility by producing a healthy son, ingratiatingly named Henry for his Tudor forebears, in early 1594. The question on both monarchs' lips was 'how did this book get into England?' It was the job of the security services, which Essex had prided himself on mastering, to root out illicit texts and the agents who carried them. He had failed to do so. More embarrassingly still, every copy of the text came emblazoned with the following dedication:

Directed to the Right Honourable the Earl of Essex of her Majesty's Privy Council & of
the noble Order of the Garter.

This was deeply embarrassing stuff. The dedication was satirical, built as it was along the same lines as the attacks that Catholic commentators had previously aimed at Burghley. It mocked Essex as the queen's puppet master – as the man who had his finger on the pulse of politics.

The sense of embarrassment went deeper. Essex's early approaches to James VI had proved otiose but the Scottish king's point of view changed with the earl's rise to political prominence. Since his pension had been cut in 1592 and he had refused to punish the Catholic earl of Huntly over the affair of the 'Spanish blanks', Elizabeth had cooled towards the man she had hoped would be a tractable client king.[131] To James, Elizabeth was now nothing more than a powerful but tiresome barrier. He had played along with her for long enough; now he simply wanted her dead. The games she played over the succession were, further, intolerable, and he would turn to whomever might be best placed to advance his claims, be they sympathetic Englishmen or Catholic Spaniards. He owed the old woman nothing; rather, she owed him assurances of his succession according to all the laws of nature and God. As a

---

[131] See Patterson, W. B. 2000. *King James VI and I and the Reunion of Christendom* (Cambridge: Cambridge University Press), pp. 14-5.

visitor to the Scottish court, Fontenay, had observed in 1584, 'he misunderstands the real extent of his poverty and weakness; he boasts too much of himself and he despises other princes'.[132] Elizabeth would one day remark that all affection was false. She might well have been thinking of her Scottish cousin.

When Prince Henry was born, the English queen ignored the birth entirely and so too did she ignore the request to stand as godmother. This was not entirely a display of wrath. She had realised that by favouring James amongst all other claimants to her throne she had effectively offered her fickle people a king-in-waiting. Paltry attempts at rebalancing the potential successors – such as Arbella Stuart's short-lived invitation to court in 1587 – had done nothing to redress that. A visible breach might.

Yet a breach between Elizabeth and James could not last forever. It might – might – keep her people guessing about the succession, but it did nothing for her international reputation and the necessity of, ultimately, keeping Scotland sweet and out of Spanish hands. She thus struck up a relationship with his inimitable young wife, Anne – the woman who would, years later, cut up Elizabeth's elaborate gowns to repurpose them for her beloved masques. Elizabeth and Anne wrote to one another as sisters and it was through the agency of the Scottish queen that Anglo-Scottish relations began to improve. James, however, was not willing to wait for his spirited wife to mend fences with England. Instead, he had begun writing seriously to Essex, with David Foulis and Anthony Bacon the respective handlers of their secret letters. All of this – Essex's growing communication with the likely heir to the throne and Elizabeth's careful cultivation of Queen Anne – was threatened by the Persons book.

Elizabeth's immediate reaction was to summon Essex to her presence. There was nothing unusual in this. When he arrived, however, it soon became clear that the book had reached the

[132] Stevenson, J. 1883. *The History of Mary Stewart: From the Murder of Riccio Until Her Flight into England* (London: W. Paterson), p. lx.

queen's eyes. What was worse was that he had indeed been warned about it by Anthony and elected to do nothing, fearful about how the cheeky dedication might be taken. But the damage was done. As Henry VIII had once worried that the availability of the bible in English would lead to the scriptures being 'jangled in alehouses', so now was the succession a matter of public conjecture. This was the fruit of Elizabeth's policy of studied silence, but she was unwilling to recognise any blame on her own part. Because she did not wish to speak of the succession, she held it true that no one else should want or be allowed to either.

Essex survived the ordeal, taking to his bed after the queen berated him – something he was to do often when events conspired to make a fool of him. His position suddenly seemed far less secure than it had done. Throughout his highly dangerous correspondence with James VI, he had prided himself that it was all conducted behind the Cecils' backs. King James was to be his correspondent, and when Elizabeth died it would be Essex who welcomed the new sovereign to court as an old friend. Yet the queen had just reminded him again that she was very much alive and not for slowing down. Nevertheless, he continued to correspond with the Scottish king, criticising Burghley when he could and discrediting Cecil as the 'little pot soon hot'.[133] The pair made excellent scapegoats – Machiavellian upstarts who, Essex hinted, had been the ones behind Elizabeth's outright rudeness and subsequent coolness.

The growing tension between the two Cecils and Essex was one that Elizabeth herself seemed eager to fan into a full-blown rivalry. When the favourite had sought to recoup the expenses he had laid out during the French campaign, the queen tartly responded that he should make his appeal through Cecil. Why she did this is not hard to guess at. Now that Essex had gained power and, more dangerously, popularity, he must have an opposite number to keep him humble. Leicester had had his Burghley and Essex must have his Cecil. In time, she probably

---

[133] Dickinson, *Court Politics*, p. 103.

supposed, they would learn to work together, as they had done in the aftermath of the Lopez affair. She did not anticipate or want all-out war, but the kind of healthy competition that had worked in the past to her and her state's advantage.

Essex's response to the threat of disgrace and the increasing respect shown to Cecil was to indulge in what might now be termed a refashioning. He lamented in the wake of the Persons book that he was 'handled by this crew of sycophants, spies, and delators'.[134] Whilst he lay in his sickbed – whether the illness was psychosomatic, faked, or genuine, we cannot know – Elizabeth came to visit him. She was in her guise as the concerned lover, not the cruel queen who had sent him there in the first place. She was always sensitive to sicknesses, both real and imagined, as Leicester had known well, and she tended to him like a nurse, spooning broth into his mouth. Entering the bedroom of her lovers was a game she had played before and would play again, but with Essex, it bordered on the erotic. It was not cynical, either. Again, the queen had intimate relationships that meant a great deal to her, and at this point in her life Essex was chief amongst them. Theirs was not built on mutual respect and admiration – she had little of that for him – but on attraction and affection. He, in turn, was always moved by displays of affection.

The queen's visit buoyed the depressed earl, moving him to begin the next stage of his campaign. Blackening the names of his attackers and those who revelled in criticising him, he set about presenting himself as the brightest star in the queen's galaxy of courtiers. Not only did he resume his networking with gusto (with the queen's blessing, albeit she probably knew nothing of his dealings with King James). The 1595 Accession Day tilts then provided an excellent opportunity to demonstrate the more glittering aspects of his character. In this Francis Bacon became paramount.

Francis Bacon was an experienced writer (though he most certainly did not publish under the name William Shakespeare). Aside from the delightful essays that would make him famous,

---

[134] Dickinson, *Court Politics*, p. 78.

he had scripted dramatic interludes for the students at Grey's Inn: he contributed, for example, to the *Gesta Grayorum* series of scenes designed to educate and delight during the revels of 1594-5. In 1592 he had written 'A Conference of Pleasure', which Essex presented to Elizabeth on that year's Accession Day. It is therefore unsurprising that the earl turned to him again in late 1595. The result was an allegory in which a variety of figures (a soldier, a hermit, and, pointedly, a secretary of state) sent by Philautia, or self-love, attempt to convince Essex to follow them. Essex, through his squire, turns them all down, preferring instead to devote himself to Elizabeth. The drama was interactive – the actors broke the fourth wall in speaking directly to Essex as both actor-playing-himself and spectator. The effect was a blurring of fiction and reality. This only served to underscore the idea that Essex, as he represented himself dramaturgically, had turned his back on the worthy soldiering life and the apolitical life of a country nobleman each out of love for the queen. Similarly, in denouncing the secretary of state as a position of self-love, a life of exclusively written work, lacking in real action, was scorned. There was, needless to say, no boy-actor playing the queen: the devotion Essex professed was directly to Elizabeth.

The skit was a hit. Its very innovativeness became a talking point in London. This was not, however, a good thing. The hermit, people supposed, was the increasingly sick and absent Burghley, the secretary his son, and the soldier the old Welshman Sir Roger Williams. As ever, the audience wished to see no nuance: they wanted to see their superiors attacking one another in the crudest possible terms. Although these readings were evidently possible – Francis Bacon was no fool and knew how to cock a snook at his master's enemies – they were unwise. The *Gesta Grayorum* had, in 'Le Prince d'Amour', noted

the perverting of honest speeches into unhonest meanings; which though he hath excused [by saying] that for [though] the words they were his, but the sence was in the Audience, and every one of them brought hither a minde of his own; and so

returned all the dishoneesty upon the hearers construction: Yet
… The fault onely [is] his; For, he hath so crept into the service
of penning some speeches … with a pernicious in-|tent of
disgracing the Government.[135]

This was a problem which would become familiar to Essex's
friend, Fulke Greville, who felt the need to burn his manuscript
play *Antony and Cleopatra* in around 1600 after showing it to
some of his circle; the readers suspected that its characters were
thinly-veiled representations of public figures. He tried the
defence that the student lawyers were warned against accepting,
lamenting that the play had to go because 'the opinion of those
few eyes which saw it, having some childish wantonness in
them apt enough to be construed or strained to a personating of
vices in the present governors and government'.[136] Essex's
attempt to laud his love of the queen fell into the same trap. And
it backfired more spectacularly.

In short, Essex had broken ranks publicly. Elizabeth
appreciated full well – as did Francis Bacon – the notion that
whatever the internecine battles fought within the realm's
governors, it was important to maintain a public façade of unity.
Essex had breached that, inviting the rabble-rousing common
folk to laugh at his peers. As Bacon had instructed the trainee
lawyers at the Inns of Court that good intentions were no excuse
for bringing the nation's governors into disrepute, one hopes
that his giving Essex such an on-the-nose piece of drama was a
bit of mischief: a thumbed nose at the man who had promised
much and delivered little. Under Essex's patronage, his career
was stultifying.

The queen did not hide her distaste. Immediately after the
drama she rose, remarking that if she had known she was to be

[135] Nelson, A. H. & Elliott Jr., J. R. (Eds.). 2011. *Inns of Court:
Records of Early English Drama, 3 Vols* (Cambridge: D. S. Brewer),
p. 176.
[136] Greville, F. 1986 [1625]. 'A Dedication to Sir Philip Sidney' in J.
Gouws (Ed.) *The Prose Works of Fulke Greville, Lord Brooke*
(Oxford: Clarendon Press), p.93

the subject she would not have bothered attending. She swept from the room in a whirl of indignation, mercifully before Bacon and Essex's script delivered its final affront: a reminder to the earl that it was only her 'unkind dealing' that might drive him into any of the self-loving professions.

Driving Elizabeth's ire was what she viewed as Essex's shameless whoring amongst the public: his pandering to the lowest common denominator. Elizabeth had always been especially jealous of her people's love. Although she undoubtedly overestimated it, she had skilfully tapped into a national mood, willingly shared by large sections of society, that she was wife to her country. On the eve of her coronation she had declared, 'I will be as good unto ye as ever a queen was unto her people ... persuade yourselves that for the safety and quietness of you all I will not spare if need be to spend my blood'. Proudly, she had asked, 'I am the most English woman of the kingdom; was I not born in this realm? Were my parents born in any foreign country?' Panegyrists such as James Aske were keen to celebrate her as the upholder of the true gospel in England in laudatory verses linking her directly to her country: 'But England joy, O England thankful be, / The night is gone, and now the day appears'.[137] Courting popularity was her prerogative, not Essex's. Playing on the national mood and occupying the position of England's face, loving and beloved, was her job. When someone else did it bordered on sedition, as did anything that threatened to stir up the emotions of crowds.[138] It is hard not to see in her attitude that of the ageing prima donna furious at the incursion of a younger, prettier actor on her stage. She cannot have been pleased when a portrait was painted of the earl to commemorate his performance. It depicted him wearing elaborate black-and-gilt, full-skirted armour, one hand provocatively on his hip and the other reaching towards a

---

[137] Nichols, J. (Ed.). 2013. *The Progresses and Public Processions of Queen* (Oxford: Oxford University Press), p. 435.
[138] Popularity, like ambition, is one of those words that has changed in meaning over the centuries, gaining positive connotations when once it was deeply negative.

helmet the plumes of which put his queen's most elaborate headdresses to shame. The motto *dum formas, minius* (in fashioning, you reduce) is prominent – yet another veiled attack on the woman who had built him up to nothing. A caparisoned horse is tended behind him, against a backdrop of England's verdant fields, and his moustaches and hair – he was beardless until his later Cadiz voyage – are carefully curled. It is a portrait of a prince standing haughtily as he waits to stride the world stage.

All was clearly not well between the pair. Essex had climbed high and fast and yet still the queen relied on men like Burghley and Cecil – men who compounded the offence of their humble births by being infuriatingly difficult to goad into anger. As a man of action, he simply did not understand his enemies. The Cecils favoured icy restraint and subtle dealing whereas Essex preferred to attack as directly, and often clumsily, as he could.

Burghley's son especially was entirely able to ignore – or pretend to ignore – jibes and insults; with a deformity in Elizabethan England he was used to them. Probably the chief minister's son knew that if he gave his enemy enough rope, he would eventually hang himself. Only when Essex was down, preferably by his own behaviour and actions, might he be pushed out. In the meantime, outward shows of tolerance and a refusal to sink into feuding demonstrated to Elizabeth that he was the mature statesman, aiming at a collegiate form of government and ready to fill his ailing father's shoes.

Essex's mood further blackened as 1595 drew to an unhappy close: his old comrade Sir Roger Williams died in December. So too did his friend Henry Hastings, 3rd earl of Huntingdon (husband to Leicester's last surviving sister, Catherine). A year that had begun in hope – the hope that he really was on his way to a position of unbreachable power, was ending in disillusionment with his fickle, needy mistress and the whole edifice of her government.

What Essex needed was to supplant the Cecil family entirely and to regain credit not in the eyes of the public – he had never lost that – but in the eyes of his queen. Proving a plot had not done it and nor had careful tending to routine business (his attendance at council, tellingly, began to decline late in 1595). In pen-pushing he could never hope to hold a candle to Cecil. It was clear too that Elizabeth was a petty and jealous woman who did not know what was good for her; she was apt to cut her nose off to spite her face, and if he had to go behind her back to get things done, so be it. It was all to her ultimate glory: as he stated himself, 'I will never do her service but against her will'.[139] His goals were not entirely selfish or born of entitlement; he had a young heir and a base son whose futures needed securing and whose father ought to be the leading man of state. Once again, his mind turned to the war – his forte based not only on experience of military matters but on his exemplary knowledge of world affairs. Spain, thankfully, had for some months indicated that it was ready to oblige.

---

[139] Birch, T. 1754. *Memoirs of the Reign of Queen Elizabeth, from the Year 1581 Till Her Death, Vol. 1* (London: A. Millar), p. 483.

14: The Empire Strikes Back

Philip of Spain was a devout man. If he had failed God in achieving a victory over the heretical English queen in 1588, he had surely reformed himself and his people enough in the years since. The first Spanish Armada had been a setback, not a killing blow. England, further, had been weakened by hard rains – both 1594 and 1595 had illustrated God's wrath towards the Protestant nation. The state of war, which had lain somewhat in abeyance, limited on England's part to piracy, must be upped to the greater glory of Spain. The island nation's ally, France, had also declared war on the Spanish empire – Henry IV might have become a Catholic to win his country, but his country had not and would not accept imperial aggression. Both countries would have to be crushed. Another Armada would have to set sail.

Essex, as the English government's unofficial foreign secretary and minister for war, had been nurturing concern about his country drifting away from France since the latter part of 1595. As a confirmed Francophile, it was his belief that only an Anglo-French alliance could stand up to the might of Spain. That might was something he shamelessly played up to the council, and which he had his spies tirelessly seek to discover; it was his goal to lead England against an empire that was 'a generall enemie to the libertie of Christendome'.[140] In the late summer of 1595 his suspicions were confirmed: a raid on Mounts Bay in Cornwall was launched by Carlos de Amésquita on patrol near Brittany, which was even then a battleground between Anglo-French and imperial forces. Thereafter Essex had an easier job in exaggerating the organisation of a second Spanish Armada, rumoured to be bigger even than that defeated in 1588. Prior to the disaster of his Accession Day drama, he had even drafted in Cecilian support: Essex could well appreciate that the war was bigger than a growing rivalry, and

[140] Essex. 1598. *An Apologie of the Earle of Essex* (sig. A3).

his desire to fight Spain relied on conciliar agreement and approval. From the Cecils' perspective, their preferred policy of subjugating Ireland might also be made cheaper and more effective if potential Spanish aggression did not require them to flood the boggy island with infantrymen.

Essex received another boon when his friend Sir Henry Unton was appointed ambassador to France. Through Unton, the earl could ensure that dispatches from France increasingly outlined the necessity of anti-Spanish aid. This, combined with the growing rumours that Philip was indeed building up a new Armada that were on the wind quite independent of Essex, had its effect. Although it remained much against her instincts, Elizabeth accepted the necessity of doing something about Spain. The empire, she was made to realise, was a sleeping dragon – but its claws had begun to flex, and the smoke issuing from its nostrils could be smelt in England.

The military strength of England lay in its navy rather than its army. Outfitting a navy was, further, cheaper: ships could be requisitioned and there were plenty of captains willing to throw in their lot with the government on the promise of loot. Drake and his fellow sea dog, John Hawkins, floated the idea of a mission which would see them attack Panama – the so-called Spanish Main from which the empire received its vast stores of treasure plundered from the Americas. Essex was not convinced, preferring to attack Spanish territory in Europe – but he was willing, even eager, to lead any ground troops that might be mustered to aid it. Plans were then written up that would see a sizeable army mustered to lead the attacks on Spanish ports with Essex leading them. Only Elizabeth, who had become far too passive in prosecuting the war for Essex's liking, dragged her feet. She was unwilling to let Essex go and months passed with him fretting, chiding, and champing at the bit for action. All she would agree to was Drake and Hawkins leading naval expeditions; these took place but were worse than disastrous. After a falling-out, the pair tried and failed to capture Las Palmas, afterwards sailing across the Atlantic where Hawkins died in November. Drake attempted to intercept the Spanish treasure fleet without him but succumbed to dysentery in

January. Less than half of the fleet managed to limp back to England in May. This, Essex could see, was the best that could be hoped from his queen's overly cautious military strategy. Even when Calais, her one white whale, was besieged in April 1596, she dilly-dallied sufficiently that the town was lost to the French and became a Spanish possession. Worse, it would give King Philip the secure base from which to launch an invasion that he had lacked in 1588.

The capture of Calais solidified all of Essex's doubts about Elizabeth's ability to understand war. It further fuelled his desire to take the fight to the Spanish before they could launch another Armada. The attack on the Spanish Main had failed. He wanted a direct raid. In this he had the support of Howard of Effingham, the lord admiral of England, as well as Raleigh, who was ever on the lookout for a chance to regain favour. Even Robert Cecil was willing to back the scheme. The only ones not happy about it were the poor sailors, and amongst them rippled some of the dissent, gossip, and vitriol that was coming to infect public discourse. Indeed, attorney-general Coke had to prosecute one poor fellow who spread false rumours about what was going on in the court:

Kuke [Coke], the Queen's Attorney moved against three for slanderous words against the Lord Admiral and the Earl of Essexe, but he proceeded only against one Smithe on his confession for spreading sclaunderous newes ... Smithe had confessed that he being a pressed soldier at Dover and the news being there that the Spaniards were on the sea (which was false, for they were Hollanders and friends of the Queen), they were shipte, bu [sic] as it turned out to be 'Grave Morris' [Maurice of Nassau, Governor of the United Provinces] they were dismissed; and he came to London and reported that the news was throughout the soldiers that the Lord Admiral's shippe beinge searchte by th'erle of Essexe & openinge divers barrelles wherein he supposed to haue been gunpowder ... & thereupon he Called him Traitor, and so theye Came bothe to the Cowrte & there the'erle of Essexe ... before the Queene tooke the Lord Admiralle by the Berde & sayde "ah thou Traytor"; and this

Smythe, trauellinge by Windsor, called at the howse of a Justice of peace thereby for drinks and reportinge the like there, was … himselfe apprehended.

It is a curious episode. The unfortunate Smith was whipped, pilloried, and had his ears cut off, the sentence recorded as unusually lenient because he was only a boy. His crime was spreading false stories about the misdoings of his betters, but the case is revealing not for its barbarity but what it tells us about the increased political climate. Amongst the common multitude, word was spreading that the nation's governors were at one another's throats over the prosecution of the war and the toll it was taking on the people. Displays of amity amongst the elite were then, as now, not entirely trusted.

Elizabeth trusted Effingham's cool head and the fleet accordingly sailed with only its leaders aware of the destination, Cadiz, chosen by the admiral. The Spanish were not the only ones who were in for a surprise, however. Before Essex had departed for Cadiz, he left a letter with his secretary, Edward Reynolds. With it was the instruction, 'which yow shall deliver butt nott till the wind hath so served us att least a weeke as yow may judg us to be in Spayne'.[141] The letter contained demands that his fellow counsellors lobby the queen to approve his plan to capture a permanent base on Spanish territory garrisoned with a stout body of English soldiers. This request directly countermanded Elizabeth's orders to destroy the Spanish fleet before returning home and preparing for the treasure raid in the Americas – she had again envisioned a defensive action which would put an end to Philip's rumoured new Armada. Essex wanted an aggressive one which would provide a state of continual battle. His letter existed in several copies, which were at first circulated amongst his friends before one was taken to the council. Cunningly, he had pre-planned a propaganda exercise which would make denial of his request more difficult.

---

[141] Daybell, J. 2012. *The Material Letter in Early Modern England: Manuscript Letters and the Culture and Practices of Letter-Writing, 1512-1635* (London: Palgrave Macmillan), p. 193.

The remaining council, led by Burghley, was not about to become Essex's instrument. After the queen had been shown the letter, he agreed with her to turn off the tap of money. Henceforth, any new financial warrants would have to be signed by himself. When Essex returned from his jolly, he would find himself forced to confront the parlous state of his finances rather than racking up yet more debt on the hope of jam tomorrow. Not only that, but she opted to negotiate an alliance with Essex's other great love, France. A month of negotiation between the two countries ensued (the Dutch not embraced until October). Two treaties were signed: a public one, which declared that neither England or France would unilaterally make peace with Spain; and a private one, which pledged 4000 English soldiers to be stationed in Picardy. Essex might have thought his venture the most critical of the war, but Elizabeth had other irons in the fire.

***

In late June the waters of the bay at Cadiz were churned by the arrival of Howard of Effingham's ships. In all, 120 English vessels were at sea. Essex attempted a daring landing, hoping to assault the town directly with his infantry, but the angry sea prevented him. The next day, however, Raleigh sailed into the bay with the vanguard of the fleet and the air was rent by the boom of gunfire. Dozens of Spanish ships were at anchor – sitting ducks for the English.

The Spanish were not complacent, but they were surprised. The alarm was raised but the English ships flooding the bay far outnumbered their own. They attempted to form a defensive formation, but the English guns bombarded them for eight hours. Panic ensued. As the Spaniards tried to manoeuvre their larger ships deeper into the bay and away from the English, they ran aground. Others exploded, their holds filled with gunpowder, in showers of sparks and torn timber. Two Spanish warships were captured, the others sinking to the bottom of the Mediterranean.

As the battle raged, it became clear to Essex that it was fast becoming Raleigh and Effingham's day. Not to be outdone, he ignored the merchant shipping and made straight for the shore, landing two thousand men led by himself and Francis Vere, one of the leading soldiers who had come over to him after Leicester's death. On landing, they proceeded to launch a ground assault, capturing the town and beginning their plunder. Fancying himself the master of England's latest possession, Essex began negotiating with the surrendering Spaniards for the ransom of those who had been captured. Unfortunately for him, the captains of the merchant ships still at anchor in the bay – the ones he should have been capturing during the battle – had decided that discretion was the better part of valour. They set light to their own vessels in a sudden scorched earth policy, having decided that if their king could not reap the benefit of the combined twelve-million ducats on board, then nor would the English queen. They went to the sea bed. Essex had won the remarkable victory he wanted, but at the direct expense – and a great expense it was – of the victory his queen had demanded. He had made no miscalculation or misjudgement – he had rather made a political statement that his way was more important than hers. In a sense he was playing to the gallery at home. The people of England expected to hear of grand military enterprises on foreign soil, not grubby piratical ambushes that enriched the coffers of already-wealthy elites. If Elizabeth was not willing to make herself queen of the ocean, he would force the role on her by establishing a permanent English presence on the Portuguese coast: a prize far above the value of the lost merchant ships' cargo.

His elation, however, came at a cost. He had defied his sovereign's orders and he knew it. He attempted to shore up support for what he had done by means of conciliar agreement with his fellow officers, but all that could be established was the necessity of receiving the queen's approval and a decision to raze the secular buildings of Cadiz. No permanent garrison would be left but nor would there be anything other than monasteries and nunneries left for the Spanish. Afterwards he wrote an account of his actions to Burghley, which left no doubt as to his views on what he had done:

My very good lord,

I shall not need to tell your L. that Cales [Cadiz] is won, and the king of Spain's great fleet ... destroyed. I shall need less to repeat the particular circumstances of either; for as Fame itself will bring the first, so this gentleman that carries my letter will perform the second. This is to crave of your L. good favour and to pray you that you will plead for me till my return; that before I be heard, I be not upon report, or misconceit, brought into H. M. displeasure, for I doubt not your L. and such honourably judges shall think I do acquit myself like an honest man.[142]

It is a confident letter, brimming with a sense of victory. But so too does it reveal Essex's anxiety about what might be going on in his absence. Playing on his favourite theme of honour, it was his attempt to manipulate and guilt the old man into, if not actually pleading for him, at least not briefing against him. What Essex knew – for he had tried to forestall it by building a network of supporters via his letters – was that Burghley and Cecil remained at home, no doubt pouring poison in Elizabeth's ear. He was right to worry. Not long after having seen and assessed the temerity of his letter, on the 5th of July she had appointed Cecil to the post of principal secretary of state: formerly Walsingham's position. More than ever she wished to cut the upstart favourite down to size.

The news of his rival's achievement sent Essex into apoplexies. His response was to attempt to raise himself up still further with martial victories, and he took his fleet to southern Portugal, winning this time only the stock of the local bishop's library. This would hardly do. He sought afterwards agreement from his fellow leaders to sail to the Portuguese Azores, about 850 miles west of the coast, there to intercept Spanish treasure ships and make good the losses of the Cadiz merchant vessels, but Raleigh could not be moved. Thus it was that he took himself back to the colder climate – in all senses – of the English

---

[142] Devereux, *Lives and Letter*, p. 372.

court.

Essex's strategy for winning the queen's approval of his actions was to divert her expected anger elsewhere. His conduct over Cadiz, he confidently believed, had been impeccable. Raleigh's, however, had cost England more than twelve-million ducats. Because of the commoner's refusal to sail with Essex to the Azores, the chance of capturing Philip's treasure ships had been lost. Rather than turning her fury elsewhere, he managed only to double it. Now she was appalled at her favourite for disobeying her and losing millions to the Spanish seabed, and Raleigh for missing an opportunity to make good on that loss. Not even the death of Essex's grandfather, the austere old Francis Knollys, softened her anger towards him. Free from any blame, of course, were safe old Burghley and his cocky son, who took great delight in detailing the financial losses incurred by the enterprise. Technically they were absolutely right to do so, but the justness of their accusations rather increased than diminished their unforgiveable nature in Essex's eyes. His response was to approach Archbishop Whitgift in the hopes of having a national, very public day of thanksgiving for the destruction of Cadiz – a request which was moderately met with a day of feasting in the capital. He then set his agent Henry Cuffe to work penning *A True Relation of the Action at Cadiz the 21st of June under the earl of Essex and the lord admiral*. Though designed primarily a means of winning Elizabeth round to the rectitude of his actions, this was also the latest of his shameless attempts to court public opinion.

That, at least, was how his queen took it when Cuffe's work was leaked to her early by Cecil, who had got an advance copy from one of Essex's less honest adherents. She had never as a leader been receptive to having her will, once it had finally been expressed, overruled. In the 1590s it became anathema. To accept a younger subject's wilful disregard would be to be to declare to the world that she was no longer an effective ruler. Age and decline had succeeded insurrection and overthrow as her chief fears.

This plan thwarted – the queen forbidding publication of the text – Essex continued his policy of the previous year.

Manuscript versions of the tract were instead circulated surreptitiously. He commissioned another portrait, this time painted by his now-favoured painter Marcus Ghreeraerts the Younger, which showed him in full regalia with Cadiz burning in the background, and with the distinctive beard – a sign of virile manhood – he had grown on display. As the previous portrait had shown him in England waiting to achieve glory, the next in what was becoming a series of visual propaganda pieces depicted him having won it. Francis Bacon warned him about the dangers of courting popularity, but he was still only too happy to praise the earl to the rafters in all of his own writings. Central to Francis' outpouring of sagacity were the recommendations that he

win the queen; if this be not the beginning, I can see not end. And I will not now speak of favour or affection, but of other correspondence and agreeableness ... [Your estate is] not grounded to his greatness, of a popular reputation, of a military dependence: I demand whether there can be a more dangerous image than this represented to any monarch living, much more to a lady, and of her Majesty's apprehension?[143]

Bacon understood Elizabeth the monarch far more than Essex, who saw only her smiling personal face and her insufferable royal one. Pointing out, rather fawningly, that 'none ascend near' the earl in competition, he exhorted him to 'take all occasions to speak against popularity and popular courses vehemently'. The advice was well meant. Bacon understood implicitly that Essex had been made by the queen and could be unmade by her, especially if she feared his influence over the hearts and minds of the people. Essex had launched himself on a dangerous course, for, as he pointed out, no monarch, either the current or the future one, would stand an overmighty

[143] Bacon, F. 1862 [1596]. 'Letter of Advice to Lord Essex' in J. Spedding (Ed.) *The Letters and the Life of Francis Bacon Including All His Occasional Works* (London: Longman, Green, Longman, and Roberts), p. 41.

subject. His military aims would not be best served by trying to win support for them in the court of public opinion.

Essex's goal, which Elizabeth was doing everything to prevent being achieved, was to breed war-fever in England, with himself the national hero. The army – his army – he argued must remain mustered and ready to bring down Calais as it had brought down Cadiz. Anyone who would help in persuading Elizabeth was drafted – the Dutch and French ambassadors, even the corporation of London. None had any effect. Elizabeth was not interested in any further grand schemes. Had Essex done purely as he was told in Portugal, she might well have been more receptive.

Yet if Cadiz had put Elizabeth off battle, it had stirred up King Philip's increasingly thin blood. Once the handsome young husband of Mary Tudor, he was now nearly seventy and in poor health. The affront of Cadiz had only confirmed his aspirations of a second naval assault on England, and he threw together the new Armada in the months following the town's destruction. Unfortunately, God once again turned his back on his most Catholic majesty, and his fleet of 126 ships was scattered by severe gales in the middle of October. The pitiful, rushed second Spanish Armada had not met the humiliating and crushing defeat of the first, but it had failed nonetheless. The survival of its ships, however, allowed the pro-war party in England, Essex amongst them, to rub their hands in glee at the thought of another year of battle. If there was one thing that never went out of fashion in England, it was military heroes.

15: Trouble in Paradise

The Christmas period of 1596-7 was a particularly cold one. Essex spent it apart from his queen. Not chosen to be one of her hosts for the round of revels, he preferred to skulk and sulk away from the court. Nor had she shown much inclination to visit him at Wanstead over the preceding months. Despite his popular victory at Cadiz, she would lend no ear to his eager protestations that another English fleet must make ready to cut Philip's ships down before they could be refitted for another attempt on England when the campaign season came around again. She had, however, been quite willing to dine with Cecil at his house on the Strand.

Often the whole decade of the 1590s is seen as one of factional fighting, chiefly between the Essex and Cecil factions. This is not, however, entirely the case, mainly because Cecil was far too aloof and clever to be drawn into spats. That did not stop those in the ever-growing Essex circle from trying. Though Essex did not plan it, those who were similarly disgruntled by the gradual accession to power of Burghley's son gravitated towards him as an opposition figure. As Burghley himself had been unpopular amongst large sections of the political community – chiefly the aristocracy – so too did his son suffer it. A number of them were thus caught up in the Essex orbit: his sisters, Penelope and Dorothy; his cousin Lord Henry Howard; Lettice and her husband, Blount; the earl of Southampton; Lord Mountjoy, Penelope's lover; and Lord Rich, her husband. One of the great tensions in the early modern period, which would simmer below the surface until the island exploded in civil war the following century, was the rightful place of nobles in the governance of the country. In the rapidly vanishing mediaeval world, there had been little questioning of it – the magnates and barons stood at the right hand of the sovereign. In the questioning, sceptical world of the renaissance, men of learning had begun to make inroads, shaking the old certainties to their foundations. Elizabeth mishandled this crisis of the nobility. As

Christopher Haigh notes, 'by 1597, the process of replacing regional magnates with reliable officers had gone further: the council had only eleven members, and although six were nobles, none were territorial magnates, and four were Elizabethan creations. The late Elizabethan council was very much a compact group of officials, and Elizabeth seems to have decided she could manage without the advice of magnates'.[144]

Naturally, this was unwelcome news to the magnates, and even those gifted with noble titles by Elizabeth had cause for suspicion of their peers in council. The aristocracy tended to fear, distrust, and dislike the new men who rose to fill their old positions; and the Tudors, from Henry VII, had done more than any other dynasty to foster that fear. The truth was that people were not looking towards Elizabeth's death, but Burghley's – he was older, had been visibly failing since the death of his wife in 1589, and as the queen's chief minister he was the archetypal 'new man'. The Essex circle wanted his successor to be their aristocratic candidate, whereas Burghley himself obviously wanted his son to assume the role. Whoever got it would have unparalleled knowledge and influence, making him invaluable to any administration.

On his return from Cadiz Essex had gradually attempted to apply Francis Bacon's advice. The lavish playing on the public fiddle decreased, and he had returned to the serious posturing he had taken up prior to the venture. Still he communicated with Henry IV and sought to strengthen the English presence in France; still his spy network sought every means possible to turn the queen to a more militant cast of mind; still the threat of Spain, his bête noire, lurked. Elizabeth approved of his behaviour. Anthony Bacon wrote in September that 'the queen used the earl most graciously, and will, no doubt, more and more ... so long as he continues his Christian zealous courses'.[145] Whilst outwardly he lived the part of the grave counsellor, privately he continued to live as he pleased. In December Francis and Anthony's redoubtable mother, Lady

---

[144] Haigh, *Elizabeth I*, p. 84.
[145] Devereux, *Lives and Letters*, p. 405.

Bacon, wrote a scathing letter to him accusing him of an adulterous affair with the pretty young countess of Derby, the daughter of Anne Cecil (and thus Burghley's granddaughter). Essex wrote back denying the charge, but his letter was so full of tongue-in-cheek high dudgeon it is hard to believe he was anything other than guilty. The one note of honesty he strikes is the complaint, 'I live in a place where I am hourly conspired against, and practiced upon … and what they cannot make probable to the queen, they give out to the world'.[146] The tensions of his double life appeared to take a toll. He fell ill in early February and this brought Elizabeth to his bedside. Likely feigned, he had managed to get what he wanted: the company of the now rapidly ageing woman who had now been a strange, fascinating, and constant presence in his life for just over ten years. What brought her was what always brought her: she found Essex and his moods every bit as annoying and engaging as ever and, although she knew of his wife and succession of pretty young bed-mates, she wished to know that she remained the magical icon who could exercise his mind where others had only his codpiece.

Part of his attempt to build a cohesive and sedate public image was an attempt at rapprochement with Robert Cecil, at least on the surface. He had managed this with Raleigh, and indeed chose Raleigh as a mediator. Towards the end of February 1597, a truce between the rivals looked likely, and Essex planned after it had been agreed to go on a progress to Wales. However, the death of Lord Cobham intervened. This was surprisingly good news. Cobham was Cecil's father-in-law and had succeeded to the post of Elizabeth's lord chamberlain in August 1596, upon the death of Lord Hunsdon. His short tenure meant one less Cecilian in the queen's immediate orbit. Bad news followed. Essex applied for the post of warden of the cinque (pronounced 'sink') ports, then a military sinecure. Instead Elizabeth told him she intended to give it to Cobham's heir, Henry Brooke: a Falstaffian figure who had never made a secret of his dislike of the earl.

---

[146] Devereux, *Lives and Letters*, p. 409.

In a huff, Essex attempted to make for Wales anyway, only to find himself apprehended and summoned to the queen's presence. He might well have hoped she had changed her mind. She had not. She did, however, award him the sop of master-general of the ordnance. This was not what he had wanted, but neither was it inconsiderable: it was a military role which gave him the challenge of organising and ordering local militias. For the rest of the month she demanded his presence, and all attempts on his part to leave for the much-deferred progress to Wales were met with offence on hers. The whole thing was a power play on both sides – his attempting to threaten her with a self-imposed exile, and her display of power in quashing the attempts. It was juvenile and it does neither of them much credit, but such was the nature of Elizabethan display politics.

More bizarre in the eyes of all observers was the continuing friendship between Essex, Raleigh, and Cecil. The trio made a point of riding together to Essex House, there to dine and hold a three-hour conference. Rumours circulated that a joke had been made at the house, evoking much wry laughter, about the parallels between the queen's recent rule and last days of Richard II, that unfortunate king whose reign sank into idle and faction-causing favouritism. What, people wondered, was going on?

The truth was that distrust, even hatred, continued between the rivals. However, as they had in previous years, they united in the realisation of a larger threat. Both men knew that Spain's Armada had gone away but not gone down. Both, further, were recipients of sheaves of secret intelligence, not just about one another, but about their common enemy. Rumours of Spanish preparations in Ferrol and Coruña, led by the adelantado of Castile, had reached them. Something had to be done, and the lord admiral, Howard of Effingham, confessed himself too old for such an undertaking. Throughout April, the unlikely trio hatched a plan, shaking hands, smiling, and distrusting each other with all the guile of the first Roman triumvirate. Another English Armada would be launched with the intention of capturing that much-coveted foothold in Spain; first the ships and armaments being assembled at Ferrol would be destroyed, and then Terceira in the mid-Atlantic Azores would be attacked and, if possible, made an English possession. The last staging post on the long sail from the Americas would therefore be seized, making future treasure ships vulnerable. In late May, Essex was given the command. Though Ferrol and Terceira were his ostensible targets, he boasted that he might take any one of King Philip's coastal outposts: 'For when I hadde defeated that force,' he wrote, 'I might go after whether I listed, and doe almost what I listed, (I meane) vpon any places vpon that coast'.[147]

The summer of 1597 looked remarkably sunny for the favourite. His colleagues on the voyage were all duly signed in, and they represented a cross-section of Essex circle members: Charles Blount, Lord Mountjoy; and Francis Vere. Even Raleigh (whom Cecil's intervention had returned to favour) got in on the act. In late June he wrote to the queen in high spirits:

Your spirit I do invoke, my most dear and most admired sovereign, to assist me, that I may express that humblest and most due thankfulness, and that high and true joy which upon the reading of your Majesty's letter my poor heart hath conceived. Upon your spirit, I say, I call, as only powerful over me, and by his infinite virtue only able to express infinite things. Or if I be too weak an instrument to be inspired with such a gift, or that words be not able to interpret for me, then to your royal dear heart I appeal, which, without my words, can fully and justly understand me.[148]

He signed the letter, 'your Majesty's humblest and most affectionate vassal'. There is no irony in the letter. Instead it offers a window into the strange relationship that had always existed between the two. Centuries before psychoanalysis, it is unlikely if Essex engaged in much introspection, but if he had, he would have found that he had become hopelessly entranced by an idea of a woman rather than the woman herself. His

[147] Essex. 1598. *An Apologie of the Earle of Essex* (sig. B1)
[148] Devereux, *Lives and Letters*, p. 413.

repeated reference to her 'spirit' indicates that he at least appreciated that theirs was a curious, almost transcendental meeting of minds. It was her 'spirit' that held him in sway. His relationships with women were as unhealthy and emotionally unrewarding as hers with men – probably more so. Only when she was giving him what he wanted did his hysterical paranoia and jealousy decline, to be replaced with overblown, loving affection. When she was Lady Bountiful, he once again fell into the pattern of adoring the woman's perplexing, labyrinthine mind, which soared above the skinny, arthritis-riddled body.

His sunny disposition, which extended still to Cecil, was not matched by the English weather. When his fleet set out for Spain, storms drove it back to England. Early July saw the bulk of them riding the waves off Plymouth. When they tried to depart again, the poor weather remained unaccommodating. Elizabeth was worried. Having decided to make Essex lord general, she immediately regretted the decision. Her young beau with his soft words and his funny moods would be in real, physical danger. Her anxiety manifested as anger, which was compounded by the fact that Essex, immured in port, was using up supplies intended to be spent during the expedition proper. As a result, he was compelled to reduce his army – already comprised of unfortunate men pressed into service – to a bare minimum necessary for a successful attack. Still contrary winds blew.

By dint of the deferral of the expedition, Essex returned to court, where Elizabeth greeted him enthusiastically. Her anger had been blown away, partly by the fact that she had just got the better of an uppity Polish ambassador, and partly by the proximity of her favourite. It was increasingly clear to all that she had developed a form of dependence on him. Primarily this was political: having made him, she was determined to make sure he came good in the end. Off on his own, he was a renegade and, worse, liable to win popularity. By her side, he was a new sweet Robin, amusing and entertaining. She was not, further, inclined to admit that she had make a mistake in making and promoting him. The queen must not be seen to have lost her touch in picking good men. Yet emotional dependence was there too, which it certainly never was with Cecil, or even his father. It is significant that she did not give such rapt attention to her other favourites either; Leicester was the only other man whose long absences she could not abide, and this alone tells us something about her private views of Essex. He was certainly amongst the first to realise it, and after his audience with her, he returned to Plymouth and favourable winds.

The fleet finally put out for Spain in mid-August. What followed bordered on fiasco as the English ships tasted a little of the gall King Philip had endured during his own attempts at naval invasion. A great tempest rose up during the attack on Ferrol, and when it subsided, it was clear that the English Armada had been scattered. Raleigh's ship and thirty more had vanished, and dark rumours grew as to their fate. These were alleviated when news arrived that they had taken shelter in the North Cape. With no hope of taking Ferrol, Essex was forced to sail down the Spanish coast in hope of upholding the second part of his commission: the capture of the treasure ships *en route* from the new world. He dispatched his uncle, Robert Knollys, with a letter explaining and excusing his actions – already he must have suspected that recriminations would be his reward.

After conferring with – and rebuking – Raleigh via a small man-of-war, the decision was made to head directly to the Azores, Essex taking his ships as the vanguard. On reaching these paradisaical islands, he passed Terceira and anchored at Flores, whereupon the Portuguese citizenry greeted him warmly. He returned their hospitality by informing them that his queen had dispatched him not to harass them, but rather to punish the wicked and tyrannous Spaniards who had manned the fortresses and garrisons which dotted their island homes. Unfortunately, he learned that Philip's main fleet was still at Ferrol, which meant that any pickings to be taken in the islands would be limited. In the middle of September Raleigh joined him and the two men reconciled, Essex apologising for the rumours of Raleigh's desertion which had followed the debacle at Ferrol. When the whole fleet regrouped, the decision was made to attempt landing on each of the islands and Essex wrote to Cecil of his hopes of surprising the treasure ships when they deigned to make across the Atlantic. He signed off with the request that Cecil 'let my dear sovereign know I do spiritually kiss her fair royal hands and think of them as a man should think of so fair flesh'.[149] The combination of the spiritual and the physical – Elizabeth's hands were her favourite feature – was designed to excite her vanity as well as emphasising his own non-physical attraction to her.

As Raleigh's ships were re-victualled with fresh water, the treasure ships were sighted. Essex flew into action. He sent word to Raleigh to meet him at Faial, where his ships could be replenished as easily, and immediately set about cruising around the islands to find and intercept the Spanish ships. Nothing was spotted. Frustrated, he laid anchor at Faial on the 22nd of September and it was then that a small number of Raleigh's ships joined him. Sir Gelli Meyrick, Essex's long-term adherent, filled his master in with embroidered tales of Raleigh's lack of obedience: his former rival had not acted as he had been commanded – most of his fleet, in fact, still sat gathering fresh water at Flores. Worse, he had landed forces without Essex's leave: a court-martialling offence. Essex, touchy of his position, egged on by the excitable Meyrick and others, and desperate to efface the fact that he was hopelessly out of his depth as a naval general, launched a pseudo-inquiry in his rival-cum-friend's conduct. The whole English fleet descended into infighting, some taking Raleigh's part and others condemning him. Whilst this unseemly farce went on, the Spanish commanders could not believe their luck. Those lodged in the island forts discreetly took what they could and retreated deeper into the islands. There followed yet more English disagreement and debate, and attempts were made to capture the abandoned Spanish forts. All was ad hoc; all was confused and messy.

The Spanish treasure ships which had been spotted and then proven so elusive were sighted again, and Essex and Raleigh elected to work together, despite the attempts by Essex's steward and his friends to sow discord. Graciosa had already

---

[149] Devereux, *Lives and Letters*, p. 457.

been invaded by the English, with the Portuguese residents submitting themselves, and it was off this beautiful island that what was called 'the Indian fleet' out of Havana was chased down. Three treasure ships were taken, one belonging to the governor of Havana and the other two support frigates, and on them was evidence that others were following. Elsewhere sixteen treasure ships were spotted by the English and an attempt made to take them. In the melee, one was fatally breached and, as the English raced to save its booty, the others escaped towards Terceira. Essex threw the dice once more, hoping to storm the ships. His fellow commanders disagreed, realising that such an action would be suicidal. The Spanish ships knew Terceira and had taken up impregnable positions. The compromise was to attack São Miguel, the 'green island', in hope of real plunder; thus far, almost nothing of value had been accomplished since leaving England.

Essex, recalling Sir Philip Sidney's supposed refusal of thigh armour which would give him an advantage, manfully embarked on a boat towards the island, refusing the helmet and breastplate Raleigh advised because the watermen who rowed him had none. It was a futile gesture. He returned to his ship with his tail between his legs, having seen first-hand that the Spanish had fortified the island and its town with snipers. Raleigh was then instructed to provide a diversion off the island whilst Essex and a 2000-strong troop slunk off in pinnaces at night and landed round the headland at Villa Franco do Compo. This scheme was put in train and Villa Franco was captured – easily, as it turned out, because again the Spanish had fled, leaving this time their stores of food and wine. As might be imagined, the troops were not inclined to leave in a hurry and there followed bouts of drunkenness and feasting as Essex tried to keep order. The plan of marching on the castle-town of São Miguel was put on ice and the fleet instead called to Villa Franco.

Essex, still out of his depth, did not discuss this with Raleigh, knowing that the older man would probably gainsay him, revealing what might be construed as buffoonery before all. His lack of experience was not his fault; no one, not even his sovereign, expected a commander of sufficient rank to need expert experience. It was simply a boon when such a man had achieved it. Further, he had been ordered to put all plans before the council of commanders, and the implied lack of trust encouraged him to rely on those of the expedition who would act as 'yes men'. Raleigh, therefore, was left to his own devices, firing intermittently at São Miguel and posturing that a landing was forthcoming. He expected any time to hear the sounds of battle and see the Spanish surprised by Essex's sneak attack. As he waited, news came instead of a great Spanish carrack – a splendid three- or four-masted vessel – bearing towards the island. Immediately he ordered all shots to be called off and flags to be hastily lowered, so as to lull the carrack into a false sense of security. One excitable Dutch ship did not get his message and fired, leading the carrack to speed towards the shore in a panic, whereupon it ran aground. Before the English-led ships could make for it, the Spanish swarmed out of the castle and began rapidly rescuing the stricken crew and their rich cargo. By the time Raleigh's forces reached the ship it had been set ablaze.

Days passed and still there was no sign of Essex or his forces. Some of the captains elected to sail around the island, and Raleigh eventually capitulated, only for a pinnace to appear bobbing around the bay. It was the lord general, bringing – finally – the message that the fleet was to attend Villa Franco immediately. Probably sighing, they left the inhabitants of São Miguel who were in gales of derisive laughter at the shambles of their attackers.

For four days the English Armada took in provisions off Villa Franco, as the waves rose. As they prepared for a humiliating return to England, reports arrived of Spanish troop movements. Plans were quickly drawn up, which used Francis Vere's ground troops to lure the Spaniards into an ambush. Essex, however, was dubious and preferred to smoke a pipe in the marketplace whilst his comrade explained the strategy. Time was of the essence and it was slipping away quickly; already the Spanish seemed to be holding back from chasing the Englishmen, who were pretending to be running in panic, into the fortified town. Thanks to Essex's foot-dragging and Spanish perception it ran out entirely. No battle took place and the English soldiers returned to the dull duty of rolling barrels to the shore and embarking. The lord general ensured that he was one of the last, making the most of the dangers of slipping away when the enemy was abroad on the island.

In October, the whole thing was at an end. A great storm had blown up and the English fleet were buffeted out of the Azores and back across the Atlantic. Essex might well have reflected on what had been achieved. In the credit column, he had taken one treasure ship and two frigates. The combined value of the haul would just about cover the cost of the expedition. On the debit side he had failed to destroy the main Spanish fleet in Ferrol. He had failed to seize a sizeable booty to enrich the queen's treasury and his own. He had failed to project the image of a sound naval commander. He had failed to gain the foothold on Spanish territory that he had insisted was necessary for years, and instead been forced to indulge in what he had once criticised as 'idle wanderings upon the sea'.[150] He had never been much of an accountant, but he did not need to be to see that his stores of favour would be very much in the red.

The return of the English Armada – which limped back scattered and confused – in October coincided with the launch of King Philip's fleet from Ferrol. It cannot rightly be described as another Spanish Armada, for by now the dying king of Spain was beyond much more than sending forth flotillas with limited aims. From his sickbed in the Escorial he had commanded, from a throat full of blisters, that his men attempt a landing in Cornwall, there to do a reverse of Essex's idea and establish an English base. Luckily for Elizabeth the storms which had prevented her favourite destroying Philip's fleet at Ferrol now conspired to prevent it leaving for Cornwall. The ships were all driven back to Spain. England had been saved, but it had been nothing to do with Essex whose failure had, in fact, left it open

---

[150] Trim, D. J. B. & Fissel, M. C. 2011. *Amphibious Warfare 1000-1700: Commerce, State Formation and European Expansion* (Leiden: Brill), p. 208.

to attack in the first place.

The war with Spain had once again reached stalemate. Philip II would die the following year, aged seventy-one, having devised no new schemes against his most persistent and irritating enemy. Essex's own dreams of a great, definitive fight with the Spaniards would never be fulfilled. He was returning from the Azores with an embarrassing record and could only imagine how furious the queen would be. No amount of hand-kissing, spiritual or otherwise, would defuse it. Beyond that he was now spent financially; for years he had banked on his ideas being fruitful if only he were allowed to put them into practice. Grudgingly, his queen had allowed him to do so, and they had been shown up for the expensive, risky fantasies she had suspected them to be. Thoroughly disillusioned, he arrived in London in November, there to face the royal mistress he had left behind.

16: Homecoming

The palace at Whitehall was one of Elizabeth's more forbidding abodes. Like Hampton Court Palace it had once been a possession of Cardinal Wolsey, and under the Tudors it had become a sprawling network of government offices, private and public gardens, and chambers for leisure and business. It was to this maze, through which he had long known the way, that Essex went after returning from the failed Azores mission.

At first the signs were good. The news of Philip's stalled fleet might well have overshadowed his expedition; he had written a long defence of his journey and the many bad hands fortune had dealt; and Elizabeth had confirmed his post as commander of her forces at the end of October. This had given him a free hand against the Spanish invaders and had been issued when the news of their defeat by Mother Nature was still to come. Nevertheless, it indicated that she was still willing to trust to her favourite. It was a false start. News had awaited him in England that Robert Cecil had been made chancellor of the duchy of Lancaster, and Howard of Effingham was being rewarded with the earldom of Nottingham for Essex's own victory at Cadiz.

In the queen's privy chamber, he was given a severe reprimand. Raleigh's supporters had reached her first and given an account of the manifold failings of the expedition – payback for what those of the Essex circle had attempted against their master in the Azores. The whole thing was unfair and humiliating. It had been the weather that had been to blame for much of the misfortunes abroad – and Raleigh, with his experience of the waves, should have had the gumption to do as he was told when necessary and do as he thought best when necessary. What Essex was also forced to confront, however unwillingly, was the reality that his self-confidence had long outweighed his ability, albeit both were hostages to nature and fortune. His response to Elizabeth's harangue was to put forward his own complaints about her behaviour – about Cecil, Effingham, and Raleigh. In his anger he was casting around for blame and burning the bridges he had built over the years. After a week, illness claimed him and he retired to Wanstead.

It is difficult to calculate how often the earl's nervous collapses were real or imagined, and if imagined whether they were wholly exaggerated or the product of some underlying mental illness. Whatever their cause, they invariably had the same effect. They moved Elizabeth to sympathy. However, she did not hasten to his bedside, though she softened somewhat and stated that his absence from court might look to his enemies like he was in disgrace, which he was not. Her lord chamberlain, Hunsdon (who had succeeded his father in the role), tactfully pointed out that the earl would be ready to do her service if she commanded it, to which she replied that 'a prince was not to be contested withal by a subject'.[151] She, at least, suspected that Essex was trying to manipulate her, and she was not to be gulled. A stalemate was reached. He would not return to court unless she begged him, and she would not demean herself by doing so.

He remained at Wanstead for two weeks before moving to Essex House. He was on strike, refusing to sit at the daily meetings of council. Likewise, he ignored the penultimate parliament of the reign, which sat from the 24th of October 1597 and which, on opening, saw 'divers people ... smothered and crushed to death, pressing betwixt Whitehall and the College Church, to have seen her Majesty and nobility riding to it'.[152] He knew that a new French ambassador, André Hurault de Maisse, had arrived in mid-November; prior to the Azores adventure he would have been doing his best to host and impress him. His refusal to do so indicates the depth of his disillusion with the politics not only of Elizabeth but the wider world.

The ambassador's mission was a tricky one and could

---

[151] Wernham, R. B. 1994. *The Return of the Armadas: The Last Years of the Elizabethan War against Spain 1595-1603* (Oxford: Clarendon Press), p. 193.
[152] Colthorpe, M. E. 2017. '1597' in M. E. Colthorpe (Ed.) *The Elizabethan Court Day by Day* (Cambridge: Folgerpedia), p. 39.

probably have done with Essex's smooth charm. Henry IV was interested in pursuing peace, but under the terms of 1596's Triple Alliance with England and the Dutch, he could not do so unilaterally. The reasons for his suddenly pacific disposition were transparent: he had managed to recover Amiens from the Spanish, the loss of which had, in March 1597, been a crushing blow. With it back in his hands, a quick peace with the dying, bankrupt Philip, who did not want to leave behind him a costly war across northern Europe either, was attractive.

Elizabeth was personally attracted to the idea of peace, as was the fast-fading Burghley, but she was under no obligation to agree with no concessions. So began a lengthy period of debate and negotiation. Chief amongst her protested concerns was the attitude of the Dutch; she could not reasonably agree to ending the war without their consent. And what would Essex, who had been the most vocal proponent of the Spanish war, think? That was an unknown as long as he maintained his troublesome and upsetting exile. Elizabeth truly did not want to make a decision without her favourite's approval. The only question was how to get him back to court without losing face. Should she relent, or would he?

***

Even without Essex, de Maisse had to be coddled, frustrated, charmed, and left hanging. Throughout the course of his six-week visit to England he met with the queen personally, in private audiences, six times. He recorded his observations of her, and these have become some of the most infamous and, as historian John Guy has recently proven, misread pen portraits of the elderly Elizabeth ever written.

A selection of these famous descriptions gives a flavour of Elizabeth at sixty-four:

[she] was strangely attired in a dress of silver cloth, white and crimson, or silver 'gauze', as they call it. This dress had slashed sleeves lined with red taffeta, and was girt about with other little sleeves that hung down to the ground, which she was for ever

twisting and untwisting. She kept the front of her dress open and one could see the whole of her bosom, and passing low, and often she would open the front of this robe with her hands as if she was too hot … On her head she wore … a great reddish-coloured wig, with a great number of spangles of gold and silver, and hanging down over her forehead some pearls, but of no great worth … her bosom is somewhat wrinkled, as well as one can see for the collar that she wears round her neck, but lower down her flesh is exceedingly white and delicate …as for her face, it appears to be very aged. It is long and thin, and her teeth are very yellow and unequal, compared with what they were formerly, so they say, and on the left side less than the right. Many of them are missing, so that one cannot understand her easily when she speaks quickly … her figure is fair and tall and graceful in whatever she does; so far as may be she keeps her dignity … she would complain that the fire was hurting her eyes, though there was a great screen before it and the she six or seven feet away … At my departure she … began to say that she was grieved that all the gentleman I had brought should see her in that condition.[153]

Guy has effectively put to bed the most scandalous of the observations: the bare bosom was based on a faulty translation and refers to her throat – what would now be called her décolletage. Yet much remains off and mysterious about the observations. One gets the impression on reading them of an aged, rather dotty and slightly shabby old woman. Elizabeth was neither of these things. She was capable of razor-sharp perception and she maintained a keen interest in her own image. Why, then, present herself in this way? The answer lies in dissimulation: a well-known diplomatic tactic of feigned powerlessness whereby one strove to appear weaker than one was. The wrinkled bosom and wattle – an inheritance from her grandfather, Henry VII – she could not hide: early modern makeup could not disguise what even modern surgery cannot.

---

[153] Martin, C. 'The Breast and Belly of a Queen: Elizabeth After Tilbury' *Early Modern Women, Vol. 2* (Fall 2007), pp. 5-28.

The poor state of her teeth is also corroborated by Paul Hentzner, a German traveller who saw her the next year. Yet a number of other red flags are apparent. The ersatz earrings, for example, clash with Henztner's observations of a woman

very majestic; her face oblong, fair, but wrinkled; her eyes small, yet black and pleasant; her nose a little hooked; her lips narrow, and her teeth black (a defect the English seem subject to, from their too great use of sugar); she had in her ears two pearls, with very rich drops; she wore false hair, and that red; upon her head she had a small crown, reported to be made of some of the gold of the celebrated Lunebourg table; her bosom was uncovered, as all the English ladies have it till they marry; and she had on a necklace of exceeding fine jewels; her hands were small, her fingers long, and her stature neither tall nor low; her air was stately, her manner of speaking mild and obliging.[154]

It seems evident that the garbled, rushed speaking voice was a ploy designed to confuse and disorientate de Maisse, as were the earrings, which were gone by Hentzner's visit. She was hoping, simply, to delay him – to keep him held in suspense as to what she intended and even whether she knew what she intended. Similarly, the tetchy, pretended complaints about heat despite the distance of the fire, the deliberate flaunting of her neck and cleavage, and the overt references to shame at being seen 'in that condition' point not to an addled and embarrassed old woman, but someone ardently over-playing the part of one. The description provided by the Swiss visitor Thomas Platter in 1599 seems to offer a different picture again, further suggesting that the queen was willing and able to act and appear old or young depending on the occasion. Her age had become a political tool, as once the possibility of her marriage had been.

---

[154] Strickland, A. 1847. *Lives of the Queens of England: From the Norman Conquest, Vols. 6-7* (Philadelphia: Lea and Blanchard), p. 167.

She was most lavishly attired in a gown of pure white satin, gold-embroidered, with a whole bird of paradise for panache, set forward on her head studded with costly jewels, wore a string of huge round pearls about her neck and elegant gloves over which were drawn costly rings. In short, she was most gorgeously apparelled, and although she was already seventy-four [sic], was very youthful still in appearance, seeming no more than twenty years of age.[155]

Crucially, none of the commentators make mention of the infamous white lead makeup, which presents a significant puzzle. Three solutions are possible. The first is that she was not wearing it, in which case Hollywood has much to answer for. The second is that her makeup was so ubiquitous amongst women of her class that it did not warrant mention (which is difficult to believe, given that even the narrowness of her lips was recorded). The third, and likeliest, is that she wore makeup so sparingly that, far from appearing clownish, her ladies managed to make it appear ordinary. No matter what the truth is of the queen's makeup, it is evident that significant reassessment is needed of the popular image we have developed of Queen Elizabeth in her sixties.

The reasons why de Maisse's observations of Elizabeth have become so celebrated is obvious: they appeal to our sense of iconoclasm. They show a faded icon parodying herself. That they have for so long been taken as accurate depictions of Elizabeth's mental and physical state in her sixties is, ironically, because she had continued to fool historians as much as she originally sought to fool the ambassador. An old woman she certainly was; a grotesque and wandering old woman she was not.

***

Elizabeth was taking her customary stroll in the palace garden

---

[155] Dunlop, I. 1970. *Palaces and Progresses of Elizabeth I* (New York: Taplinger Publishing Co.), p. 108.

in early December. Although a few months over sixty-four, she had an extraordinary constitution which she was determined to flaunt before her courtiers as often as she could. What she did not know was that a man had concealed himself in the garden and was waiting for her to pass by.

She recognised him instantly – occasionally she wore spectacles for reading but she was far from blind. It was Francis Vere, the gentleman soldier who had been under Leicester and latterly under Essex. She called out to him and, still bitter about her missing-in-action favourite, berated him about the earl's antics abroad. Vere was loyal. Patiently and humbly, but loud enough that others could hear it, he delivered his own, exculpatory, version of events. She nodded, became animated, and called those in her train to hear the man's words and explain themselves for badmouthing him. She led Vere out of the garden, conversing cheerfully and closing with fond words about his master. The loyal soldier had given her the excuse she needed to break the stalemate. She summoned Essex to court in December. He had won the contest of wills.

Yet Essex would not be gracious in victory. In his absence rumours had swirled around the court that he had in fact been suffering from syphilis or some other venereal disease – the same embarrassing allegations that had circulated and been mentioned by Elizabeth when he had pursued Dr Lopez. There is likely no truth to these rumours, though their basis is clearly the earl's own licentious lifestyle. He would, in fact, soon return to bedding one Mistress Bridges, a royal attendant, within months – which indicates both his louche living and the paucity of evidence that he was truly diseased. Even Essex lacked such magnetism that a woman would willingly risk the infamous French pox to enjoy his embraces. Allegations of sexual disease were simply well-worn means of defaming people of both sexes, and syphilis had by the 1590s become a byword for corruption and decay. Rather than trying to diagnose the earl's alleged ailment, they were intended as metaphors for his descent from the top. The people behind it, he suspected, were his old enemies: the Cecils and all those who opposed the Essex circle. Factionalism, that grouping together of opposing parties behind key individuals that had so long been held at bay, was beginning to poison the Elizabethan body politic. It would see political players of various hues throw in their lots together when either short- or long-term aims converged, and it would lead to what one historian has labelled 'the nasty nineties'.[156]

Although he returned to court, he would not sit at the daily meetings of the privy council, citing as his reasons the range of men who conspired against him. Having beaten Elizabeth in their battle of wills, he was determined to press home his advantage. There ensued a farcical series of withdrawals and returns: he attended on her, returned to Essex House, and then haunted the court again at night. In response to the rumours of his disease he fostered fear that violence was forthcoming, thanks to the peacocking of old Effingham, now the earl of Nottingham and lord steward, who had the right to precedence over Essex in parliament. A quarrel developed between the sixty-odd-year-old and his embittered young colleague, with Nottingham pulling Essex's trick of feigning illness and retiring from court. After another round of withdrawal and return, the queen more firmly took his part, proposing to make him her earl marshal: another considerable office with military applications and responsibilities.

Elizabeth's role throughout Essex's petulant quarrelling is mysterious. What had she to gain? It has been suggested and was suggested by Essex at the time that she was interested in keeping dissent amongst her courtiers alive. This would not be out of character. Throughout her reign she had fostered rivalries, disliking only those which she had not manufactured and which she could not control. Further, although she wanted Essex back at court, his Francophilia and diplomatic skills being beyond question, it served her well to foment disagreement. As long as her counsellors were split and disinclined to speak to one another she might spin out the negotiations with de Maisse

---

[156] Collinson, P. 1995. 'Ecclesiastical vitriol: religious satire in the 1590s and the invention of puritanism' in J. Guy (Ed.) *The Reign of Elizabeth I: Court and Culture in the Last Decade* (Cambridge: Cambridge University Press), pp. 150-70.

that much longer. It was, however, a mistake this time. What she did not realise was that the short-term fostering of division would have longer-term results. Burghley was too close to death, and so, potentially, was she, for her to be able to divide men safe in the knowledge that they would ultimately have to come together under an immutable administration. The stakes of the late 1590s were far too high for her time-honoured politicking.

Whatever the nature of her strategic summons and benefaction, Essex was mollified. With the new office planned, he even made his peace with Nottingham. Worryingly, however, he had once again achieved something by means of defiance and recalcitrance. He had again been shown that he might get his own way by sheer force of will. He fooled himself even further that his own charms were so irresistible to Elizabeth that she would bend heaven and earth to keep him by her side. There was, quite simply, no other man at court who could behave as he had done and come up in clover. He did not see the politics behind her actions, though we can safely discount the argument of G. B. Harrison that he failed 'to realise that being a woman she acted on the instinct of the moment, and therefore was incalculable'.[157] She acted when moments were thrust upon her, and it was not instinct that drove her but an outmoded political strategy.

Neither did Essex have 'a mere lust for power'.[158] The gossip and slander which echoed the streets of London and the chambers of Whitehall had brought home to him the fact that he had enemies. That was not surprising: all great men had enemies and he had complained often enough about 'delators' conspiring against him. Yet the worry was that those enemies might topple him. In order to stay safe, relevant, and have at least a reasonable chance at a long and prosperous life, the Elizabethan courtier, whether favourite or statesman, had to achieve a measure of what would now be called 'job security'. Countless men had fallen from great heights during the

---

[157] Harrison, *Life and Death*, p. 181
[158] *Ibid.*

sixteenth century: Norfolk, Buckingham, Surrey, Northumberland, Suffolk – one could almost entirely shade in a map of the regions of England with the titles of dead noblemen. Many more still had fallen out of favour and into obscurity and penury. There were no guarantees against failure and the surest means of success lay in making oneself necessary to the state and the monarch. To that Essex had added, unwisely, 'beloved of the people'.

***

The wrangling over the peace with Spain continued. Essex, flush with success and feeling generous, opted to join in. The French ambassador was invited to the council – a signal of friendly intent – although Elizabeth did not attend.[159] A piece of stagecraft then took place, with Burghley asking Essex to deliver the queen's judgement on the peace between Spain, France, England, and the Dutch states. He said nothing. Elizabeth and England had no official opinion. Burghley then explained that Elizabeth proposed sending commissioners to France, there to join with Dutch commissioners to thrash out a solution. Throughout, Essex's only contribution was that Protestantism might be under threat in the event of peace between Catholic Spain and France.

What is interesting is just how much Essex toed the government line during the meeting. There were no rambunctious interventions, none of his own unasked-for suggestions. On the one hand this was indicative of a mature ability to restrain himself. On the other, it illustrates that his disillusion with international politics had not fully been dispelled; even his former pet subjects of France and Spain could not rouse much interest.

---

[159] The invitation of foreign ambassadors into council meetings is a fascinating and under-researched area. Not only did Elizabeth do it occasionally, but Mary Queen of Scots repeatedly invited the English ambassador, Thomas Randolph, to sit in on meetings of her privy council.

This was hardly encouraging to de Maisse, who had sought a simple embracing of peace from the English queen. Following the council meeting he was conducted to her presence, leaving Burghley to ruminate on the pro-peace and anti-peace divisions in the council. Elizabeth, when de Maisse came to her, gave another tour de force performance. As Maisse recorded, she stated 'that she was a woman, old and capable of nothing by herself; she had to deal with nobles of divers humours, and peoples who, although they made great demonstration of love towards her, nevertheless were fickle and inconstant'.[160] This gave verbal reinforcement to the visual message she had sought to impress upon him during his previous audiences. It was textbook dissimulation, though played masterfully.

Before leaving England, de Maisse consulted first with Burghley and then Essex. The choice was revealing: first the chief minister and then the man who hoped to succeed him. Essex was careful to point out that he had been invited to stand as a commissioner, but that his personal affairs precluded him from so august a mission. In reality he had no wish to go, as he neither wished for peace nor saw anything to be gained by entangling himself in the affair. He criticised the inconstancy of Elizabeth the queen – always a source of irritation to him, but a dangerous one to voice – and won the following approbation from de Maisse: 'he is a man who in no wise contents himself with a petty fortune and aspires to greatness'.[161] Essex was positioning himself for a life after Burghley and after Elizabeth.

If Essex would not lead a delegation of commissioners to France, the question remained as to who would. To his confusion – whether he ought to be angry or relieved about the thankless but prominent role going to him was unclear – Robert Cecil was chosen.

---

[160] de Maisse, A. H., cited in Haigh, *Elizabeth I*, p. 179.

[161] Pringle, R. 1980. *Portrait of Elizabeth I: In the Words of the Queen and Her Contemporaries* (New York: Barnes & Noble Books), p. 99.

17: Little Cecil Tripping Up and Down

Secretary Cecil left court in February 1598. In the preceding months his rival Essex had been mothing but friendliness. This raised his anxiety. There was more to be feared in his rival's false smiles than in the outright, hair-trigger hostility he had long known to be the man's weakness. He had attempted to keep the earl sweet prior to leaving by persuading the queen to allow him the purchase of booty taken from the Azores expedition at a very low price. Knowing Essex's financial situation, which Burghley had exacerbated, this was shrewd; still, it was no guarantee that the unpredictable favourite would not make hay politically whilst his back was turned. A letter from the earl which included the line, 'I value [you] in judgement [and] with affection and therefore I must be doubly careful [worried] about yourself' looked promising, for it contained the very true words, 'these glustering tempestuous days that are past do awaken and increase my care [troubles], which ever shall be constant'.[162]

Cecil need not have worried unduly. Rather than honestly keeping his promise of not making mischief for his rival, he was forced to do so by circumstances. Those in his circle were proving to be a handful in themselves, and he was coming to realise the difficulties of maintaining a following. For starters, securing positions was proving to be as difficult in Cecil's absence as it had been in his presence. Elizabeth steadfastly refused to grant Sir Robert Sidney the post of vice-chamberlain, and there was little that could dishearten loyal supporters more than being unable to gain them favours.

Beyond his faction, he threw himself into parliamentary affairs, making up for his calculated absence at the outset, and once more saw to his conciliar work. If he had planned on

---

[162] Roberts, R. A. (Ed.) 1899. 'Cecil Papers: Feburary 1598, 1-15', in *Calendar of the Cecil Papers in Hatfield House: Volume 8, 1598* (London, 1899), pp. 36-49. British History Online http://www.british-history.ac.uk/cal-cecil-papers/vol8/pp36-49.

ruining Cecil, there was simply no time to do so. In addition to all that occupied him, the issue of Ireland, which had been on the periphery of Essex's life and career since childhood, flared up and dominated discussion at court. The colonised kingdom had been in open revolt under Hugh O'Neill, earl of Tyrone, since 1593, and the lord deputy, Lord Burgh, had died – rumours said of poisoning by the corrupt English soldiery – in October 1597.

Scotland, too, was giving cause for concern. In January James VI had criticised Elizabeth in parliament and, after she wrote berating him, he simply chose to ignore her. His wife Anne, too, was flirting with Catholicism and encouraging the king to court the Spanish and the Irish and thereby gain international approval for his succession to England's throne. Elizabeth saw conspiracy ringing her country. If the Scottish border was England's back door, Ireland was a neighbouring park, run-down, dense, and full of strangers, with only a shallow pond separating it. It was, further, a money pit, into which successive monarchs and nobles had poured money and men in an attempt to stamp the authority of English dominion. In subsequent years Essex would fall prey, as his father had done, to the queen's obsession with Anglicising Ireland and thereby removing it as a source of threat. Doing so would, further, prevent the still-worryingly-independent James VI from making overtures to Irish rebels and their Spanish backers.

Cecil returned warmth to Essex after arriving at Dieppe, hoping no doubt that the earl's sense of chivalry would keep him inactive. 'I confess to you I do not only conceive inward contentment in the knowledge of your care and affection, but am apt to let it appear externally, here to my company, how much I am valued by you'.[163] Burghley's son outdid his father in having a delicious sense of irony.

In the absence of a secretary, the role fell, naturally, to Essex. He set to work, as men and women often will, trying to make the most of the sudden and temporary promotion. His first order

---

[163] Doran, S. 2015. *Elizabeth I and her Circle* (Oxford: Oxford University Press), p. 286.

of business was to try and mend fences between his beloved mother and the queen. Lettice had never got over being banished from court – she saw it as her rightful place as a dowager countess, cousin to the queen, and mother of arguably the third person in the realm (after Elizabeth and Burghley). Elizabeth knew of this and delighted in it. One of the few pleasures left to her was the knowledge that whilst Lettice had won Leicester, she had had the last laugh, taking both the court and her son's attention from her. She was not going to waste the opportunity to enjoy a little more of the insufferable matriarch's misery.

There followed a period of cruel but rather amusing maliciousness on the queen's part. Lettice was invited to court and allowed to stand waiting in the privy gallery, through which Elizabeth would pass on the way to the presence chamber. Made up, perfumed, and clasping a jewel as a gift, the dowager waited. And waited. Elizabeth did not appear, having found reason to remain immured in the more private space reserved for her special friends and subjects. Lettice went home disappointed.

The summons was again issued, and again Lettice took up her post. Again, she was disappointed. Elizabeth did not come out. The farce was repeated as many times as Elizabeth felt she could manage – which, in effect, was as long as it continued to amuse her without alienating Essex too much. In March she let it be known that she would be setting out in her coach and accordingly Lettice appeared, still clutching her present. Elizabeth found reason not to ride out that day. This finally stirred Essex who, obviously incensed at the way his mother was being made a laughing stock, threw on his nightgown (he had been ill and keeping to his chamber at court) and remonstrated with Elizabeth. Like a sulky child caught doing something naughty, Elizabeth agreed to meet with Lettice the next day, and, to her credit, she did so. The two women, who had bitterly despised one another for two decades, kissed and embraced, much to Essex's delight. He would be less delighted when, a week later, Lettice pushed her luck by requesting to kiss the queen's hand in public, in order to demonstrate before the world her return to favour, only to be refused.

The entire thing had been a bit of nasty fun. It is tempting to criticise the queen for her delight in such an absurd and petty bit of mockery of a woman whose punishment already was, and would continue to be, an enforced exile from the public stage. However, there is no need to be moralistic about it. Elizabeth hated Lettice and was willing only to tolerate her for Essex's sake. In some matters, her habitual vacillation could illustrate her amusingly malicious streak, and her behaviour demonstrates that, although approaching sixty-five, she had not lost the wicked sense of humour that is often overlooked when one focuses only on her statecraft.

***

One man who had been less and less encouraged by Essex's behaviour since his return from the Azores, and who had had reservations about it before even that, was Francis Bacon. The often-disappointed lawyer did, however, seize advantage of Cecil's absence by directing his friend and would-be benefactor's attention to the Irish question (that question being 'what on earth is to be done about Ireland?'). He set out a list of reasons why Essex should involve himself directly in the country's affairs – something which the earl had never shown much inclination to do. Chief amongst them were his father, the late earl of Essex's, interests there; the general focus of English debate being Ireland; the opportunity it represented for those who could bring the confusion and rebellion there into order; and the honour attendant on those willing to engage themselves in what one later historian has called Tudor England's Siberia.[164]

The last reason touched Essex particularly. Honour had always been one of his obsessions. Francis further shot at the ideal target when he declared to Essex that 'if your lordship doubts to put a sickle in another man's harvest; time brings it to you in Mr Secretary's absence; next being mixt with matter of

---

[164] Guy, *Elizabeth*, p. 283.

war it is fittest for you; and lastly, I know that your lordship will carry it with that modesty … and good correspondence towards my dear kinsman and your good friend now abroad, as no inconvenience may grow that way'.[165] Francis was saying, essentially, that engaging with Ireland was a gold-plated means of winning credit which would otherwise fall to Cecil. It might be done, too, with a smile, under the guise of saving the absent secretary the trouble. Nothing could have been calculated to better appeal to Essex.

Unfortunately, events conspired to ignite only a spark of interest; whether they would later catch flame only time would tell. Tyrone called for a truce and was granted a general pardon in April and Cecil's mission proved to be all too short-lived. After trekking hundreds of miles across France, he and his colleagues had met the French king. Elizabeth, however, had discovered evidence that Henry IV had already made an illegal separate peace with Philip. This was thanks to Burghley, who had secured spies in the court of the governor general of the Spanish Netherlands, and Phelippes, who had left Essex's employ and become a jobbing spy with a chequered criminal record. Henry, probably knowing that he had been rumbled, then began moving his court around, leaving the English commission to trail him. By the middle of April Cecil realised that the French king had hoodwinked him as he had hoodwinked Essex during the Rouen campaign and, defeated and annoyed, he asked leave to return to England.

Essex received news of Cecil's return six days after the garter feast. Cecil wrote him secretly, promising that only the earl, to whom he 'professed entirely love and service' knew of his return – even Burghley was unaware. In reality it was his father's health that had sped his flight out of France. The old man was on his last legs, albeit the queen rallied him with personal attendance on his sickbed. Having lived through the

---

[165] Bacon, F. 1826 [1598]. 'Considerations touching the queens service in Ireland' in C. Rivington & J. Rivington (Eds.) *The Works of Francis Bacon, Baron of Verulam, Viscount St. Alban, and Lord High Chancellor of England* (London: C. & J. Rivington), p. 244.

reigns of Henry VIII, Edward VI, Protector Somerset, Jane Grey, Mary I, and Elizabeth, the seventy-seven-year-old wanted to leave England in a measure of peace. Palsied but still vehement, he argued strongly in favour of joining France in making peace with Spain.

Essex would have none of this. Partly this was because he truly did not believe that it could be honourably achieved, and partly it was because he had staked his entire career to date on being the warlike voice of aggression. To accede to a Cecilian peace would be to throw down the gauntlet to his rivals. He was, however, mistaken. If he had hoped to court public opinion by playing on English xenophobia against the Spanish, he misjudged the public mood. Even the most popular wars lose their lustre when the economy is in the doldrums and the human cost intensifies. A war of propaganda therefore broke out, in which the earl was satirised as having learnt 'to entrench himself with popularity, / And for a writhen face, and body's move / be barracadoed in [protected by] the people's love'.[166] His response was an open letter to Anthony Bacon defending his position (open letters being both a fashionable means of disseminating information and in keeping with his earlier attempt to justify his planned raid on Cadiz). It was known as Essex's *Apologie*, and this latest early modern social media campaign aimed to prove that Essex was no warmonger for glory's sake, but for England's. Instead, the ploy was seen through, Elizabeth was annoyed, and he had to pretend that the missive had been copied and those copies fallen into the wrong hands. His stock was plummeting.

But the Spanish theatre of war was not the only or even the most pressing one in 1598. The mysterious death of Lord Burgh in Ireland had left a vacancy for a trusted lord deputy and, as usual, nomination to the post meant competition amongst the rivals' candidates. However, it was not a competition in the usual sense, because none wished their friends to be sent into the land that had ruined so many fortunes and claimed so many

---

[166] Cox, J. D. 2014. *Shakespeare and the Dramaturgy of Power* (Princeton: Princeton University Press), p. 114.

lives. In July it became critical; the rebellion of the Irish had not dissipated with Tyrone's truce. Passions flared in the council chamber with Essex favouring the dispatch of Sir George Carew – a Cecil adherent whom he despised. Elizabeth wanted Sir William Knollys, Lettice's brother and Essex's uncle. This was intolerable and Essex grew angry. In a fit of explosive pique, he narrowed his eyes in scorn at the queen's arguments and turned his back on her. Elizabeth could not let such a flagrant display of lèse-majesté slide and she cuffed his ear before telling him to go hang. The earl's hand flew to his sword. Nottingham jumped forward and stood between them. Elizabeth and Essex glared at one another, she in shock and he in rage. He would not, he announced, have taken such an insult even from her father. Taking advantage of the stunned silence, he stamped out of the council and court.

Essex's behaviour was extreme. Yet it is not hard to discern what lay behind it. Elizabeth had taken a cocksure young man and created a monster of ego. Worse, she had indulged and forgiven his behaviour to such an extent over the years that he must have felt untouchable. The troubling thing about bad behaviour is that those who sufficiently and consistently get away with it invariably becomes sloppy and overconfident.

To her credit, the queen seems to have realised her role in enabling and encouraging Essex's behaviour. In raising Essex high, she had discovered an age-old problem: that an exciting young lover can become a shrill and demanding spouse. It was a lesson her father had learnt after raising her mother first to marchioness and then to queen. The favourite received no punishment and instead was allowed to wallow in his own sense of injustice at Wanstead. What she wanted was a graceful and peaceful reconciliation and, accordingly, Essex was bombarded with letters from his peers begging him to return and smooth matters over. This was precisely the wrong thing for them and their sovereign to do; it simply encouraged him in the belief that he was in the right and that they all knew it. He replied to the lord keeper, Egerton's, request with the haughty words, 'What, cannot princes err? Cannot subjects receive wrong? Is an earthly power or authority infinite? Pardon me, pardon me, my good lord, I can never subscribe to these principles'.[167] This was not just self-pity and injured pride: it was disillusion turned into dangerous political dissent. By denigrating and questioning the queen's status and authority he was as good as calling for the overthrow of a monarch and the rights of subjects. It was born of anger rather than any ideological realisation, but it nevertheless represented a rupture in the system which kept the nobility and the monarchy in mutual support.

Paranoia, always so close to the surface now, also made its presence known, as he lamented that 'in this course [his behaviour and actions] do I do anything for mine enemies? When I was in the court, I found them absolute; and, therefore, I had rather they should triumph alone, than that they should have me attendant on their chariots'.[168] The image he invoked tells us something of his own self-awareness in the period and explains both his outburst and his shocking behaviour towards the queen. He feared eclipse. More than that, he feared the success of his enemies. These feelings had been simmering since the Azores and had simply reached boiling point.

To the queen herself he was both lofty and fawning – an uncomfortable mix:

Madam,

When I think how I have preferred your beauty above all things and received no pleasure in life but by the increase of your favour towards me, I wonder at myself what cause there could be to make me absent myself one day from you. But when I remember that your Majesty hath, by the intolerable wrong you have done both me and yourself, not only broken all laws of affection, but done against the honour of your sex, I think all places better than that where I am, and all dangers well undertaken, so I might retire myself from the memory of my false, inconstant, and beguiling pleasures … I was never proud,

---

[167] Devereux, *Lives and Letters*, p. 501.
[168] Devereux, *Lives and Letters*, p. 500.

till your Majesty made me so base.[169]

This was strong stuff. It is tempting to write it off as another attempt to win the queen's favour by flattery and rebuke – yet the rambling nature of his thoughts as recorded is instead indicative of his state of confusion. Essex truly thought that he had done no wrong. As such, he could barely understand his situation and he had never understood his feelings for the queen, so warped were they by division between hatred of her politics, chaste attraction to her mind and image, and the required, mawkish expostulation of physical attraction to her person. At any rate it did nothing to warm Elizabeth to him. 'He hath played long enough upon me. I mean to play upon him,' she is said to have hissed.[170]

As Essex stewed in his own neuroses, worrying over enemies at court both real and imagined, one of the chief pillars of the age was crumbling. In August, agonising trips to the council chamber were beyond Burghley and he took to what would be his deathbed. He slipped away peacefully on the 4th of August and with his passing it is fair to say that the queen remained the last remnant of the already-faint Elizabethan age. She was beginning to look, too, like a sad reminder of a dead era at best, and a choke on progress at worst. The world had changed so dramatically since the heydays of the 1560s, 70s and 80s that the Jacobean era was already measuring for curtains: it is telling that Robert Greene's *The Scottish History of James the Fourth*, with its subtle look ahead to what might be needed in the event of a Scottish succession, was published the same year. Portents hung in the air itself – in early September 'two great cracks of lighting and thunder' struck London, 'whereby some men were smitten at the postern by the Tower, and one man slain at the bridgehouse in Southwark'.[171] 1598 saw also the publication of

---

[169] Devereux, *Lives and Letters*, p. 493.
[170] Williams, W. 1998. *Elizabeth I* (New York: Welcome Rain), p. 200.
[171] Harrison, G. B. 1938. *The Elizabethan Journals, 1591-1603* (London: Routledge & Sons), p. 305.

the late Peter Wentworth's *A Pithy Exhortation to Her Majesty for Establishing her Successor to the Crown* and *A Treatise Containing Mr Wentworth's Judgement Concerning the Person of the True and Lawful Successor to these Realms of England and Ireland.* Elizabeth was becoming yesterday's woman.

***

Burghley was dead but England still had to be governed. In the aftermath of his death, Essex found himself pressed again to return to court. He attended a meeting of the council but, on learning that Elizabeth would not give him a personal audience, he went home in a huff.

The earl's absence from matters of state was not simply an annoyance or even an embarrassment, though it was undoubtedly both; he had been laden with offices and, without him, the business of the realm could not operate smoothly. There were decisions to be made, documents to sign, debates to be had, and intelligence from his network of spies and foreign friends to be discussed. He knew this and, like a modern-day cabinet minister refusing to sign off on key government legislation, he revelled in holding things up. This was what he wanted: to show the world and the queen that he was invaluable.

Burghley was barely cold and the relationship between Elizabeth and Essex still frosty when Cecil received news from his own intelligence sources of disaster in Ireland. Tyrone had turned traitor again, and was 'digginge deep hoales in the rivers, the more to distresse the armye that shold come to releive yt'. Worse was to come. In the middle of August an English army was sent to revictual the fort at Blackwater, only to find itself trapped in ambush. Over 800 English soldiers were massacred including Marshal Henry Bagenal; 400 more were wounded; and 300 defected to the Irish confederates. The Irish seized Blackwater two weeks later, on the day that Burghley was laid to rest in Westminster Abbey. Most of Ulster now lay open to Tyrone and his men, who were riding high on what had become the greatest victory over the English in the entire Tudor era.[172] The Irish earl demanded nothing less than freedom of religion for all Catholic Irish, and he was now in a position to press for it.

Ireland and war-talk brought Essex back to court. The queen continued to refuse to see him, but for once he persevered, even showing a measure of contrition. When she rejected both his presence and a letter, he took up his pen again. Ireland had fired him up: the spark which Francis Bacon had struck was kindling. 'Duty', he wrote, 'was strong enough to rouse me out of my deadest melancholy'.[173] It was true. His obsessive personality had struck again and this time it had fixed upon Ireland. Just as importantly, Burghley's death had left vacant a number of plum offices which he was losing the opportunity to lobby for, for both himself and his friends. Mastery of the wards – the position that had once made Burghley his legal guardian – was a particularly delectable one.

Another tiresome game of power ensued, Essex desiring to return to service, the queen eager for him back but only with suitable shows of supplication. Strategic illness on his part made a recurrence, and he was carried to Wanstead in a litter – always a good means of publicising one's poor state of health. Elizabeth sent her physicians (who were presumably nervous of the earl) and, miraculously, he recovered enough to return to court and council.

With the death of Philip II and the accession of his son, the Spanish war looked like falling into abeyance – at least until the new king made his feelings known. What Philip III knew was that Ireland was England's weak spot, and the island was still in chaos. In arguing against the appointment of Lord Mountjoy as lord deputy, Essex was, either by accident or design, putting himself forward for the job. As autumn marched on, he found himself warming more and more to the idea: his ideas on Ireland were, after all, coming to dominate his thoughts. The only

---

[172] Maginn, C. 2012. *William Cecil, Ireland, and the Tudor State* (Oxford: Oxford University Press), pp. 191-214.

[173] Devereux, *Lives and Letters*, p. 496.

trouble was the distance it would put between him and the court, to which he had only just returned and where his enemies might well conspire against him in any absence. As it became clear that he would become the new lord deputy, experienced captains began approaching him, no doubt digging into their meagre reserves to buy positions in his new army. He began planning the expedition eagerly, putting forward his friend Southampton for the role of master of horse, but this was refused: Southampton had been banished from court for brawling with Ambrose Willoughby earlier in the year and gone on a tour of the continent, returning only for the birth of his son by his mistress, the queen's maid of honour, Elizabeth Vernon. The wild-natured young man was in deep disgrace and would only manage to accompany the expedition in an unofficial capacity. Still, this was a minor inconvenience.

What Essex wanted from his latest, most dangerous military adventure was quite different from what he had sought in Rouen, Cadiz, and the Azores. In each of those he had thirsted for glory: for a chance to make his name and achieve fame. Despite the mistakes he made, especially on the last of the three, he had achieved it – he had become the people's earl, champion of queen and country, hero of Cadiz. Since the Azores, however, he had fallen, thanks, he thought, to his enemies. In reality it was due mainly to his own rash and irreverent behaviour and his history of pressing the Spanish war. Popularity, he was coming to learn, was fickle mistress: no sooner had he gained it than people were eager to watch him fall. Having tasted glory and flirted dangerously with disfavour, Ireland would prove his chance to recover the former and banish all traces of the latter.

To Elizabeth, her favourite had one last chance. She had few qualms about him putting his life in danger this time. Having insulted her so egregiously, it was time for him to do or die.

18: An Té Nach Bhfuil Láidir, Ní Foláir Dó Bheith Glic

In September 1599 the earl of Tyrone rode into the River Glyde, the water rising to his horse's belly. It was a gesture of humility. From a hill overlooking the river, Essex rode down to meet him. The two men put their heads together and spoke for half an hour. What they said is unrecorded. They withdrew from one another before later meeting again, more formally, and having another conference, this time with six witnesses on either side. A date was fixed for a further discussion the following day. Essex did not make it, but Tyrone did. The result was a renewable six-week truce. It was probably the smartest thing the favourite had ever done on any campaign. It was also against his queen's express orders. He knew this and, after dismissing his army and recovering his health at Drogheda, he abdicated responsibility for Ireland to two lord justices and sailed for England, knowing that he had been forbidden to do so. He knew exactly what kind of reception he might expect and thought he knew how he might forestall and defuse it. But what on earth had happened to his attempts to bring Ireland to heel? What possessed him to make peace with a rebellious traitor?

***

The trials and tribulations of Essex's Irish expedition might fill this book in its entirety; certainly, several excellent studies of the campaign already exist.[174] There is no need to rehearse

---

[174] See Morgan, H. 1993. *Tyrone's Rebellion: The Outbreak of the Nine Years War in Tudor Ireland* (London: Royal Historical Society); Falls, C. 1997. *Elizabeth's Irish Wars* (Syracuse: Syracuse University Press); Hammer, P. E. J. 2014. ' "Base rogues" and "gentlemen of quality": the earl of Essex's Irish Knights and royal displeasure in 1599' in B. Kane & V. McGowan-Doyle (Eds.) *Elizabeth I and Ireland* (Cambridge: Cambridge University Press), pp. 184-208.

every detail of them here. However, consideration of the ways in which his relationship with Elizabeth was impacted during his time in Ireland is necessary.

The festive period of 1598-9 was an uncomfortable one. Edmund Spenser, who would die in January, made one of his rare visits to court with dire warnings from English settlers in Munster. Elizabeth was also forced to write to a ruffled James VI, who had been falsely accused by a rogue called Valentine Thomas of employing him to assassinate her. It was not the only plot doing the rounds. In December Cecil was advised to tell the queen

that a Jesuit and a Franciscan friar, by order from the Pope and the King of Spain, are in England to kill her. The Pope has absolved them, and promised that the Church will pray for them, as for holy martyrs. When the Queen goeth forth to walk or on hunting, they shall come in the apparel of country fellows or poor men, with their weapons, which are two books … within each of them is conveyed two pistol barrels, which with unclasping the book go off … and within each of them are a dozen bullets.[175]

Francis Bacon, who was even then advising Essex against leading the Irish expedition, noted in the same month that

the Council did make remonstrance unto Queen Elizabeth of the continual conspiracies against her life; and namely of a late one: and showed her a rapier, taken from a conspirator, that had a false chape [point], being of brown paper, but gilt over, as it could not be known from a chape of metal; which was devised to the end that without drawing the rapier might give a stab; and upon this occasion advised her that she should go less abroad to take the air, weakly accompanied, as she used. But the Queen

---

[175] Colthorpe, M. E. 2017. '1598' in M. E. Colthorpe (Ed.) *The Elizabethan Court Day by Day* (Cambridge: Folgerpedia), p. 45.

answered: That she had rather be dead, than put in custody.[176]

Such conspiracies had always existed, and Elizabeth had always rose to meet them. At least some of her people, growing 'weary of an old woman's government' were certainly looking forward to seeing her go. Any administration will grow stale over time, and Elizabeth had now governed England for forty years. Lately the harvests had been bad, inflation had increased wildly, and the Irish and Spanish wars were costly and unpopular. It is no surprise that two women in Dorset were arrested and confessed that one Edward Francis had claimed the queen had

had three bastards by noblemen of the court, two sons and a daughter, and was herself base born; and added that the land had been happy if her Majesty had been cut off 20 years since, so that some noble prince might have reigned in her stead.[177]

These were ugly times. In January St James' Palace was burgled whilst the queen was in residence and several pounds' worth of linen stolen. One Thomas Cholcroft was later examined for saying, 'they that hated not the queen, I would they were hanged'.[178] He was found not guilty. Less lucky was Joan Botting, who was sentenced to hang for stating that

it would never be better until there were a change that rich men's throats were cut and then poor men should be rich. And said that she did pray uprising and down lying to God to take away the Queen's Majesty, and that she would be one that should help to cut the rich men's throats and she hoped that this informer would do the like, and help the Queen's enemies.[179]

---

[176] Colthorpe, '1598', p. 47.

[177] *Ibid.*

[178] Colthorpe, M. E. 2017. '1599' in M. E. Colthorpe (Ed.) *The Elizabethan Court Day by Day* (Cambridge: Folgerpedia), p. 2.

[179] Colthorpe, '*1599*', p. 6.

To the gallows too went Edward Tedder of Strood for 'intending to compass the queen's death' and declaring that he, having been born at Whitehall and believing it his house, was king. Treasonous words against Elizabeth had always been spoken and the speakers always punished when they could be found and prosecuted. The slanders had graduated beyond mere abuse to vocal desire for and full expectation of her imminent death. It was now not only likely but a certainty, whether it came in a few weeks, months, or a very few years.

More dangerous still – and more bizarre – was the execution in late 1598 of Edward Squires, who was found guilty of spreading poison on the pommel of the queen's horse. Squires having sailed with Essex on the mission to the Azores the previous year, it emerged that he had also smeared poison on the earl's seat in an attempt to kill him too. The solution to both the attempts on her and her favourite's lives, and the overall decline of the people into licentious and scurrilous grumbling, was gory execution and state-sanctioned prayers of thanksgiving. Still, Squires' death only sped a general descent into invective between Catholics and Protestants to add to the internecine conflict between Protestants and Protestants.

But the story of the year, and of Elizabeth's last years, more generally, is not one of wholesale decline. Attempting to challenge the narrative of weak governance, favouritism, and a waning age, the queen did what she could to refresh her reign. She reopened a diplomatic relationship with the Ottoman empire; she maintained a public presence, and 'was to be seen in her old age dancing three or four galliards'; and she continued to patronise the growing Merchant Adventurers Company. In his commonplace book – an early modern form of journal for the safekeeping of phrases, prayers, recipes, and all manner of delightful ephemera, Henry Stanford recorded lines from the courtly epilogue to Shakespeare's *As You Like It*:

As the dial hand tells ore
The same hours it had before,
Still beginning in the ending,
Circular account still lending,

So most mighty Queen we pray,
Like the Dial day by day,
You may lead the seasons on,
Making new when old are gone.
That the babe which now is young
And hath yet no use of tongue,
Many a Shrovetide here may bow
To that Empress I do now,
That the children of these lords
Sitting at your Council Boards
May be grave and aged seen
Of her that was their fathers' Queen.[180]

Stafford was, it should be noted, of the late lord chamberlain's household; he had a vested interest in the maintenance of the Elizabethan administration. Opinions in England were starkly divided on the longevity of the nation's ruler. Unlike in constitutional monarchies, a long-lived sovereign did not necessarily inspire affection amongst swathes of the population as a kind of apolitical mascot; because their role was deeply political, they were to blame when the nation's fortunes ebbed as well as when they flowed.

Increasing the febrile political climate still further was the publication of a book by young lawyer and amateur historian John Hayward: *The First Part of the Life and Raigne of King Henrie IV*. That king had, of course, assumed the throne after the deposition of Richard II. The book had a Latin prefatory epistle dedicated to Essex. For months the queen would grit her already-crumbling teeth over the book, seeking all means available – including the legal skills of Francis Bacon – to have it suppressed. It was not the first time she had been compared to Richard II; not only had Essex, Raleigh, and Cecil made some joke about the historical parallels between her reign and his, but Essex's grandfather had lamented those who compared her

---

[180] MacFaul, T. 2012. *Problem Fathers in Shakespeare and Renaissance Drama* (Cambridge: Cambridge University Press), p. 106.

system of favourites with King Richard's back in the late 70s. Shakespeare's play, too, had been published in 1597, inviting the public to draw parallels between the historical and the current monarch, albeit the deposition scene was omitted from official print runs.

Thanks to Hayward, it was a bad time to be leaving, for who knew what political capital his opponents might make of the dedication. But it was hardly his choice, and so it was against this backdrop that Essex received his instructions as leader of the campaign to be launched in Ireland. He was to learn the state of the country, assemble a council, monitor religion and justice, reform corruption, and confer knighthoods only in exceptional circumstances. Tyrone was to be received only on the grounds of full submission and security against further misbehaviour. He was, essentially, being asked to root out the weeds and bring Ireland into some semblance of English-dominated order. All this was to be accomplished and Essex might return only with good cause, having left two trusted lord justices in control. As an added boon, he was discharged of £10,000 of debt to the crown.

On setting out, he received his customary shouts of praise and approbation from the people. A whole host of men had, further, joined him in the hope of adventure and profit: Southampton, Lord Grey, John Harington, the returning earl of Kildare (who would perish when his ship foundered in the Irish sea). All was set for a grand and suitably illustrious campaign. However, Elizabeth, from the outset, showed herself uncooperative with regard to his wishes. His request that his stepfather, Christopher Blount, should be made a member of his Irish council was refused. This dampened any enthusiasm he had mustered for the trip; he had by now come to understand his queen's arbitrary and distrustful attitude towards her military leaders' autonomy. It had also begun to enter into his mind that the chance to reclaim glory was, on her part, a kind of exile – a cold dish of revenge for his behaviour the previous year.

Essex arrived at Dublin in April after a stormy passage – two of his ships narrowly missed ramming each other – and was sworn in with the sword of state. With him were 20,000 foot-soldiers and 2000 cavalry. His plan was to establish a new English garrison in the far north; as always, he believed in establishing coastal bases from which to then launch attacks on the enemy. However, the English council in London, now headed by Cecil, had effectively scuppered the strategy by focusing resources in the south of the island rather than in Ulster in the north. Any attempt to attack the north in the optimal month of June would be impossible. One can imagine the smugness with which Cecil wrote to Essex informing him that if he wanted men, he might recruit them from the wandering, dispossessed English colonists who had been driven south by Tyrone. It was a calculated move. The secretary was hoping that Essex would fail – he was ever on the lookout for a great fall – but not to the extent that state security might be compromised. Moreover, he could only hobble the expedition subtly, careful that his excuses for not providing aid in the north were entirely explicable and backed by conciliar agreement. This was not the only sour note. Essex soon quarrelled with Lord Grey, whom he accused of being bound to Cecil rather than himself. Although a minor incident, it would have lasting repercussions.

The earl did manage to increase his force by marching out of Dublin and joining with the earl of Ormond and his men, and May saw a skirmish with the Irish near Rheban Castle, during which the rebels fled into the safety of the forest. A more serious fight erupted a few days later near Ballyknockan, in what became to the Irish 'the Battle of the Pass of the Plumes'. As the English attempted to make their way through a narrow pass on the way to Kilkenny (having already reinforced the garrison at Maryborough), the Irish set upon them. Irish and English chroniclers differ in their accounts, the latter claim that Essex acted with bravery and lost only two officers and six lesser men; the former insist that he lost 500 and that their plumed helmets littered the pass. One suspects that the truth lies somewhere in the middle – Essex likely behaved with courage and fortitude, and likely lost more men than he was willing to allow into written dispatches.

From Kilkenny, where he wrote in exasperation and admiration at the boldness of the Irish, he moved to Waterford, arriving in late May. His goal, pursued with his usual single-minded determination, was the capture of Cahir Castle. This he managed, but not without further losses of men and damage to his cannon. It was a minor victory, outweighed by the losses incurred by the portion of the army he had sent to Wicklow under Sir Henry Harington. There, over 200 men were killed in action.

In June he briefly met with his old enemy, Sir George Carew, who was acting as the campaign's treasurer-at-war, at Limerick, before setting off to engage the Irish. He met the rebels in arms but pursued them too far, before camping at Crumme Castle and, the next day, reaching Killmalough in Country Cavan. By late June Essex had formulated a plan with Carew, which would see Ireland put to the flame. It was a scorched earth policy, its goal being to make the land as uninhabitable as possible for the rebels and to secure the south against the possibility of Spanish naval support. A path of destruction was therefore planned throughout the southern part of Ireland as Essex sought to relieve the defeated and disordered Harington.

The march was not without incident. The Irish had no intention of letting Essex and his army despoil their land or beat it into submission. As the English marched north, the rebels harassed them all the way, striking no major blows but tiring and diverting them. It had an effect on Essex, at least. By the time he reached Wicklow, where Harington's forces had been so comprehensively routed, he wrote to the privy council of the declining state of his health. This time it was not at all exaggerated or political. For the first time he had been put in absolute charge of the unrelenting grind of real warfare rather than working under Leicester, traipsing around Spanish-fortified French territory, raiding poorly defended garrisons, or invading abandoned forts. It was messy, stressful, painful, and crushing.

On returning to Dublin with the remnants of his and Harington's forces, Essex set about the distasteful job of punishment. One in ten of the soldiers who had disappointed at Wicklow were hanged for cowardice and Harington was imprisoned. He then wrote back to England of the surprising power of the Irish – reinforced, he suggested, by Spanish support. More men were necessary, not only because he was engaged in killing some of them for discipline, but because disease was swiftly sweeping through the ranks of the poorly-fed and densely-packed soldiery. Everything was in short supply: clothing, edible food, and arms. The government in London, he bemoaned, simply did not understand the conditions in Ireland. In that he was right. He had by now been three months in Ireland and was no closer to taking Ulster than he had been at the start.

***

Elizabeth had no time for failure. Essex was in Ireland as her servant not her favourite. The island was the possession of her crown and it was up to him to secure it quickly, cheaply, and preferably without a plethora of excuses. She took up her pen and wrote a scathing letter in late July, tartly pointing out that if he had time to write he had time to capture the country:

We have perceived … that you have arrived at Dublin after your journey into Munster; where, though it seemeth, by the words of your letter, that you have spent divers days in taking an account of all things that have passed since you left that place, yet have you in this despatch given us small light either when, or in what order, you intend particularly to proceed to the northern action.[181]

She wanted a plan, and a plan in train, not excuses. Cuttingly, she rebuked him for having brought no rebels into custody, made light of the capture of Cahir Castle, and condemned him for allowing Tyrone to lord it over him, herself, and England. 'You are disgraced,' she blazed, 'from hence in your friends' fortune, that poor Ireland suffers in you; still exclaiming against

---

[181] Elizabeth I. 1870 [1599]. 'Letter to Essex' in J. S. Brewer & W. Bullen (Eds.) *Calendar of the Carew Manuscripts, 1601-1603* (London: Longman, Green, & Co.), p. lx.

the effects of your own causes'. These were feelings Elizabeth had been brewing towards Essex for some years now, and it is ironic that on this occasion she was wrong. The unravelling of his Irish campaign was not, for once, due to his own hubris or vainglory. Her letter was so stinging that the council felt the need to send a more moderate message of their own.

Elizabeth's censorious words were a display of her power over him as a subject and a man. All they did, however, was reenergise the feeling he had always had towards her in her monarchical role: she was an ignoramus and a termagant – a puffed-up figure who had no understanding of the realities of warfare but was happy to make all manner of pronouncements on it and judgements about its conduct nonetheless. At the end of July, she had the temerity to write again, peremptorily telling him to 'assail the northern traitor, and to plant garrisons in his country, it being ever your firm opinion, amongst others of our council, to conclude that all that was done in any other kind in Ireland, was but waste and consumption'.[182] Suspecting that he might use the excuse of ill health and lack of provisions to return and beg her in person for aid, she added a note rescinding the clause in his initial instructions that he might return leaving two lord justices in charge of the country. He was thereby formally disbarred from returning to England until 'the northern action be tried'. She did not want him back; she knew that if he came, she might be susceptible to his personal entreaties and thereby lose the few remaining campaigning months.

Despite her hard words, the privy council did decide to increase Essex's army. Before news of this development could reach him, however, Sir Conyers Clifford, governor of Connaught, was ambushed by the Irish rebels on his way to create a diversion allowing the English army to march into Ulster. Hundreds of Englishmen were slain by a comparatively small number of Irishmen. This latest disaster compounded the decision of Essex's Irish council, made only days before, that

---

[182] Elizabeth I. 1980 [1599] 'Letter to Essex' in A. Plowden (Ed.) *Elizabeth Regina: The Age of Triumph, 1588-1603* (London: Macmillan), p. 144.

Elizabeth's demands were unachievable. The invasion of the north could not and would not be undertaken. In order to keep his men's morale up, he disobeyed her further by conferring knighthoods on fifty-nine men. To Elizabeth, this was pure favour-currying and a direct contravention of her will; to Essex it was necessary to prevent desertion.

In an attempt to divide the queen's anger, Essex drew up a resolution signed and approved by all members of his council at Dublin. It laid out their opposition to the invasion of Ulster. Then, surprisingly, he changed his mind and, at the end of August, sent his secretary, Henry Cuffe, to England with both the resolution and a note indicating that he was making the attempt despite it. What did he hope to gain by this? The likeliest explanation is that the Irish council's decision and subsequent resolution were feints: together they created an insurance policy. If he failed, as he expected he might, reality having long-since broken his usual fantasies, he could rightly point out that the mission had been one discouraged by his council but forced upon him by his queen. It would not be his fault but hers.

Essex took his army to Kells in County Meath. In early September, at Ardee, he got his first glimpse of the famous Tyrone and his army across the Lagan. The enemy forces glared at one across the river but did not engage. Boldly, Essex opted instead to march his men straight into Louth. Tyrone followed but, after the council had decided that it would be hazardous to do so, the rebel himself sent word that he wished to speak to Essex rather than battle him. At length Essex agreed.

***

The meeting and subsequent truce which opened this chapter was therefore undertaken and concluded. The reasons for it are not hard to find. For the first time in his military career, Essex had come to realise his own strengths – diplomacy and interpersonal charm – and both his weaknesses and those of the English army. Elizabeth had decided that he must attack the north of Ireland and bring Tyrone to heel, but Elizabeth had never set foot in Ireland and had no idea of Tyrone's strength. He and his Irish council did and, upon realising the conditions on the island, knew that her demands were impossible. Peace was preferable, both because of the cold water of reality that had been poured on him and because he was now seeking to be known as a man who thought on his feet rather than a hot-head.

Elizabeth was predictably furious, and she aired her opinion in another fiery letter. Running over several pages, it decried Essex, his men, and especially those – like Southampton, whom she despised and had not wanted to go to Ireland in any capacity – of the officer class who had had the cheek to subscribe their names to a policy which ran contrary to her will.

Essex received her latest insulting and, in his opinion, wholly ignorant message after returning to Dublin from Drogheda. At first, he was so angry that he, egged on by Southampton, spoke of rebellion – of taking their best soldiers across the Irish Sea and marching upon London. Cooler heads – his stepfather's, mainly – prevailed. He decided to ignore Elizabeth's revocation of his permission to leave two trusted men in charge and return home. Taking a small band of men to prevent him from being arrested on landing, he named Adam Loftus, the Irish lord chancellor, and Sir George Carew as Ireland's governors, and fled Ireland in late September. If Elizabeth would not see him, he would see her. What he actually saw would transform his relationship with her forever.

19: Whither Shall I Wander?

Elizabeth I's bedchambers were the inner sanctums of her royal palaces. Unlike her French and Scottish peers, she did not treat bedrooms as spaces for private political exchanges. Men were not permitted to mill around Elizabeth's great state beds as they had been around Mary Queen of Scots'. In the female-only space of her bedchamber, the most private functions of her body could be attended to. She could be washed down with linens, perfumed, clothed, coiffed, and painted. Only when the sixty-six-year-old face and body had been decked out in finery and splendour would she allow anyone outside her immediate circle of female attendants to see her.

That all changed on the morning of September the 28th, 1599. Elizabeth was not long up – she was a late riser – and still in a state of déshabillé. She was dressed only in her shift, her wig not yet on and her grey hair hanging loose. No makeup had been applied and the wrinkles that she usually covered over – unless it was politically necessary not to do so – were thus visible. She had no warning when the door burst open and Essex strode in, his boots and clothing still splattered with mud from his ride through the city.

She cannot have known what brought him – whether it was rebellion, madness, or deep repentance. In August alarms had been given that the Spanish were in the Isle of Wight and Southampton; later in the month they had been rumoured off the French coast; anything might have happened. Amazingly, she gave no sign of surprise or shame at being seen as she truly was. Nor did Essex betray any surprise at seeing her, for the first time in their long friendship, looking other than the glamourous, red-headed Gloriana of Spenser's *The Faerie Queene*. He fell to his knees and kissed her hands and she, whatever she felt inside, patted him, greeting him with warm words and begging only a little time to finish dressing.

Essex could not believe his luck, though his glimpse of the undressed queen had left an impression that would burst forth later. He had banked on a personal interview warming what he suddenly, and probably for the first time, realised was only a fragile old woman, and her kindly attitude convinced him that he had won. The whole thing had been calculated from the start as a display of overflowing passion – the muddy boots and the element of surprise were the stuff of courtly romance, meant to convey an inability to go another moment without his seeing the object of his affections. He was following a hoary model, as had Henry VIII on his impromptu ride to meet Anne of Cleves at Rochester. Essex was even more appalled by the reality of the woman than Henry had been, but the misguided gallantry appeared to serve his purpose. He withdrew, loudly expostulating about his gladness at finding such sweet calm after his storm of troubles. The half-naked old woman had become an indulgent and loving schoolmaster. He could push, break rules, and do as he pleased; invariably she would forgive. By virtue of his having once loved her, he believed that she was hopelessly in love with him. To Essex, love did not mean never having to say he was sorry - but he did appear to think it meant always being forgiven.

Later in the morning Elizabeth was ready for a proper welcome in her privy chamber – the proper setting for private audiences. Still she remained friendly, inviting him to relate his experiences. This he did for over an hour. Afterwards, at the noontime dinner, he regaled all who would listen about his adventures, and looked for all the world like a man on top of it. By the afternoon, however, Elizabeth had had time to gather her thoughts.

Why, she asked him, had he left Ireland against orders? The smiles were gone. What followed was a harangue about the dangers he had caused across the Irish sea. His enemies began to scent blood: Cecil, Nottingham, even Raleigh all realised that he would soon be called to explain himself before the council, and Elizabeth would expect him to be raked across the coals. This was what she did indeed command, and he was hauled before all those members who were in attendance at Nonsuch. As messengers were sent out to those who were absent, Essex was ordered to keep to his chamber. A long and frightening night at court followed, during which Francis Bacon visited him to warn him of what lay ahead and what he ought to do: appear modest, demand nothing, and above all seek further personal interviews with Elizabeth. Only she, both men knew, could shield him and only if he could secure her favour.

The next morning Essex was obliged to attend the council, his head uncovered as a mark of respect. Cecil led the discussion, reading out the litany of offences the earl had committed. It was rapidly becoming an inquiry into his behaviour. For three hours he endured it, nodding, and refusing to rise to the bait. Afterwards, he was allowed to return to his chamber whilst his peers deliberated on his actions, writing up a report and delivering it to the queen. Elizabeth gave out that she would consider what to do. It is likely that she was genuinely in a quandary. The latest example of Essex's lèse-majesté had touched her personally. Beyond that, gossip held that his conference with Tyrone had touched on some kind of illicit agreement about Spain, adding political impetus to the necessity of knowing exactly what he had been up to. She continued to mull the matter over until the following Monday, whereupon she summoned Essex to her. In the presence of the lord keeper, the treasurer, the admiral, and Cecil, she announced that he was to remain in ward at York House. He was a prisoner of the state.

News of this spread quickly and illicitly: 'it was a world ... so full of danger that a man must take good heed of what he say or write'.[183] London was rapidly filling up with the men Essex had abandoned in Ireland; like lost puppies they chased after their master. This was intolerable to Elizabeth – these dispossessed Essex adherents were a security risk. She had the entire court packed up and moved to Richmond.

Essex fell into a state of depression, exacerbated by the dysentery which had plagued him during and after his time in Ireland. For weeks he was left to suffer at York House, and he refused to turn his mind to any matter of business. The stress and fear must have been acute. Despite his quiver of state positions, he could easily be unmade. His friends attempted to

---

[183] Harrison, *The Elizabethan Journals*, p. 43.

intercede for him, with the queen and with Cecil, but it was to no avail. He had burnt his boat. When these approaches failed wild plans were invented by Mountjoy to spring him from York House and send him abroad – but Essex would not agree to them. When Frances attempted to see her husband – she was willing, in fact, to join him in imprisonment, despite having only given birth to their daughter, another Frances, in September – Essex coldly refused to see her. He refused to see anyone unless they came directly from the queen. Still unfailingly loyal, despite her husband's history of adultery, Frances tried to gain approval from Elizabeth to join Essex. Dressed in black, she pled her case with the countess of Huntingdon, but was rebuffed and sent packing from the court. This only sped up rumours that the earl's ultimate destination was the Tower, where he would be held at the queen's pleasure. The queen was furious at Essex and her anger 'appeased in nothing'.

Yet Elizabeth did not hold all the cards. The longer, she knew, that the favourite – or rather the former favourite – was held in unofficial custody, the more the public would clamour for information. He remained a popular man and any whispers of unjust treatment would redound on her. He was no Mary Queen of Scots, foreign and Catholic. Something must be done to satisfy the people, and at the end of November the Star Chamber, which was in effect the name given to the privy council operating as a judicial body – gave out a public declaration of Essex' s misdeeds and the sorry state of Ireland which he had done nothing to help and everything to make safe for Spanish soldiers. The favourite had fallen.

***

Or had he? Essex's depression brought him to what he believed was his deathbed and he received communion. However, when he sent the patents of his offices back to the queen, she returned them. Thereafter Elizabeth granted Frances leave to visit him. The mixed messages coming from the queen, piling on top of months of stress and fear, caused some kind of nervous breakdown in the earl.

His mental collapse led him to God. His problems, he proclaimed, were God's judgement on his manifold sins, including but not limited to his failure to observe the Sabbath. But God was forgiving. He wrote to Southampton of his religious discovery, exhorting the licentious earl to repent and be forgiven. 'There is not peace,' he warned, 'for the wicked and ungodly'.[184] Unsurprisingly, doctors were sent in. Elizabeth herself dispatched eight for a conference, and when they returned the news that there was no hope for a man as far gone in his wits and wasted in body, she wept. If one was to be overly cynical, it might be suggested that Essex was faking the whole thing, but this time his illnesses, mental and physical, were real. His legs filled with fluid and, confined to bed, he made his will.

False rumours circulated that he had died in his confinement but, as the Christmas period arrived, he in fact began to recover. This seemed to disappoint rather than cheer the queen, who sent back his present. When Lettice attempted to intercede on his behalf – this being one of the few ways in which women could make politically-charged speeches – Elizabeth refused her access, and likewise refused to acknowledge the expensive gown the dowager countess tried to give her. She did, however, accept Francis Bacon's present of a white petticoat embroidered with feathers. It seems she had accustomed herself to Essex's death, seeing it as a sad but necessary end; she had even allowed his sisters, Penelope and Dorothy, to attend upon her.

When it became clear that Essex would not quietly die, in early 1600 it was determined that he should at last face a public trial. This was a dangerous time for him, the expectation being that he would be held up to public condemnation and thereby lose his stores of popular affection. When his health had suitably recovered, he commissioned an engraving to be made, depicting him in full armour as a war hero – the better to make it difficult for the crown and its agents to try him. The date was set for the 7th of February but, at Cecil's importuning him to write a letter of supplication to the queen, which Cecil himself

---

[184] Harrison, *Life and Death*, p. 255.

carried, it was cancelled. The secretary did not do this out of any sense of affection or honour. The truth was that he wanted Essex stripped of power, not tried. Star Chamber trials were open to the public and he knew that he would be blamed for bringing down a popular man. This kind of negative opinion was something Cecil wanted to avoid, being already an unpopular one himself: cruel opponents scrawled 'here lieth the Toad' and 'here lieth the toad at London' on the doors of his lodgings.[185]

Still Essex remained immured, albeit with permission to play tennis and walk in the gardens, and still his friends conspired at his release. Lord Mountjoy (whom Elizabeth selected to succeed to Essex's role in Ireland), Southampton, and Sir Charles Danvers all secretly wrote to James VI, encouraging his belief that Cecil was against his succession and that, if he made ready an army on the border, they would have their English soldiers ensure his claim to the throne was recognised in London. This was pie-in-the-sky stuff, but it reveals the depth of political machination and wild-eyed ambition that orbited the imprisoned Essex. The earl threw himself into it. He had seen from the state of Elizabeth's natural body that she was far gone – if James VI was going to become James I, then he had an opportunity to secure the incoming king's favour. Much therefore depended upon Essex and his friends being able to assure James that his disgrace was temporary and that he would still be available – and hopefully still relatively young and handsome – for high office when the new age began. This was more important than ever, because he could no longer count on his absence from court stalling state business as he had during the French ambassador's visit. Then his exile had been self-imposed. He was in control. Now that it was thrust upon him the government had every reason to strip him of all offices and conduct affairs without him.

The scheme to woo King James was still in operation when

[185] Croft, P. 1991. 'The Reputation of Robert Cecil: Libels, Political Opinion and Popular Awareness in the Early Seventeenth Century', *Transactions of the Royal Historical Society, Vol. 1*, pp. 43-69.

Mountjoy was dispatched to Ireland, where he soon began proving himself a more able general than his friend. Sir Henry Lee had been dispatched to Edinburgh and returned with only noncommittal statements from the Scottish king. This did not stop him being arrested; Cecil had known all along what was going on.

Two things were now going on simultaneously. Essex was, like a spider, spinning a very small and insubstantial web. His agent throughout was Henry Cuffe, the Machiavellian secretary who had penned his defence after the Cadiz affair. The goal was to restore the earl to some measure of respectability and favour, and Essex played his part by soliciting not only James VI, but Elizabeth, to whom he sent a letter reminding her that she had once promised only to correct rather than ruin him. The other thing was a careful investigation into the earl on the part of the council, led, naturally, by Cecil. This culminated, in June, in an inquiry not under the painted ceiling of the public Star Chamber, but at Essex's place of house arrest. Yet the crown and Cecil were up to something else. In May, Essex's *Apologie*, written in 1598 as an open letter in defence of his attitudes towards Spain, reappeared in print in 292 copies without his authorisation. This text, when it first appeared in manuscript, had irritated Elizabeth and so did its revival, causing Essex to write to her, 'I am gnawed on and torn by the basest creatures upon earth. The tavern-haunter speaks of me what he lists; the frantic libeller write of me what he lists; they print me and make me speak to the world; and shortly they will play me in what forms they list upon the stage'.[186] A bootleg printer was blamed, but it was apparent that someone was out to get him, and they were doing it secretly and scurrilously by means of the printed word.

The fruits of the crown's investigation had yielded much. Facing his accusers, who did not trouble to stand or doff their caps, Essex was given a cushion on which to kneel whilst the charges were read out. The attorney-general, Edward Coke, laid

---

[186] Raymond, J. 1999. *News, Newspapers and Society in Early Modern Britain* (London: Frank Cass), p. 19.

them out with verve. Despite his having had so high a trust reposed in him, Essex had made Southampton the master of his horse (against the queen's commands); toured Leinster and Munster rather than Ulster; conferred knighthoods without good cause; met with Tyrone and agreed a truce rather than fighting and arresting him; and returned from Ireland against his sovereign's orders. His greatest crimes, Coke added with a flourish, were being 'proud and ambitious … disobedient and contemptuous … notorious and dangerous'.[187]

This was not, for Essex, the most hurtful part of the trial. The crown had summoned another witness for the prosecution: the earl's own friend and adviser, Francis Bacon. This was an awkward and deeply unpleasant moment for both men, as it was intended to be, and Francis had begged the queen to excuse him from it. Not only did the earl have to see a friend disclose his secrets, but Francis had to follow up his rival and superior, Coke, in doing so. Because he had been tasked with investigating the Hayward book, he was told that his testimony was absolutely necessary. He gave a short speech, adumbrating Essex's actions across the Irish sea, and commending the fact that the inquiry was not given over the Star Chamber. He then quoted the earl's private letters, including his criticisms of Elizabeth – 'her heart', he said, 'was obdurate' – before making clear that such words breached the laws of England. He went on to condemn his friend for his tardiness in bringing Hayward's book, with its dangerous Latin dedication, to the attention of the archbishop of Canterbury (who then had authority over printed material).

In his defence, Essex assumed the role of a penitent and thanked the queen – who was not present – for sparing him the Star Chamber. In his characteristic style he apologised profusely for all his errors and misdeeds, before stating his desire to do Elizabeth service, promising to reach into his chest and tear out his own heart if he should fail. The treasurer, keeper, and Cecil then took turns delivering their official censures. The punishment agreed upon was Essex's dismissal

[187] Harrison, *Life and Death*, p. 263.

from the council, the loss of his position of earl marshal, and that he should return to his own house to await the queen's further pleasure.

The following day Bacon had an audience with the queen during which she requested his full report on the preceding day's assembly. On reading it, she said, 'You speak his part well. I perceive that old love does not easily die.'

'I hope by that, madam, you mean your own,' he replied.

***

Essex continued a prisoner whilst Elizabeth first removed, then reinstated, his keeper. She was in a confusion at to what the former favourite's future should be; never before had one of her men behaved in such a manner and been brought to such a pass. He had not committed clear treason nor been tried and, further, she still felt responsible for him. The ongoing inquiry into the conduct of John Hayward was a dead end: under questioning the printer, Wolfe, revealed that the book had initially contained no dedication and it was only added after he and Hayward decided to capitalise on the earl's martial fame and his upcoming journey to Ireland – a country of some importance to the text. This had worked – the book had sold like hotcakes. In the long run it did Hayward little good. At the conclusion of the investigation he was sent to the Tower. Much to the council's chagrin, however, no treasonous link could be found between Hayward, *The First Part of the Life and Raigne of King Henrie IV*, and Essex.

Happily, Francis Bacon wrote to Essex apologising for having had to testify against him, and Essex in turn wrote that he neither commended nor censured his actions. This gave Francis leave to promote his own ideas for remedying the situation. It involved the earl and Anthony Bacon writing a series of letters back and forth, building upon one another to present an image of contrition and continued respect for Elizabeth. These would, when the time was right, be accidentally brought to the queen's attention. It was a neat trick, but it would require a long game.

Cecil, in tandem with the keeper and treasurer (the secretary had learnt that there was power in numbers) interrupted the enactment of the plan, summoning Essex and informing him that he was to be set at liberty, albeit barred from the court. Elizabeth's motives for doing so stemmed mainly from the fact that she had no wish to punish him for matters that had been dealt with. Ireland was under the surprisingly steady hand of Mountjoy, the Hayward book had had no real connection to Essex, and if she did not suffer his presence – which had become anathema to her since he had broken into her bedroom – then he might retire quietly. It was the equivalent, one might argue, of the life Henry VIII had offered the discarded Katherine of Aragon – distant seclusion in a nunnery.

Essex received the news with equanimity. He was quite prepared to retire in something like honour. It need not be forever. He was still in the prime of his life, and Elizabeth was an old and spent woman. He might return to public life under a favourable monarch – the Scottish king whom he had long strove to court – albeit from the disadvantageous position of a humbled man. The men around him, however, were not content to let matters lie; if he retired even for the short term then their own hopes of preferment were dead. Henry Cuffe, especially, taunted his master for his weakness, especially against men of meaner minds and wits. His steward, Gelli Meyrick, shared this view. Essex simply could not be allowed to go quietly. They brought home the dangers of retirement by playing up his finances, and in truth these had partly contributed to his desire to appear quiet, humble, and sorrowful.

The inability to move to the country – his uncle, Sir William Knollys's house was his preferred retreat – was almost immediately thrown into relief. His monopoly on the farm of sweet wines was due for renewal and he knew that, should the queen not grant it, he was undone and his house – and his heirs' house - ruined. This, he suspected, was Cecil's intention, for surely it was the secretary who was poisoning the queen's mind, looking to ruin him, and taking advantage of his disgrace to do it.

Elizabeth probably initially intended to renew it, but she was not minded to make the decision quickly – she made few decisions quickly. In truth, she wanted to extract a final few drops of apology and humility from him. He realised this and bombarded her with desperate letters full of the most abject, ostentatious words of vassalage and faithfulness. All he needed, he protested, was the farm on the customs and he might truly live a quiet life free of intrigue. His entreaties were not quite enough. He locked himself up in Essex House, his fragile mental health again at breaking point.

Elizabeth ignored the request right through October. It was about this time that Francis revealed the complimentary letters about her which had passed between Essex and Anthony. She was unmoved, recognising them for what they were: blatant attempts to get her to renew the monopoly. The scheme failed. She was watching carefully to see what Essex would do – his own behaviour would prove or disprove the sincerity of his soft and flattering words. He fumbled. In desperation he readmitted Cuffe to his household, having dismissed him for his previous remarks. Worse, he activated his network of malcontents and adherents – Charles Danvers was dispatched to pressure Mountjoy into scheming; Southampton returned from the Netherlands, where Essex had sent him earlier in the year to drum up support against Elizabeth's government. These men were, to Elizabeth, desperadoes. Each had been involved in all manner of illicit schemes, from inviting James VI to assemble an army to trying to ferry the English army in Ireland over to London to force Essex back into favour. He had learnt nothing. At the beginning of November, she let it be known that she would retain the monopoly for herself.

In Essex's mind, fed by an ever-present paranoia, he was merely doing what must be done to keep himself and his friends safe from the parasitical insects who buzzed around the queen. They were to blame for his predicament. The inquiry at York House had shown him who his enemies were and, if he lacked access to the court and queen, he would find other means of ridding England of them. He was down, but he would not be out. His embracing of obscure retirement had lasted about two months.

20: A Very British Coup

The earl of Essex never launched a rebellion. Contrary to what is frequently reported in histories of Elizabeth's reign and Essex's life, the action he planned in late 1600 and early 1601 had a much narrower, very different aim.

It all began in the days and weeks following the news of Elizabeth's decision not to renew the monopoly on sweet wines, and it fed off of various stillborn schemes which had briefly emerged during Essex's confinement. Elizabeth – loathsome as she had made herself to him – was not to blame for her actions. It was clear to the earl that her death and the accession of a new monarch would solve nothing as long as Cecil and his faction were England's premier players. A whole host of them were now making hay: Lord Cobham, warden of the cinque ports; Raleigh; Lord Grey, with whom he had quarrelled in Ireland; Buckhurst, the lord treasurer; and old Nottingham. But it was the secretary, as puffed up with spite and jealousy as the toad people called him, who was behind the latest affront. The new king – and Essex calculated that it would be James VI – would simply fall prey to Cecil as Elizabeth had done.

At Essex House the speculation ran wild. These were dark times. Elizabeth was surely soon for the grave. What then? She had never named her heir and there was no guarantee that King James would smoothly succeed. Surely the fact that Cecil, like his father, had approved peace with Spain suggested that he would gift the English throne to the Spanish infanta, whose descent from John of Gaunt her late father never failed to trumpet. It is difficult to believe that Essex truly believed this – but he very much hoped that others would. He was looking over Elizabeth's shoulder, and attempting to get his bid in early as the mastermind, premier noble, and valued minister behind his favoured candidate as her successor.

As a result, these were the notions on which Essex and his partisans fed. Deprived of access to the court they embroidered the tidbits that drifted around London. They suspected, and were right, that the secretary was now actively anticipating the earl's downfall, and to some extent they were also right that Elizabeth was in thrall to him. Cecil, it should also be acknowledged, certainly had been treating with the new Spanish king as part of the abortive peace negotiations at Boulogne in May. It was a short step from this to claiming that the secretary had darker motives.[188] Hoping to convince others that the men who surrounded Elizabeth were preparing for a Spanish succession, Essex elected to deepen his overtures to the Protestant King James. If this seems ridiculous – we know that James VI became James I with relative ease – it is important to remind ourselves that, in 1600, no one knew that his succession would be so easy, least of all James himself. Scotland's king was the odds-on favourite, but it was a still a jump race. Essentially, events had forced Essex to pick this moment to build a pro-Jacobean party with himself at its head. To help construct it, he sought to make of Cecil and his colleagues an opposing, pro-Spanish party. As he was in disgrace and his enemies in high favour, there was no time to lose. James was the man he supposed would command the greatest public support as the next monarch and so he wished to beat his opponents to the Scottish king's door.

In the chilly northern kingdom, the king was in a perpetual state of aggrieved anxiety when it came to the question of his English rights. He had always fancied himself bigger and better than his dreary and relatively poor realm. Although he had ruled it skilfully, he had found the barons and the clergy overmighty, and the proto-republican views of its most cherished thinkers unpalatable. England, to James, was a promised land with a bottomless treasury. Its throne was his by right, and it aggravated him, as it had once aggravated his mother, that the old harridan down south preferred to play games than acknowledge the principle of primogeniture. He had no interest in the challenges of her reign; he did not care if she had had to ban the succession question for the sake of her own political longevity; he just wanted her to die and leave the throne

---

[188] Loades, *The Cecils*, p. 248.

unquestioningly to him. His nervousness about what might happen when Elizabeth died had manifested throughout the previous decade in his tentative approach to Spain, which he hoped he might induce to support his claim, his increasing tolerance of Catholicism, and his establishing contact with leading English courtiers. Essex was chief amongst the latter.

At the end of the year the earl wrote to James warning him of Cecil's alleged Spanish sympathies and asking him to send the earl of Mar southwards to treat directly with Elizabeth about the succession. Included also were complaints that the secretary was stealing his papers and forging letters – and on this he was probably right. Did Essex, one wonders, suspect that it was Cecil who had been behind the publication of a printed version of his *Apologie*? The letter went via a circuitous route – first through the governor of Berwick, Lord Willoughby, and then through a printer travelling to Edinburgh. Essex was not stupid. He knew that secrecy was of the essence and that Cecil's spies were everywhere.

James replied, and immediately Essex knew that he had caught his mark. The Scottish king did not have an in-depth knowledge of the goings on in England, chiefly because the reports which reached him were inevitably highly coloured and contradictory. As a consequence, he believed Essex to be in a much stronger position than he was. Proud of his catch and terrified of its discovery, the earl kept James' letter in a black silken bag which he wore around his neck.

If he thought that his behaviour and the talk that was going on at Essex House were a secret, he was mistaken. It was too dangerous to be kept from Elizabeth and, moreover, those around her were eager to blacken his name. He was, of course, giving them plenty to work with. Walter Raleigh would later report that he had said to the queen, 'her conditions! Her conditions are as crooked as her carcass!' There is disagreement as to the precise date at which he made this statement, with some historians reporting, implausibly, that Raleigh was correct in stating he spoke the words to her or in her hearing.[189] 'The conditions' would then appear to refer to the conditions by which he might return to court, which would imply they had been spoken much earlier, before the decision had been made to banish him. Others date them to late 1600 – the weeks presently under discussion, when his house was a hotbed of angry talk.[190] Alternatively, then, 'conditions' might have been meant in the older sense – her state of being and behaviours. Whenever precisely Essex voiced these sentiments, they are incredibly important. For the first time in their long relationship, he had reconciled the queen and the woman. Whether 'conditions' explicitly meant her behaviours or her terms, they touched upon her regal status – on Elizabeth the queen. 'Her carcass' directly compared them to her body – Elizabeth the decayed and enfeebled woman. He now knew both, understood both, and was disgusted by both.

***

The Accession Day celebrations of 1600 passed joyfully enough without Essex and his circle of friends and hangers-on. A particularly execrable piece of verse, 'A Pleasant New Ballad' was sung 'for the joy and comfort of all her Majesty's faithful subjects':

Ring out your bells!
What should you do else?
Strike up your drums for joy!
The Noblest Queen
that ever was seen,
In England doth Reign this day!

Now let us pray,

---

[189] Edwards, E. P. 1868. *The Letters of Raleigh, Vol. II* (London: Macmillan), p. 217.
[190] Levin, C. 2001. *The Reign of Elizabeth* (London: Palgrave), p. 101.

and keep holy-day,
The seventeenth day of November;
For joy of her Grace,
in every place,
Let us great praises render![191]

It was a false picture of what Elizabethan England had
become after the years of dearth. Still the people starved. Ireland
continued to be a nuisance despite Mountjoy doing
commendable English service – so good, in fact, that the queen
jokingly called him her 'kitchen-maid' for his dutiful burning
of the crops of the rebellious Irish. Foreigners were still blamed
for the nation's ills. Indeed, at the start of the year, Elizabeth
had professed herself

greatly distressed in these hard times of dearth [and] highly
discontented to understand the great number of Negroes and
blackamoors which are crept into this realm since the troubles
between her Highness and the King of Spain.[192]

The queen, like her subjects, was quite willing to blame the
other for the problems of her kingdom.

When the new year dawned, Essex was not allowed to be
forgotten. Francis Bacon remained loyal, albeit he was far too
intelligent to involve himself in the goings on at Essex House.
Because of his continually pressing Elizabeth to restore Essex
to favour, she 'became utterly alienated' from him and, she
wrote, 'would not as much as look on me, but turned away from
me wheresoever she saw me'. When business compelled her to
acknowledge him, he told her, 'a great many love me not,
because they think I have been against my Lord of Essex; and
you love me not, because you know I have been for him …
Upon which speeches of mine [she] was exceedingly moved
and accumulated a number of kind and gracious words upon

[191] Plowden, *Elizabeth Regina*, p. 49.
[192] Vaughan, V. M. 2005. *Performing Blackness on English Stages,
1500-1800* (Cambridge: Cambridge University Press), p.76.

me'.[193] This tells us two important things: Essex remained popular amongst the people; and the queen, despite her heart having hardened towards her old favourite, retained a shred of regret. Unlike her father, the queen's bark was worse than her bite. Even when she disposed of those she had once loved, she had a conscience, and her scapegoats, when she chose to make them, were only political.

The wise Francis, however, was not now the type from whom Essex was taking advice. His orbit was filled now with discontented refugees from court and religious radicals who preached the overthrow of bad monarchs. In fact, the Essex circle had really ceased to be that: it became a broad coalition of people willing to have him as leader, however temporarily, whether due to religious or political disaffection. The earls of Bedford, Rutland (married to Frances's daughter by Philip Sidney), Worcester, and Sussex all flocked to Essex House to hear the gossip, commiserate with the fallen favourite, and complain about the primacy of Cecil and his friends. The growth in his party refuelled his old self-confidence. A corpus of nobles was on his side and those who remained in thrall to the son of a jumped-up lawyer were nothing less than class traitors. 1601 would see a reckoning. It is often suggested that the earl was bounced into action by the Iago-like goading of these men, but this is not necessarily the case. Essex was no pliable lump of clay: he had been quite happy to temporarily dismiss Henry Cuffe when the insolent secretary had called him weak. The decision to strike would be his own.

Southampton, ever the hothead, met that enemy of the Essex camp, Lord Grey, in January, and Grey drew his sword. The pair had been feuding since Grey had ignored Southampton's orders not to attack a rebel force when they had been in Ireland under Essex; but Essex did not see this as an eruption of the vendetta. Instead, he thought it an attempt on the life of his friend, probably ordered by Cecil. No doubt he supposed he was on the imaginary hit-list too. That was all but confirmed when news leaked that John Hayward, still languishing in the Tower,

---

[193] Bacon, *The Letters and the Life of Francis Bacon*, p. 158

had again been interrogated about his dedication of *Henrie IV*. It was clear that Cecil's council – for it was surely all his now – was plotting his destruction, so frightened were its members of the growing body of noble opposition. Something would have to be done and quickly.

The move to action was swift. Essex made enquiries in London about opponents of the Cecil-led regime, and they began to meet secretly. In addition to those already in the loop were the impoverished Lords Mounteagle, Cromwell, and Sandys. Less august gentlemen, such as Charles Danvers, John Davies, and Ferdinando Gorges, joined too. Without Essex present, his followers met at Southampton's Drury House in February to thrash out exactly what was to be done. It was Davies (who was not the celebrated poet of the same name) who codified the group's plan, which had long been simmering: discreetly invade the court at Whitehall with a small number of conspirators, overwhelming the guards and allowing Essex and his noble adherents passage to the queen; send men into London to explain and justify their actions; seize Raleigh and the most egregious of the counsellors and proclaim the opening of a parliament at which those taken might be tried.

For avid readers of history this type of plan might seem familiar. It was no rebellion, but a court coup, almost identical to that which had been attempted in 1566 upon Mary Queen of Scots, whose husband, Darnley, had joined up with a clique of disgruntled nobles and surprised her, dragging away her unpopular secretary, David Riccio. The men had not been rebels, but politicians trying to enact a bloody coup. Their aim had not been to kill Mary, but to force a change in her government and restore the place of the old nobility. Scottish politics also threw up the example of James III, whose favourites were hanged at Lauder; and in England Edward II had been forcefully separated from his great favourite, Piers Gaveston. Palace coups had a tradition in British history. It was a triply British endeavour by dint of Essex's links with James VI of Scotland, and the crew of Welshman brought into the ever-expanding circle by his Welsh steward, Meyrick.

Yet there was one key difference between Essex's plan and

the actions of previous generations. His relied in large part on riding a public wave of weariness and disaffection. Whereas the older coups had mainly involved a select group of aristocrats banding together to unify their networks of adherents as early opposition parties, Essex hoped to do this as well as mobilising popular sentiment in his favour. In this way he was positioning himself as both a conservative – in his defence of the traditional rights of the nobility to advise their sovereign – and a radical – in engaging with growing ideas about the subject's right to question, criticise, and oppose the state. He would be a beacon for malcontents who yearned for a time before the 'new men' as well as for those who hated the stale government and its autocratic head. None of this was accidental. Essex's history of courting the public, which had been born after Rouen and grown year upon year, had led him to the ineluctable conclusion that the public were a force to be marshalled, even if he would never embrace even nascent republicanism.

Disagreement amongst the company prevented the plan from being agreed upon: it was decided to leave it to Essex to decide what was and was not feasible. His mind was not on the recent Scottish example of a coup, but on the theatrical depiction of one. Only days after the discussion of how best to take the queen and court, Lord Mounteagle, along with Charles and Jocelyn Percy, paid a visit to the Globe theatre in Southwark. The Essex crowd, including the earl himself, were avid theatregoers and knew the power of the written and spoken word – indeed, the aspiring poet and playwright Thomas Middleton had dedicated his dull *The Wisdom of Solomon Paraphrased* to Essex in 1597.

At the theatre, they asked a favour of the players, The Lord Chamberlain's Men – the premier acting company in the capital. Would they consider putting on a performance of their actor-playwright's old drama, *Richard II*? Shakespeare and company were unwilling – the play was old. Forty shillings bought the command performance. The next afternoon, the play was performed before a large company, amongst which Essex's friends were prominent. Doubts must have crossed the actors' minds, but money was money and, besides, the play had long since been licensed as acceptable for performance by the queen's own master of the revels.

Essex's purpose in having *Richard II* performed has been debated for centuries. Almost every historian and literary critic has cited the playing of its climactic scenes – the deposition of the unpopular king, the slaughter of his favourites, and the accession of Henry Bolingroke as Henry IV – as a call to arms. It is accordingly argued that Richard II was Elizabeth (this was certainly her opinion of the affair); his favourites, Bushy, Bagot, and Green, were Cecil, Raleigh, and Cobham; and Bolingbroke was Essex. Some of the resonances are accurate enough – Elizabeth and the favourites were there. The performance was not, however, intended to raise rebellion.

Those familiar with *Richard II* will recall its most stirring lines, spoken by the bishop of Carlisle:

My Lord of Hereford here, whom you call king,
Is a foul traitor to proud Hereford's king:
And if you crown him, let me prophesy:
The blood of English shall manure the ground,
And future ages groan for this foul act;
Peace shall go sleep with Turks and infidels,
And in this seat of peace tumultuous wars
Shall kin with kin and kind with kind confound;
Disorder, horror, fear and mutiny
Shall here inhabit, and this land be call'd
The field of Golgotha and dead men's skulls.
O, if you raise this house against this house,
It will the woefullest division prove
That ever fell upon this cursed earth.
Prevent it, resist it, let it not be so,
Lest child, child's children, cry against you woe!

These are hardly words to strike up desire for a rebellion, still less for the murder of a monarch – which the play obviously never advocates. Neither *Richard II* or any of the period's popular plays show monarchs as they actually spoke and behaved, but rather how the common people thought they should or should not behave. In common with most of

Shakespeare's work, the play is deeply suspicious of rebellion and is careful to show that Bolingbroke's troubles do not end with his accession. Still factional nobles importune him. But if the staging was not intended to fire up the London playgoers with blood-thirst against an unpopular monarch and her sycophants, why the command performance?

Richard II, Essex hoped, would serve as a warning. There but for the removal of Cecil and company would go England. In the play was the greatest of terrors – a bloody deposition, their queen undone, if the people did not support the removal of the parasites and protect her from infamy in as smooth and orderly a fashion as possible. He was not seeking to destroy Elizabeth, but rather positioning himself and his men as her saviours. If they did not act, her reign would end – as all knew it soon would end – in ignominy. Only by the destruction of the Bushys, Bagots, and Greens of her court might her fame be preserved. If they did not go, she would indeed become another Richard II and factional politics would continue into the next administration. Disorder, horror, fear, blood, tears, division, woe, and curses: these were England's fate if the current government was allowed to continue. The threat, too, was that the queen might have to be ignominiously deposed if Cecil and his faction were not cut out of the body politic by loyal and right-minded heroes. In staging Shakespeare's play, both threat and warning were intended – not bloody uprising.

The problem was that the play's subject matter was far too close to the recent anxieties over Hayward's book. This was obviously why Essex had chosen it out of all the plays which depicted a fallen England, but it also aroused the attention of the court and council; Elizabeth peremptorily summoned Essex and his fellow noble conspirators to her presence to account for it. He was not about to obey her – especially not when another messenger warned him that he would be walking into an ambush. From where had he got this talk of an ambush? The sources are silent. What seems possible, even likely, is that the council knew what was in the offing and decided to feed Essex's paranoia, thereby hoping to goad him into precipitate action. If so, it was a neat reversal of the years in which the earl had attempted to goad Cecil into open feud.

Essex refused the summons, only to be issued with another one. Again, he refused. The repeated summonses did, however, spook his party, and opinion immediately divided as to what ought to be done. Against advice that he should immediately flee to Wales or abroad, he elected that he would muster the city the next day. His confidence, which had grown over the months, had expanded to embrace his ever-reliable popularity with the common people. He was the hero of Rouen and Cadiz, multiple-times champion of the queen's Accession Day tilts. The public knew that he had been unfairly treated and the same public hated Cecil and his cronies as much as he did. Having lived away from the court he had seen the general disaffection with the turn Elizabeth's reign had taken and, further, he was absolutely in the right: England was suffering, and he was its saviour.

All through the night, men slipped in and out of Essex House. An air of excitement and unreality descended. When Raleigh sent a message to Ferdinando Gorges requesting to meet on the Thames, Christopher Blount suggested that the captain of the guard might be assassinated on his boat. As the sun broke over the jagged London skyline, Essex's followers began to arrive.

Little of what was happening went unreported to the council, and Cecil began defensive preparations. For years now he had expected a reckoning with Essex. His approach to his rival had always been to watch and wait. Finally, the earl had rope enough to hang himself – it must just be paid out a little longer: allow him too much and he might actually hang Cecil.

Gorges left Essex House and met with Raleigh on the Thames. He did not attack him, but instead haughtily told him to return to court, for he would 'have a bloody day of it'. The morning was drawing on. The courtyard of Essex House jangled with horses' harnesses and the ground was awash with gathering men's spittle. Essex strode around, clapping backs and shaking hands, and was as surprised as anyone when someone began battering the outer gate.

Chief Justice Popham, Sir William Knollys, Sir Thomas Egerton, and the earl of Worcester – recently an Essex man –

were all demanding entry in the queen's name. They were admitted and demanded of Essex the reason for his sudden display of men. Essex did not miss the opportunity for melodrama, shouting for all to hear that his life was in danger and the assembly his bodyguard. Again, he repeated that his signature had been forged and letters written in his name – an echo of his claim the previous year that he had been 'deeply wounded by practising libellers'.[194] He might well have been looking at Worcester. The paranoia Essex had developed was well-founded – Elizabethan politics had become a mire of backbiting, false-dealing, and personal attacks whispered, handwritten, printed, nailed upon doors, and thrown down streets. Writing during the Jacobean period, Essex's kinsman Fulke Greville would go so far as to suggest that 'under the ... cloud [of disfavour] his enemies took audacity to cast libels abroad in his name against the state, made by themselves; set papers upon posts, to bring his innocent friends in question'.[195] Greville blamed the Catholics, and was seeking to absolve his dead relative of all guilt, but the fractious nature of the times he recalled faithfully enough. He was, further, probably correct in assuming that Cecil, who had long waited for Essex to be out of favour, was active in using his own network of agents in London to foment unrest in Essex's name. If so, Cecil's then-establishment party anticipated and actively aided the earl's attempts to foster public anxiety, knowing that it could later be used as a means of inflating what was brewing into a full-scale rebellion.

Egerton announced that if Essex had any just complaint, he should make it properly and let justice take its course. Southampton tartly raised the matter of Lord Grey's attack upon him, to which the lord keeper answered that Grey had been imprisoned for his drawn sword. This fell rather flat, as the lord's commitment to the Fleet Prison had been so brief it was

---

[194] Irish, B. J., Keller, M., McClure, E., & Mohamed, F. 2018. *Emotion in the Tudor Court: Literature, History, and Early Modern Feeling* (Evanston: Northwestern University Press), p. 152.
[195] Greville, *Life of Sidney*, p. 157.

already over. Egerton and the other queen's men were fighting a losing battle. The mob of Essex supporters began turning ugly, heckling and jeering. Seemingly graciously, Essex led the deputation into the house, cries of 'kill them' at their back.

The earl did not kill them. Instead, he bid them wait in his study whilst he saw to his security by speaking with the lord mayor and the city's sheriffs. Promising to return shortly, he left the room, telling Sir John Davies and one of Meyrick's Welsh friends, Owen Salisbury, to keep them in honourable confinement. His plan was indeed to confer with the mayor of London and his sheriff, but not for safeguarding his person; he expected to recruit them to his cause. Returning to the courtyard, he was met with the jubilant cries of his followers who demanded to march upon the court, which was still at Whitehall less than a mile west of his house on the Strand. Instead, Essex led them east into the city. It was a fatal error of judgement.

About 200 men went with Essex, carrying only swords and rapiers. Others of his company joined as they passed through Fleet Street and through the Ludgate. 'For the queen,' cried Essex repeatedly. He meant it. Still he believed he was saving Elizabeth from her own weaknesses, of body, mind, and monarchy. 'A plot is laid for my life!'

As they marched, people hung out of windows, some cheering and others laughing. This was the kind of show they normally had to pay a penny each to see acted upon the stage. Crucially, however, none disappeared from their windows and emerged on the street with weapons. Things were already going badly. All the way past St Paul's Cathedral, along Lombard Street, and to the home of Thomas Smythe, London's sheriff, the Essex train marched, Lord Cromwell arriving first. Smythe was no idiot. Dissimulating like an actor himself, he told Cromwell that if his life were in danger, Sir William Ryder, the lord mayor, could offer better protection. At this point Essex caught up and made to burst into Smythe's house; at this, Smythe promised to go and fetch Ryder himself. He slipped out a back door and so escaped the whole unfolding fiasco.

Essex realised the jig was up. He collapsed in Smythe's house, sweating so much that he had to remove his shirt. It is difficult to imagine his thoughts at the time. He knew that he was now staring death in the face, and on a day that had started with so much promise. He had no idea what to do next and, in the absence of anything else, he allowed dinner to be served. During his meal news arrived that he was proclaimed a traitor across London. At first he refused to believe it. Delusion had set in. He went out into the street to see what was happening and began crying out wildly that he was acting in good faith – he was trying to save England and the queen from the corrupt minions who were selling the country to Spain. No one paid much attention to what must have looked like a madman.

He mounted a nearby horse and rode to Gracechurch Street where he met Smythe. The sheriff asked him to attend on the lord mayor; Essex refused and, pathetically, told Smythe, 'you shall go with me ... and I shall take the gates for the safety of the city'. He barely understood that he was being viewed as the enemy rather than the saviour. In desperation he rode off for Essex House, thinking only of returning home, as though a return would somehow eradicate the nightmare-like day.

On reaching Ludgate, Essex found that the city was under martial law. At first the queen had reportedly wished to go 'out in person to see what any rebel of them all durst do against me', but she was dissuaded. Stymied, she decided to ignore the failing coup, leaving Cecil and the council to swing into action. They dispatched loyal men to lock London down. The earl of Cumberland and the bishop of London had taken over the part of it in which Essex found himself, putting an old commander, Sir John Leveson, in charge. When Essex reached him, he sent Gorges forward to seek safe passage home. He was refused. He tried again, and again, pleading to send a message to the queen – all to no avail.

Essex's mind might have been descending into chaos, but it was a gentler kind of madness than that of his followers. One amongst his company shot off a pistol and Leveson's men returned fire. A bullet carried off Essex's hat and another struck and killed his young page boy. Two bystanders were also killed in the affray. The sudden eruption of violence spurred him out of his stupor and into stupidity. He drew his sword, raised it, and commanded Blount to charge.

A short skirmish was all that they managed. When Leveson's men raised and trained their weapons directly at the party, Essex called a retreat and fled, leaving Blount at the head of the party and in the soldiers' hands. Departing, unfollowed, he sent Gorges home to release Chief Justice Popham from Essex House. His diminished band of men made straight for the river, where he commandeered a boat and took the watery highway home. There he discovered that not only had Gorges indeed beaten him, but he had released all the prisoners and made for court – another betrayal.

Essex saw no other choice but to make a stand. He locked up the house and began barricading himself and his friends in – another pathetic and rather sad gesture. He began burning his correspondence, including the letter from James VI that he had kept all along in its little black bag around his neck. 'This bag' he said, 'should tell no tales'. As darkness fell, Nottingham and his troupe of queen's men – deliberately composed of loyal earls and lords in order to give the lie to Essex's pretended monopoly on noble support – approached. Essex and his remaining friends walked out onto the roof leads, held up their swords in defiance, and then retreated back indoors. From inside the house came occasional gunshots and cries from the women – Frances, Penelope, and their attendants. Frances had given birth to Essex's last child, Dorothy, in December, and it is possible that the baby, her one-year-old sister, and their nurses were also present.

As Robert Sidney, loyal to the queen, demanded surrender, Southampton reappeared on the roof, where he refused to yield, promising that he and those inside would rather die fighting than accept accusations of treachery. It was a display of pure bravado. He achieved only the safe release of the women. Left alone, the men, now declared traitors, debated what to do. Essex wished to die – better to go down fighting like a soldier than have his head lopped off like a traitor. The rest of his company were less enthusiastic. Ultimately, they opted to parley, securing only the right to be fairly treated, heard judicially, and given spiritual comfort. On receiving as warm an affirmation as Nottingham could give as to their conditions, they surrendered, filtering out and handing over their swords.

Essex's attempted coup had ended in farce, as had so many of his military campaigns. It was not a stupid idea in itself, but it had been badly handled. He had time to reflect on this as, during the cold, dark February night, he was rowed to Lambeth Palace a prisoner. There was no way out for him now but death, unless he could somehow win the queen's mercy. At every previous point in his life and every mistake and crossed word he had been able to do just that – from the moment he had met her, aged twelve, and refused to doff his cap. Everything banked on whether, as she had indicated to Francis Bacon, she still had some tenderness towards him.

21: Final Fantasies

On the 19th of February Essex was brought to trial, along with Southampton, at Westminster Hall. From Lambeth he had been taken to the Tower, and there he had waited whilst the smaller fry were rounded up and punished, and the city reassured with prayers of thanksgiving and public proclamations against sedition. The times were unsettled, but Elizabeth gave no sign of it; even when one of Essex's captains, Thomas Lee, was found to be planning to break into the privy chamber and force out of her a warrant for the earl's release, the man was allowed to stand outside the door until he could be arrested. He was swiftly tried, found guilty, and executed at Tyburn on the 14th.

Whether Essex had deluded himself that the queen would save him or whether instead he welcomed death is difficult to gauge. His words indicate the latter but his spirited defence and his attempts to spin out proceedings suggest the former. If he hoped for some kind of royal intervention he was indulging simply in fantasy. In fact, all of the fantasies he had conceived and given voice to – the success and godliness of his actions, the conspiring of Cecil and his friends to secure a Spanish succession – were all going to be deflated during the course of the day.

The result was a foregone conclusion. The trial's purpose was a public demonstration of the full, united panoply of state ranged against the traitors.[196] Essex and Southampton, as the declared ringleaders, were accompanied to the court in Westminster Hall by the lieutenant and constable of the Tower: Lord Thomas Howard and Sir John Peyton. The two prisoners

---

[196] Lord Treasurer Buckhurst presiders as lord high steward; before him sat the clerk of the crown and his assistants. At two long tables were seated the peers and the law officers of state: the lord chief justice; Sir the lord chief baron; the master justices; the lord high steward; the queen's sergeant; the attorney-general; the solicitor-general; the recorder of London; and Francis Bacon.

were dressed entirely in black. The famous axe, which would be turned on the delivery of the verdict, was carried by the gentleman porter. All was done with great ceremony. Again, the message to be sent out was that the accused were enemies of a fully functioning state.

Defiantly, Essex laughed and asked about the possibility of personal challenge when the roll of peers was read out. Lord Grey, seated at one of the long tables, was present and Southampton might wish to settle the score. Chief Justice Popham was in no mood for games and adroitly turned the earl's joke upon him: peers, he tartly pointed out, were immune from the privilege of personal challenge. Aristocrats who did not dabble in treason were well protected. The state had won, and Essex asked that the grim spectacle should continue.

The charges were read out, and they focused on Essex, Southampton, Rutland, Sandys, and others conspiring to 'deprive and depose' Elizabeth, and to 'procure her death and destruction'. This was untrue. Essex had sought to deprive the existing council of its leaders, installing himself as chief political adviser to a puppet queen, who might be allowed to live out the little time remaining to her whilst he fixed the next succession on James VI. The earl was a man of feeling - shallow but expressed in extremes. He had been an intimate of Elizabeth for over well over a decade - he had loved and loathed her, expressing himself far more vocally than he ever did towards his wife. He certainly did not want her murdered and was offended even by the accusation. Rather he wanted her to accept his pre-eminent position in her council in what were patently her last years. Only he could smooth the way for what would follow her death.

He and Southampton accordingly pled not guilty, Essex declaring, 'I call God to witness, before whom I hope shortly to appear, that I bear a true heart to her Majesty and my country, and have done nothing but that which the law of nature commanded me to do in my own defence, and which any reasonable would have done in the like case'. This was a mistake. His egotistical focus on himself and the ostensible danger in which he had lived negated his claims to be acting in

239

the public good.

For the prosecution spoke the queen's sergeant, Yelverton. He professed himself shocked that Essex and Southampton did not blush at pleading not guilty following so notorious a rebellion. Already the spin-doctors of the council had made clear throughout the country and abroad that the attempted coup had indeed been a rebellion. Coke spoke next, and in his baroque style he went on at length about the definition of treason, citing numerous precedent cases. Their behaviour, he expounded, 'must needs imply the death and destruction of the queen and [was] higher than the highest treason'.

This, Essex protested, was slander. He begged leave to speak and accused Coke of embodying the kind of justice one expected in corrupt states. He knew, of course, that he had been pre-judged guilty, and during his time in the Tower it must have dawned on him that there would be no royal pardon. The best that he might hope for was that the queen would drag her feet over signing his death warrant, and perhaps die in the interim. On hearing the lord high steward's answer – that the evidence must be presented before the accused could launch a defence – Essex begged to be allowed to respond to each piece of individual evidence. His goal was to rubbish the court's proceedings. It would not deliver a favourable verdict, but it would greatly disturb the public mood, which the council was working so hard to turn against him.

To the evidence of planning at Essex House on the morning of the coup, he pointed out that the crown witness had only heard about it rather than witnessed it. To the charge of false imprisonment of Popham, Egerton, Knollys, and Worcester, to which the lord chief justice himself attested, he claimed that he had locked them in his study only for their own safety. When asked why he did not dissolve his assembly on being ordered to, he pointed out the multitude of armed men which had converged on Essex House, making those inside fear for their lives and refuse to disperse.

After this Southampton and Grey began arguing and the whole trial threatened to dissolve into name-calling. The lord high steward put a stop to the argument and called forth Sir

Walter Raleigh. As he was sworn in, Essex loudly asked, 'what booteth it to swear the fox?' What use, he meant, was there in swearing in a notorious and sly liar? Hearing this hardly induced Raleigh to warmth and he revealed Ferdinando Gorge's words on the Thames on the morning of the coup: 'you are like to have a bloody day of it'. Essex claimed that this was not what Gorges had told him.

Gorges had, however, turned queen's evidence via a written confession which was read out, first on his behalf and then by Gorges himself. The quavering turncoat claimed that he had begged his friend and master to submit himself to Elizabeth, but that the earl had been resolute in his rebellion. 'My lords,' cried Essex, alarmed by the plainly terrified appearance of Gorges, 'look upon Sir Ferdinando, and see if he looks like himself. All the world shall see, by my death and his life, whose testimony is the truest'. Still he was thinking of the public's reaction to the affair.

Southampton then stood to speak, and although he admitted that there had been talk at his house of a palace coup, nothing had been determined upon. Talk, he insisted, was not treason, and the launching of men on the morning of the so-called rebellion had been a surprise to him. The pistol he had been carrying had come from a man in the street and lacked any flint to fire it. After Southampton's speech, the judges conferred before delivering their conclusions. In doing so they would cover all bases.

Essex, they declared, had committed treason even if he intended only to remove those enemies of himself he perceived to surround the queen. His march into the city, whatever he thought of it, was tantamount to rebellion. That being so, Southampton's sticking by him, whether he knew exactly what Essex's plan of action was or not, was also treason. All who had accompanied the earl into the city were traitors and only those who joined him on his march but went home when the council's proclamations were read might be pardoned.

There followed the testimony of Charles Danvers, Christopher Blount, Rutland, and Lord Sandys. All confirmed Essex's action on re-entering Essex House: he had burnt his papers and destroyed the mysterious black bag he carried on a string around his neck. Coke took the opportunity to accurately say of the earl, 'you were confident in London, having been persuaded by your sycophants that all the city was on your part'. The narrative the court was now spinning was that Essex had coveted the crown of England for himself – which was a nonsense – and the earl responded:

I do charge you all, my lords, that notwithstanding all eloquence is used to call me a traitor, a papist, a sectary, and an atheist [then a catch-all term of any objection to Anglicanism], and to have aspired to the crown, that you have a true regard to your consciences, and judge of me as a good Christian, and as one that never sought to exceed the degree of a subject … howsoever I have been dealt withal, I had sought to appease all humours of revenge in me, and for confirmation thereof was resolved to receive the sacrament, until the attempt upon the earl of Southampton by the Lord Grey.[197]

This was partly true. It was Grey's attack on Southampton that had spurred him into believing that Cecil and his enemies might aim at his own life. Yet the fact that he carried James VI's letter around before and during the coup suggests that his chief motivation was ensuring his premiership in what he would ensure was the next reign.

After Mounteagle's testimony, which Coke pointed out comported with the rest without the speakers having any fear of torture, Essex declared, 'I was drawn into this hazard by those who have the queen's ear, and abuse it, informing her of falsehoods against many of us'. This was definitely true. It indicates also his ongoing need to present himself as the only one with the courage to stand up for the old ways. The aristocracy was being abused by a queen beholden to favourites and it was his intent to restore long-established order rather than destroy Elizabeth. He named Cecil, Cobham, and Raleigh as the

[197] Jardine, D. 1835. *The Lives and Criminal Trials of Celebrated Men* (Philadelphia), p. 348.

chief architects of the reign's decay. His protests again raised a tumult – which was to be expected given that the court was designed explicitly to show that he was not a noble protector but a traitor. The twenty-five assembled peers began voicing their objections vociferously.

When the lord steward had again calmed the hall, Francis Bacon rose to speak. His presence seems odd and can only be attributed to the queen's desire to have him speak against the man she knew he still loved. She had never especially liked Francis – his conduct at the first parliament after Essex had been elevated to the privy council always rankled – and this was her opportunity to make him sweat. It has been suggested also that he was blackmailed into taking part by the threat of his invalid brother, who had remained in charge of Essex's spy network, being taken into custody.[198] More likely is that, as a court lawyer with intimate knowledge of the defendant, the crown simply expected his testimony to cement its case, and Francis was in no position to refuse. Writing in 1604 of his involvement in the trial, he refused to admit what exactly placed him in Westminster Hall in February 1601.

Francis Bacon laid out damning charges against his friend, pointing out that if his fear was of Cobham, Raleigh, and Cecil, there was no justification for imprisoning Popham and the others. Rather than acting on the spur of the moment, the assembly and rebellion had been at least three months in the making. It would be better, he concluded, that Essex confess rather than try and justify his actions. As he sat and Essex rose, the tension must have been unbearable. This was far greater a breach than the inquiry which had been undertaken at York House into Essex's conduct in Ireland. Francis knew that his words would help kill his friend, as did Essex; and after the inevitable execution, the name Francis Bacon would likely become tainted in the public imagination.

Essex launched into a tirade against Francis and his words are extremely interesting. 'Mr Bacon,' he said, 'a daily courtier

<hr />

[198] See in particularly Daphne du Maurier's discussion in *The Golden Lads*.

[who] had free access to her Majesty, pretending to be my friend … undertook to go to the queen on my behalf. And he drew for me a letter most artificially in my name, and another in his brother Mr Anthony Bacon's name; which letters he purposed to show to the queen, and he showed them both to me … by [those letters] it will appear what conceit Mr Bacon at that time had of those men and of me'.[199] The letters were those Francis had cooked up to attempt to win Essex Elizabeth's favour. What the earl was trying to do, and he was throwing Francis to the wolves in doing it, was reiterate a general feeling amongst the Elizabethan court that Cecil, Cobham, and Raleigh were denigrating queen and country.

Francis sidestepped the issue neatly, refusing to deny his part in trying to restore his friend to favour. The attorney-general took his part. This led Essex to indulge his accusations against Cecil. He had heard, he revealed, the chief secretary say to another counsellor that 'the infanta's title is as good as any'. This was true – but Essex had wilfully misread the context; Cecil had been raising the Spanish claim to England's throne in order to argue against it.

Hearing his name, Cecil dramatically revealed himself. Like a miniature Polonius, he had been hiding behind an arras as the trial went on. Essex's attack had roused him to fury, and he fell to his knees, despite Popham rubbishing the accusations. This was his moment to shine. It was the moment for which he had been waiting for many years and he did not miss the opportunity to release the floodgates of hostility:

My lord of Essex, the difference between you and me is great. For wit I give you the pre-eminence … for nobility I also give you place. I am not noble, yet a gentleman; I am no swordsman – there you have the odds; but I have innocence, conscience, truth, and honesty, to defend me against the scandal and sting of slanderous tongues, and in this court, I stand as an upright man and your lordship as a delinquent … you have a wolf's head in a sheep's garment, in appearance humble and religious,

[199] Jardine, *Lives and Criminal Trials*, p. 352.

but in disposition ambitious and aspiring. God be thanked, we know you now.[200]

This was worthy of Shakespeare's pen. Undoubtedly Cecil had prepared it in advance. Essex seemed to realise this. Wryly, he replied, 'I thank God for my humiliation that you, in the ruff of all your bravery, have come hither to make your oration against me'. The rivalry was now over. Cecil had won.

The trial continued with Cecil asking Essex to name the counsellor to whom he had spoken of the Spanish infanta. Southampton volunteered the name: Essex's uncle, Sir William Knollys, comptroller of the queen's household. Cecil was not willing to give up, and Knollys was sent for. When he arrived, he gave the devastating answer that the secretary had said only, 'is it not a strange impudence that Doleman [Robert Persons, who had released the racy book on the succession in the summer of 1595] gives as equal right in the succession of the crown to the infanta of Spain as any other?' In so short a space of time, Cecil had won again.

Thereafter the trial was all but over. Coke played it out, returning over the minutiae of what constituted treason, and Essex continued to protest the innocence and goodwill of his intentions. He repeated that he aimed no higher than a subject might, and Francis Bacon again rose to speak against him. Eventually the long day began to wind down and the lord high steward invited the peers to confer privately about the verdict. After they had done so, they returned to the hall to deliver it. There had never been any doubt about that. Both Essex and Southampton were declared guilty. Each peer repeated the same.

On being invited to give any evidence as to why he might be spared death, Essex professed to welcome it, asking only that his fellow nobles might speak with the queen on Southampton's behalf. Southampton was less altruistic, and opted to plead for his own life, asking the peers also to speak to the queen for him. Their official fate as decided at the moment, however, was that

---

[200] Jardine, *Lives and Criminal Trials*, p. 353.

they be imprisoned until such a time as they might be hanged, drawn, and quartered. This was the legal fate of traitors, as Essex knew, having ensured that Dr Lopez had met it. Customarily, however, the aristocracy were spared its full horrors and instead beheaded.

Before being taken back to the Tower to await death, Essex asked only that Elizabeth might grant him a suitable preacher to give him spiritual comfort before the end, and that the officers of the Tower might take the sacrament with him. He was promised that all would be done to make this happen. The court was then dissolved, and Essex and Southampton led away, the former apologising to those men whose sons he had involved in his coup.

As Essex was taken back to the Tower of London, people thronged the streets to see him go. These were the same people he had imagined would rally to his cause – the poor, dispossessed Londoners who had been exhausted by a government fallen into corruption. They commiserated with their fallen hero now, but none had been willing to risk their necks in joining his coup. He ignored them, keeping his head down.

The earl had given a spirited performance throughout the day. If he expected to live, he would be disappointed, but if he expected to die, he could be sure that his name would not be spattered with the kind of mud that Cecil and his friends had hoped. It is difficult to find much sympathy for him. Like Dr Lopez, whose death he had sought with all the determination of a terrier, he had played a foolish and dangerous game and lost. Death was the price of failure in early modern politics. There was no real hope that he might expect anything from Elizabeth other than her own sudden death. Rumours have abounded in the centuries since that she had gifted him a ring after his return from Cadiz, promising that if ever he sent it to her in a time of danger, she would not fail to rescue him. The story goes that he tried to send this ring to her via Catherine Carey, the countess of Nottingham after his trial, but that the countess failed to deliver it. After confessing to not having done so shortly before her death in February 1603, Elizabeth is reported to have replied, 'may God forgive you, madam, but I never can.' This story is almost certainly apocryphal. Elizabeth brazened out the trial and its aftermath as she had brazened out the day of the coup, refusing to accept or acknowledge that anything was going on. *Semper eadem* remained her motto. Another favourite had departed – the last of her courtly lovers and probably the most ardent and naively adoring – but nothing had changed. When information was brought to her about his conversations in the Tower, such news always being eagerly reported, she might have expected or even hoped for a few final protestations of love and contrition. If that were the case, she would be disappointed.

The truth was that by this stage Elizabeth and Essex had finally seen through one another, and neither much liked what they saw: he a tired and inconstant old woman and she a vainglorious and ambitious fool.

***

The earl of Essex was led out onto Tower Hill on the 25th of February. His last few days on earth had not been entirely without incident. The day after the trial he was attended on by the dean of Norwich, Thomas Dove, who had been instructed by the council to try and get something more out of him. An admission of guilt would be good, a confession as to the content of the black silk bag better. The news of the common people rallying round him on his journey from Westminster had disturbed the counsellors, particularly the unpopular Cecil.

Dove failed, but the chaplain who next arrived, Reverend Ashton, one of the Puritan ministers who had preached at Essex House during the winter, met with more success. Ashton was no longer fomenting fear of God's wrath. Instead he had been turned by the council. Although Essex tried at first to revive the spirit of his trial, waxing lyrical on his innocence and honourable intentions, the man of God lugubriously played on his fear of the afterlife. The earl admitted what he had previously kept only to himself: his desire to settle the succession question in favour of King James. Further, he revealed the names of those who had agreed with him. As he repeated the confession at Ashton's request, it is hard not to believe that Essex smelled a rat, and it is very likely that, facing death, he intended for those who had been his conspirators to go down with him. Further evidence of this can be found in his next request, which was made to the queen. It was no attempt at salvation, but a plea that she would send members of the privy council to her, Cecil included, that he might unburden himself.

This request was met the following day. Cecil and Nottingham arrived, no doubt full of excitement. He acidly informed them of his thanks that Elizabeth had granted him Ashton, who 'hath made me know my sins unto her Majesty'. He then gave a full confession, revealing that he had intended, like the Riccio plotters decades before and 300 miles away, to seize the queen and use her authority to force a change in the government. Cecil and Nottingham were not mollified. This was not the blazing confession they had hoped for – here was no attempt to murder them and Elizabeth and take the crown of England. They drew from him apologies for his accusations against Cecil, Cobham, and Raleigh. He also supposedly asked for the right to die privately within the precincts of the Tower, though some doubt has been cast on this claim (even immediately afterwards by the French king) – which might lead us to wonder what else reported of his words and actions in his final captivity were massaged.[201] This, they assured him, could be arranged, if he would put his words down in writing with the names of his accomplices. This he did, laying charges against his stepfather, Blount; his secretaries; Mountjoy; and, most shockingly of all, his sister, Penelope, who he claimed had urged him by calling him a coward, so possessed was she 'of a proud spirit'. In this he was probably telling the truth; it is safe to assume that Lady Rich really had been exercising political influence through her brother and her lover, Mountjoy (she had, it will be remembered, sought to steal a march on the rest of the elite by courting James VI back in 1589). It was still an ugly truth. He was taking no prisoners.

---

[201] Jardine, *Lives and Criminal Trials*, pp. 371-2.

Essex's behaviour was shocking and ugly. There was certainly a degree of malice in it. It must be set against both the conditions of his imprisonment – he was facing death and might have felt a genuine need to unburden his soul – and his lifelong attachment to notions of chivalry, which held that a man ought to protect his friends and relatives. Chivalry had availed him of nothing in end, and so he opted for the spiteful pleasure of truly unburdening his soul. This should not be overly surprising. He had had Godly fits before – for example, on his return for Ireland, during his brush with death and his first taste of real disfavour. When Cuffe was sent for he made no secret of his disgust at the earl's unchivalrous behaviour.

Following his confessions, Essex parleyed with two more divines, Mountford and Barlow. To them he made the extraordinary claim that he greatly desired death, because the queen would not be safe as long as he lived. He had retreated again into wild, grandiloquent fantasies, which in future centuries would likely have rendered the confessions themselves suspect. He raved about dying for a bad cause, unlike the celebrated Protestant martyrs. An air of unreality had fallen over the Tower and its prisoner. If he had any thoughts of his wife and children, he gave no sign of it, and certainly he did not accuse Frances of anything. One hopes that he had finally grown to appreciate her loyalty and did not want to trouble her, after a decade of giving his body to other women and his mind and expressions of passion to the queen. This is, unfortunately, supposition.

Preparations for the execution were begun on Shrove Tuesday. Two men were hired to sever his head, in case one lost his courage. Careful instructions were sent to the Tower detailing the death itself. He was to be accompanied to the scaffold, given spiritual succour, but allowed only to speak of redemption and repentance. Any other words, particularly accusations or justifications, were to be swiftly silenced. It is reasonable to ask why, given that the official version of events, as outlined above, depicted a changed man who had made full confessions willingly.

The writ commanding the execution was sent to the Tower,

only to be rescinded immediately by Elizabeth. It is tempting here to think that she was hoping even at the last moment, knowing of his words to Cecil and the divines, that he would beg for his life and she might hold the whole thing in suspense. This is possible. Equally possible is that, as with Mary Queen of Scots, she simply did not want to be responsible for his death. Elizabeth had never easily or smoothly ordered the death of high-ranking figures. The insecurity which had always permeated her personality and reign simply made it impossible. At sixty-seven she was not about to break the habit of a lifetime.

Throughout the events of late-1600 and early-1601, she had assumed a passive role, even allowing herself to be persuaded to adopt inaction during the coup. The trial, too, was stage-managed by her council. Whatever her own feelings were, she guarded them. The truth was that she had finally been trapped between factions – a thing she had always managed to avoid in the past. To pardon or show mercy to Essex would mean destabilising her government and tacitly encouraging dissent. Cecil and his friends were now firmly in control of affairs, and it was they who wove the narrative of rebellion. She, whether believing the crown's case or not, accepted that the secretary's party had won, and there was nothing she could do about it. Her days of managing opposing parties was over. The winning party would now seek to manage her.

The queen picked at her food at the Shrovetide Feast – she always ate like a bird – and thereafter watched a play by the Lord Chamberlain's Men. Evidently, she bore no ill will towards them for having staged *Richard II*. Augustine Philips, the company's spokesman, had been examined following the failed coup and nothing incriminating had been found against the players. It is not surprising: they had simply performed a state-authorised play – to condemn them for that would be to highlight the authorities' own weak system of licensing. Having them appear before the queen so soon afterwards went some way towards showing that, despite Essex's actions and fall, nothing had changed.

Again, the writ of execution went out, and this time there was no faltering. Essex spent the night praying and, in the morning, he was ready for death. He was led down and out to the scaffold, which was enclosed by a railing. Around it stood over a hundred men, from nobility and officials to knights, gentlemen, and aldermen of London. Essex moved through them, accompanied by three men of God, Sir John Peyton, and a small body of guards. He wore a black satin suit with a black velvet over-gown, and a black hat was perched on his head. After mounting the scaffold, he turned and cried, 'God be merciful to me, the most wretched creature on the earth'.[202] To the assembled crowd he then turned and delivered his final speech, which focused upon the condign nature of his punishment, and his multitude of sins (their number being greater than the hairs upon his head). His last sin, especially, he hoped would be forgiven: the co-opting of so many men to 'venture their lives and souls' in challenging the divinely ordained order. Although he added a token hope of forgiveness from the queen and council, his words aimed at mercy from a higher power.

He could not resist slight barbs. 'The lord grant her Majesty a prosperous reign,' he said, 'and a long one, if it be His will'.[203] The conditional was loaded. He could not resist either repeating his protestations that he had never intended Elizabeth's death or violence to her person. These were all the more convincing because they were true. He was justly condemned, he admitted – for Tudor justice had been done – albeit for his religion, and in that religion he was ready to die. His intent here was two-fold. He hoped to achieve a measure of martyrdom, and again sought to underscore that he had been acting in the Protestant faith against those who dealt with Catholic Spain. The words were all carefully measured to say much by saying little – the

---

[202] Green, M. A. E. (Ed.). 1869. *Calendar of State Papers: Preserved in the State Paper Department of Her Majesty's Public Record Office. Reign of Elizabeth: 1598 - 1601, Volume 5* (London: H. M. S. O.), p. 592.

[203] Green, M. A. E., & Lemon, R. (Eds.). 1869. *Calendar of State Papers, Domestic Series, of the Reigns of Edward VI, Mary, Elizabeth, 1547-1625: 1598-1601: Elizabeth* (Longman, Brown, Green, Longmans, & Roberts), p. 593.

opposite of Elizabeth's style of rhetoric.

After a few minutes of private prayer, he removed his outer garments, and when one of the divines told him not to be afraid, he answered that he had faced danger and death on the field before. God would give him strength of mind over body now as He had done then. When the executioner then begged for forgiveness, as was customary, he said, 'I forgive thee. Thou art the minister of justice'.[204]

Essex knelt down on the straw, the block before him. He began his final, loud prayers, begging for the comfort of God and condemning the omnipresent forces of Satan. After this came the Lord's Prayer, the last lines of which he repeated. On being instructed to, he loudly forgave his enemies – like him, they were God's creatures – and then he removed his doublet. He stood and bowed to the block, before asking the executioner to strike when he held out his arms. He was intent on giving a good show, knowing that his end would be spoken of throughout London and the courts of Europe.

'O God, I prostrate myself to your deserved punishment,' he cried, lowering himself again to the straw. With his neck on the block he recited the 51st Psalm and, when he reached the words, 'cleanse me from my sin,' he paused to shout, 'executioner, strike home!' He raised his arms and held them out, away from his body. As the axe was raised to the sky, the metal glinting in the wintry light, he resumed the Psalm. He did not finish it. The words were cut off abruptly as the metal bit into the back of his neck.

The first strike did not sever his head, but it undoubtedly erased his consciousness. Even sharpened Tudor-era axes killed by the heavy crushing of the blade. Up it went, and down it came again. The unconscious Essex lay there, blood pouring from his wounds. Still his head remained stubbornly attached to his body. For a final time, the executioner swung the bloody axe into the mangled flesh and at last his head fell to the rushes with a thump.

---

[204] Harrison, G. B. 1933. *A Last Elizabethan Journal* (London: Routledge & Kegan Paul), p. 164.

The last of the queen's great favourites, after so many years of trying his luck – sometimes winning, often losing – was dead.

***

Southampton's execution was commuted to life imprisonment, which was revoked after Elizabeth's death. Cecil won this concession from the queen. Neither she or the secretary wished to see Tower Green awash in aristocratic blood. That would only give weight to Essex's claims that his actions had been born of a noble assault on base and low-born favourites. Similarly, the earl of Rutland was able to buy his freedom by promising to pay a stiff fine, which he was never able to make good on. Lords Sandys, Mounteagle, Cromwell also got away with spilling their purses rather than their blood. Penelope and her illegitimate children by Mountjoy were thrown out by her husband, Lord Rich, but Elizabeth did not proceed against either the sister Essex had accused or her lover. Essex's Tower confessions did, however, lead Penelope to say, 'I have been more like a slave than a sister, which proceeded out of my exceeding love rather than his authority'.[205] These were politically astute sentiments.

Others fared less well, having less credit and being of lower rank. Although John Davies was reprieved, Gelli Meyrick and Henry Cuffe suffered the full horror of disembowelling at Tyburn. Sir Charles Danvers and Christopher Blount were granted the axe. Blount's death left Lettice widowed again, but the canny dowager had begun distancing herself from him anyway and spent the entire coup and its aftermath at her home, Drayton Bassett. She was saddened by the death of her son, but more saddened still at the wounds he had opened up in the family by accusing Penelope. She remained close to her daughters, outliving both by some margin. She died at ninety-one in a comfortable chair on Christmas Day 1634.

---

[205] Goodman, G. 1839. *The Court of King James I. of the Most Distinguished Characters in the Court of that Monarch* (London: Richard Bentley), p. 19.

Essex's countess continued to be loyal. She entrusted a casket containing Essex's more incriminating letters to the safety of a trusted former servant. That servant's husband was less honest and attempted to blackmail her. On hearing of this, Elizabeth had the blackmailer punished and his fine given to Frances. She had never had anything against her former favourite's wife, and she wanted the whole matter buried with Essex. Frances would go on to marry the 4th earl of Clanricarde, by whom she had three further children.

Of Essex's own children, little Robert succeeded to the earldom when the new king, a self-proclaimed Solomon, reversed the attainder under which his father had died. He became later an active parliamentarian and fought against the royalists in the civil war, dying only in 1646. He is probably most famous for his disastrous marriage to Frances Howard and the Jacobean poisoning scandal involving his wife, her lover, and Thomas Overbury. His sister, Frances, became the duchess of Somerset; her husband was the widower of Arbella Stewart and became a royalist commander in the middle of the seventeenth century. She lived a long life, not dying until 1674. The last legitimate child, Dorothy Devereux, had a less public life, marrying Sir Henry Shirley and living only until 1636. Finally, the illegitimate Walter, born to Essex and Elizabeth Southwell, formed a close bond with his half-brother and joined him in fighting in the name of parliament. He died suddenly in 1641.

Loyal also were Francis and Anthony Bacon. For Anthony it hardly mattered – he died shortly after Essex, his long suffering as an invalid at an end. Francis enjoyed greater successes than he ever had under Elizabeth during the next reign. He wrote his many excellent and still-relevant works, on everything from history to philosophy. In his writings he spoke fondly of his executed friend. His career blossomed without Elizabeth to foil him, and he eventually made it to the post of lord chancellor. Like Essex, he flew too high. He was accused of corruption in 1621 and his old enemy, Edward Coke, took great pleasure in overseeing his downfall. He died in 1626 after catching a chill when experimenting with freezing chicken. Not for nothing has be become known as one of the founding fathers of empirical science.

Essex's name almost immediately passed into legend, as he probably hoped it would. He became a martyr, although not for his religion. Over a year after his death Londoners were to be found singing ballads about him, and his old *impresas* at Whitehall became tourist attractions. He was the warrior who had fallen victim to the odious Cecil and his minions. The room at the Tower in which he had been kept, in a tower in the north-west corner of the inner curtain wall, lost its name, 'the Devil's tower' and became 'the Devereux tower' after its famous, glamorous, doomed inmate. Rumours circulated that a lucky man had acquired a bone from the dead man's neck and wore it as a charmed relic, and his blood had supposedly seeped into the ground of Tower Green leaving a patch where no grass would grow.[206] Fulke Greville would celebrate him as 'free from … unnatural crime … he suffered England to stand alone, in her ancient degrees of freedom, and integrities, and so reserved that absolute power of creation sacred in his sovereign, without any mercenary stain'.[207]

The lionisation was shameless. If this seems difficult to understand, given his career, it is necessary to consider the way in which heroes are constructed throughout the ages. Just as those of Ancient Greece seem alien to us – often monstrous, in fact – so did the Elizabethan age have a very different conception of heroism. His legend endured not because he was a brilliant commander but because he was passionate, direct, and noble: and because he carefully cultivated an image of greatness via poetry, portraiture, and personal charisma amongst the people. What was and remains problematic is that his posthumous reputation hinged so strongly on a single character trait – his dedication to the idea of chivalry, which he renounced in the Tower when he betrayed his friends and sister. Essex was not a chivalric knight in anything like the medieval sense. He was an aspirant renaissance knight: a poet and patron;

---

[206] Hiscock, 'Achilles Alter', p. 117.
[207] Greville, *Life of Sidney*, p. 159.

a military enthusiast and soldier; a spymaster; a player on the world stage.

Why he remains a figure of such astonishing interest is easier to see. Essex represented the best and worst of the Elizabethan age. Indeed, one can scarcely imagine him inhabiting any other era - under Henry VIII he would have been swiftly cut down; under James he would have been a civic-minded cynic. In his disrespect towards authority he appears remarkably modern, almost frustrated by the limitations of his age. In other ways he seems a throwback to a distant and imaginary past. Unique amongst his contemporaries, he took the rebirth of chivalric ideals to extremes because he truly believed in them. He wrote poetry, engaged in complex politics (to varying degrees of success), and took part in numerous European campaigns. Yet he was also vengeful, spiteful, obsessed with warfare and in thrall to the idea that his birth gifted ability. It is reasonable to wonder why he, uniquely amongst his contemporaries, took the teachings of the age so seriously. Those teachings were, after all, contradictory and strange: men were expected to count themselves superior to women and yet passionately love their mistresses, especially their sovereign lady. Many men managed one or the other, but for years Essex juggled both.

Partly this is down to the uniqueness of personality and personal circumstances, but it is more due to the fact that Elizabeth's other favourites – Leicester, Hatton, Raleigh, Oxford, and a whole slew of others – were either too old by the time of the high renaissance, too low in rank, too dependent on her goodwill, too unpopular amongst the people, or some other combination of all. Essex matured at the height of Shakespeare's nationalistic history plays; at the beginning of the end of Elizabeth's reign; he was of ancient and noble lineage; and he had the extraordinary qualities that might make anyone popular – good looks, easy charm, and the common touch. If his letters and attitudes do little to convey this, it is important to realise that the former are very much of their period, stylistically flowery, and mostly written during crises; and the latter were largely attractive to people governed by an ageing woman.

22: Requiem for a Queen

Crowds of mourners lined the streets outside the sprawling palace of Whitehall, each hoping for a glimpse of the magnificent funeral procession. Few could recall having seen the last royal funeral for an English monarch; it had taken place nearly forty-five years before. Eventually a hush descended. Weighted down with black velvet and led by two royal equerries, a great horse appeared, and behind them followed the long, winding procession of the royal household. It was Elizabeth's funeral. She had died 'mildly, like a lamb' rather than 'like a thunder-clap' on the 24th of March, only a month before, and a little over two years after Essex had went to the block.[208] Her final days, according to the French ambassador, saw the first retreat into infantilism she had engaged in since infancy itself. She sat 'holding her finger almost continually in her mouth, with her eyes open and fix'd upon the ground'.[209] This followed what Lady Southwell described as an end to the vanity which had long sustained her:

Afterwards, in the melancholy of her sickness she desired to see a true looking -- glass, which in twenty years before she had not seen, but only such a one as on purpose was made to deceive her sight, which true looking-glass being brought her, she presently fell exclaiming at all those flatterers which had so much commended her, and they durst not after come into her presence.[210]

Reality, and the passage of time, which she had always tried

---

[208] Perry, M. 1999. *The Word of a Prince: A Lie of Elizabeth I Through Contemporary Documents* (Cambridge: Boydell Press), p. 238; Dekker, T. 2011 [1604]. *The Wonderful Yeare* 1603 (Oxford: Benediction Classics), p. 3.

[209] Birch, *Memoirs of the Reign of Queen Elizabeth*, p. 507.

[210] Strickland, *Lives of the Queens of England*, p. 217.

to deny, became unavoidable with the approach of death. Inscrutable to the last, however, she gave no indication of whom she wished to succeed to her throne. Her ministers, Cecil chief amongst them, would have to manufacture her wishes which, unsurprisingly, comported with their own.

In the aftermath of Essex's death, her godson and former member of Essex's Irish campaign, Sir John Harington, visited her and noted that 'she walks much in her privy chamber, and stamps with her feet at ill news, and thrusts her rusty sword at times into the arras in great rage'.[211] The image is arresting: the queen is again a cracked and broken woman, full of fear and fury. It is not, however, accurate. At other times she put on her old displays of splendour – not least when she addressed parliament and delivered her so-called 'golden speech' in November. What, then, was she – the polished queen or the crazed old woman?

Elizabeth was both. What followed Essex's death and persisted until her own was a deep distrust and dislike of youth and the young people who now populated her court. As she had put on a politic display of feebleness before the French ambassador in 1597, she again used her age as a weapon. This time the tetchiness and bouts of mad fury were aimed at the young pups who occasionally stirred her ire. Essex's legacy to the queen was an intolerance for empty-headed youth.

No favourites succeeded Essex in her affections. Walter Raleigh continued acting as governor of Jersey, the role which he had been given in 1600 and which had allowed Essex to suggest at the time of the coup would make him an overly lax gatekeeper to Cecil's Spanish friends. Raleigh had never been a popular man amongst the people, which was why Elizabeth had liked him. He did not win any after Essex's death. Instead, rumours dogged him that he had sat blowing smoke in a gesture of disdain towards the condemned man. More dangerous, and deeply unfair, gossip continued about his penchant for the Spanish, and after Elizabeth's death he was accused of having plotted to thwart the succession in favour of Arbella Stewart,

---

[211] Strickland, *Lives of the Queens of England*, p. 198.

with Spanish money greasing his palms. The agent who was truly behind this plot, known as the Main Plot, was his old colleague Cobham. Raleigh lived a prisoner in the Tower for years under James VI and I, emerging briefly in 1617 to attempt a lucrative voyage to Guiana. This failed and he went to the block in 1618, protesting at the last that he did not blow smoke on Essex's death. Cobham was clapped in the Tower for the Main Plot, where he remained until 1618, being released only to die in penury the same year. Lord Grey, Southampton's great enemy, was also implicated and similarly confined to the Tower, where he died in 1614.

Of the trio of Essex's last enemies, Cecil fared the best. The intelligent little secretary was elevated to the peerage as Baron Cecil of Essendon in 1603, Viscount Cranborne in 1604, and finally Earl of Salisbury in 1605. Although Essex had done everything he could to blacken Cecil's name and win the role of the new king's chief adviser for himself, he could do little to halt his rival's ascent from beyond the grave. Cecil, however, found that high office under James VI and I was even more ruinous to the health than his father had found it under Elizabeth. Overworked by the spendthrift king, he died in agony of mind and body in May 1612.

The king who succeeded Elizabeth and who had been so assiduously courted by Essex got what he wanted, and smoothly. As the author Thomas Dekker colourfully put it, 'upon Thursday it was treason to cry 'God save King James, King of England, and upon Friday high treason not to cry so'.[212] His reign coincided with a severe outbreak of plague in London, which delayed his coronation, but thereafter he set about pursuing peace with the Spanish. This was both his policy and Cecil's. The problems in Ireland continued, but the Anglo-Spanish war drew to a close in 1604. More capable a king than he is usually given credit for, he nevertheless never managed to bring about his pet project – the amalgamation of England and Scotland into one nation of Great Britain, with the names of Scotland and England whitewashed out of the histories. Even in

---

[212] Dekker, *The Wonderful Yeare*, p. 10.

the next century, when the treaty of union passed under the last Stewart monarch, Queen Anne, it would not go quite as far as James had envisioned. His son Henry, a promising young man, died suddenly in 1612 and his wife, Anne of Denmark, in 1619. James would die in 1625, leaving the throne to his ill-fated and incompetent son, Charles I.

It was not long into James' reign that the people, at first joyful at the end of the old administration, realised that they were getting more of the same. Accordingly, they began to eulogise the late queen's rule. She was celebrated in plays, such as Thomas Heywood's *If You Know Not Me, You Know Nobody; or The Troubles of Queen Elizabeth* of 1605 and Shakespeare and Fletcher's *All is True or Henry VIII*, the climax of which is her christening. The crop failures, factionalism, and favouritism were forgotten in the welter of racier scandals unfolding under the new king. Retrospectively, her reign became a golden age. Greville had even more to say on the late queen than he did on her dead favourite:

This lady … by an humble and constant temper, had already with true obedience triumphed over the curious examinations of ascending flattery, or descending tyranny, even in the tendernesse of princes' successions … This she-David of ours ventured to undertake the great Goliath amongst the philistines abroad, I mean Spain and the Pope; despiseth their multitudes, not of men, but of hosts; scornfully rejecteth that holy father's wind-blown superstitions, and takes the (almost solitary) truth for her leading-star … Even at the height of Essex his credit with her, how far was she from permitting him (like Remus) to leap over any wall of her new-built anti-Rome.[213]

He reached his apogee when he apologised to the reader for turning their minds to 'all those glories of life which he formerly enjoyed, under the blessed, and blessing presence of this unmatchable queen and woman'.[214] Under Greville's gold-

---

[213] Greville, *Life of Sidney*, p. 163.
[214] Greville, *Life of Sidney*, p. 215.

dipped pen, the queen never embraced favouritism. His text, it should be noted, is intended as a warning to his then and future monarchs. The glitter which was rapidly sprinkled over Elizabeth's reign in the years after its close was not simple nostalgia; it was hoped that rewriting it as a glorious and error-free age would give her successors a model of kingship to emulate.

It is as a golden age that people tend to still think of Elizabeth's reign. To some extent, and for some people, it was. It was also, however, an age of insecurity and pain for many. Her system of favouritism and patronage worked well for the majority of it, but it provided fertile ground for a man like Essex to rise and fall. In many ways, it is only surprising that more of her favourites did not push as far as he did. So blinded are we by the mythos of the incomparable Gloriana – probably the most iconic of queens in history – that it is easy to forget that, to those living under her in the late sixteenth century, she was rapidly becoming an old woman in charge of a stale and corrupt administration. As he lies in the shadow of her posthumous ascent to brilliance, we often overlook the fact that Essex was a noble, young, and immensely popular figure who represented everything that the elderly queen was not. He might have worked in tandem with her government as its smiling face, but he was too headstrong and she too jealous for that type of relationship to last, despite both trying.

One of the questions I have sought to tackle in this book is whether or not, ultimately, the strange pair loved one another. In writing it, I hope I have demonstrated that he certainly loved her in the early days of their association – albeit via a form of courtly love that is very different to our own. She was the untouchable mistress, ethereal and, when the sun shone, bountiful – quite unlike the women he pursued for casual sex and even the steely woman whom honour compelled him to make his wife. His infatuation was, to complicate matters further, aimed at the woman as an icon. The woman as a queen he could never love and seldom if ever respected. He was, in this strange duality, a victim of his age's contradictions.

Elizabeth's feelings towards him are far more difficult to

gauge, for she was never as open or as transparent as he was. The fact that she made a patronage system out of ties of affection and attraction makes her feelings almost impossible to discern – as probably she intended it to do. The queen was human, and she was given to favouritism and irrational likes and dislikes as much as she was a politician given to shrewd wisdom and cunning. The men she favoured were human, and given to avarice, cupidity, and stupidity as much as they were loyal Englishmen given to respect, gratitude, and admiration.

At best, it is fair to say that she held him in deep affection. He excited her, frustrated her, and defied her in ways that she was unused to. She most certainly loved his lavish attentions, his private conversation, his protestations of love; but she did not love anything deeper than that. His developing political outlook and his streak of independence she abhorred, and probably she hoped that time would cure him of these, as it had cured others. This was a blunder. His attitudes and beliefs largely solidified with the passing years, and the questioning of royal power, which would explode in the next century, was starting to invite criticism and give vitality to debates about the role of the subject. She failed, too, to realise that men were less inclined to break and become her vassals as her end approached. Her conscience, though, compelled her to forgive him often for his transgressions, knowing that she had made him and bore the lion's share of responsibility for the man he became. It helped enormously that he said all the right things. The problem was that he often did all the wrong ones. In the end, though, policy came first. His attempt to force a change in her council failed and his means of carrying it out sealed his fate. By the time it happened, there was nothing between them but mutual contempt. He was a rebel and she made tyrannical by sycophants. This does not efface what had gone before, during the decade-and-a-half of close personal contact. Elizabeth and Essex did not have one of history's great romances, but they did have one of its most misunderstood.

NOTES & REFERENCES

Full details are given for the first citation of a book or article. Thereafter, short references are used.

21918748R00163

Printed in Great Britain
by Amazon